THE TESTAMENT OF GOD

By the same author

Barbarism with a Human Face (1979)

Bernard-Henri Lévy

THE
TESTAMENT
OF GOD

TRANSLATED FROM THE FRENCH

BY George Holoch

HARPER & ROW, PUBLISHERS, New York
Cambridge, Hagerstown, Philadelphia, San Francisco,
London, Mexico City, São Paulo, Sydney
1817

This work was first published in France under the title *Le Testament de Dieu*. © Editions Grasset & Fasquelle, 1979.

THE TESTAMENT OF GOD. English translation copyright © 1980 by Harper & Row, Publishers, Inc. All rights reserved. Printed in the United States of America. No part of this book may be used or reproduced in any manner whatsoever without written permission except in the case of brief quotations embodied in critical articles and reviews. For information address Harper & Row, Publishers, Inc., 10 East 53rd Street, New York, N.Y. 10022. Published simultaneously in Canada by Fitzhenry & Whiteside Limited, Toronto.

FIRST EDITION

Designer: Sidney Feinberg

ISBN: 0-06-012616-7

LIBRARY OF CONGRESS CATALOG CARD NUMBER: 80-7589

80 81 82 83 84 10 9 8 7 6 5 4 3 2 1

To Sylvie
To Justine

Contents

Foreword

It takes some insolence to continue to speak of hope in the century of the gas chamber and the concentration camp. Like all men of my time, I know the grandiloquence and profusion of joyful wisdom with which the executioners of every country display the banners floating over their slaughterhouses. Everything about this age militates against that optimism which, always from the topmost towers, gives voice to the suffering of the galley slaves, prisoners, or slum dwellers of the world. Not long ago, I myself wrote *Barbarism with a Human Face,* in which, confronted by so many fascisms hawking their smiling monsters in the great marketplace of hope, I concluded with a call for the most intransigent and perhaps the most "negative" kind of critical lucidity. This book, of course, does not in any way retract that demand. But it begins, simply, with the doubt and uncertainty which that demand confronted. It posits, assumes, wagers, that the time of disarray has in a sense gone by. Put simply, it proposes to follow a single, inexhaustible, and impossible question: Since the horror is what it is, in the name of what can men, here and now, concretely, oppose and reject it?

For it is a fact that they reject it. Everywhere in the world, in the West as well as the East, more and more men and women have arisen who are infinitely weary with secular mystification and are embarking on the adventure of a Name and a singular revolt. Thousands, indeed, millions of solitary individuals are proclaiming to the world the proud and enormous certainty that Truth, Good, Justice are not the idle words the technicians of sorrow and suffering believe them to be. They form vast crowds of a new kind of fool, their lips sealed and their souls on fire, who have only contempt for "revolution," "liberation," and "socialism" when those forces, wearing the colors of Science, History, and now of Islam, conspire to degrade and humiliate the human body. You can hear the chains of lies rattling from Moscow to Buenos Aires, see the resistance stiffening from Hanoi to Teheran. Can it have been so soon forgotten that even in Auschwitz and Buchenwald, at the farthest reaches of suffering, there were those who revolted, stood by themselves, and said no to the inevitable?[1] I certainly do not presume to stand by the side of those heroes and martyrs. Yet it is true that, were it not for them, I would probably not have risked this new undertaking. It is certain that, thanks to them, the works of freedom have maintained a meaning and an urgency that a vagabond century has quite blithely given up. Antifascism is a new idea, in the West and in the East. Modestly but firmly, I would like to take up that idea, that challenge.

It is also certain that this project could hardly have been considered had I not borne in mind a more ancient and perhaps more elevated tradition: an ageless, properly speaking, immemorial rebelliousness, which has constantly affirmed for two thousand years the most continuous, stubborn, persistent refusal that has, until now, illustrated the human chronicle. An absolutely unique case, resistant alike to logic, to obsolescence, even to genocide; a determination to say no, to contradict the verdict of the facts, to defy the mechanism of the centuries with its procession of warnings and murderous necessities. So singular, so unprecedented an experience, that it is inscribed on the tablets of a sacred Law; and time has changed it so little that the Law has rather continually tested, troubled, and disinherited history itself and its so-called imperatives. I am speaking of the Jewish people, of course, of that indomitable people whose perseverance in existing remains one of the deepest mysteries confronting contemporary consciousness. A community of wandering but also of light and confidence which, carried by fate to the very limits of sorrow, never surrendered the simple pride of being human. Without ambiguity, I recognize myself in that community. Ardently, proudly, I choose to carry and exalt its colors. I claim— and I will prove—that the authors of the Book are also the inventers of the modern idea of Resistance.

For I claim above all that in the Book itself, in that clear and spare word, chiseled in its letters, recorded on the stones of memory, there lies an immense legacy, an invaluable document whose vital contemporary importance is just beginning to be discovered. Should we reread the Bible? Several teachers have showed me the way, among whom it is enough for me to name the distinguished philosopher Emmanuel Levinas and the Catholic René Girard[2] to express all the value I attach to Judeo-Christian dialogue, a dialogue whose traces the spirit of the age seems determined to obliterate as rapidly as possible. A return to monotheism? Monotheism, it will soon be clear, is neither a monism nor a theism, but a concrete ethics, a celebration of Law, a pledge on the Universal, and a miracle of Reason, whose impossible figure is perhaps the surest and the last recourse against the dangers of voluntary surrender and submission. God is dead? "God is unconscious" rather, as Jacques Lacan says; and He has left us a last will and testament whose lesson will appear, gently at first, then more and more harshly as the guiding thread of this study becomes clearer. For at botton, this is the central hypothesis: The morality of resistance, the systematic antifascism which the century has forced us to adopt, may find its only chance to take on reality in the memory of the One God and His passion for the Law.

To conclude a preamble already grown too long, is it necessary to explain that this reference is a recourse rather than a return, as one might hastily imagine? That there is nothing in common between meditation on a text whose real aim was always the struggle against "idolatry," and the periodic resurgence of the "sacred" which has become a theme song of modernity? That it is even *against* those resurgences, those regressions, against the romanticisms in which modernity indulges, that the wager on the Name and the cold glitter of the flame in which I place all my hope have any value? The Mosaic law is not an archaism, and nothing is in fact more foreign to it than the search for "roots" and the nostalgia for "sources" wherein always lurks that hideous "spirit of the woods" already denounced by the Prophets. Primacy of the Law does not mean theocracy but, on the contrary, mistrust of all embodied norms, of all profane gods, of all gods, in which there has appeared once again, at the end of the twentieth century, the cowardly obscurantism of ancient polytheism. The Bible is the book of resistance of our time; that also means that the principal contradiction around which the age turns is the contradiction between paganism and monotheism. The Testament of God is again the death of God, still the death of God, carried to the end of the road, through all its consequences and symptoms—to the conclusion of a desanctification beginning, for example, with the cult of the Political.

THE TESTAMENT OF GOD

PART ONE:
LIMIT POLITICS TO MAKE ROOM
FOR ETHICS

Must we really go back, yet again, to politics—to all those wordy commonplaces with which the choristers of modernity continue to commune, to the eternal "problem" everywhere discussed and celebrated ad nauseam? Politics is on its deathbed, they say, and yet it has rarely taken so long to lay out a corpse. It is merely a ghost, a shadow of its former self; but the ghosts must surely be real since they are suddenly making so much noise. Has the illusion been destroyed? It would rather seem to resemble the Messiah described by Kafka, who endlessly dies and is resurrected among the dead.[1]

This is why what is really urgent is to dispense with the principle behind the whole business; to reduce, to limit, to desanctify a concern that renews the ceremonies of its worship through those very acts that would deny it; to consider precisely those repudiations that contain the most discreet, and the most deceptive, forms of the old idolatry. Politics is not, or should no longer be, a "problem" at all. It is neither the sun it claims to be nor the infernal horror some believe it to be. Hating it is like worshipping it—the other side of the same religion. This is what the remarks that follow will attempt to establish. They should be read as efforts to clear a path that can open onto or at least point the way toward the urgent demands of ethics.

1

In Praise of the State

To begin with, there is the celebrated and hackneyed "question of the state"—a perfect example of the perennial pendulum swings of idolatrous worship. The history of Western intellectuals for the past two centuries could almost be summed up in this singular and enigmatic movement. For two centuries they have been divided—better, they have oscillated—between blind fascination and a no less blind and horrified repulsion. At times, they swear by the noonday ideologies which, following the lead of Marxism and classic Jacobinism, can conceive of no salvation outside gigantic mechanisms designed to program, socialize, and establish happiness. At other times, as though they had come through some catastrophe, they turn toward twilight notions, imitating anarchism, suddenly brandished like a charm, for which the most urgent task is to deny the state as such since it has become the source of all evils, an image of absolute evil, and absolutely hateful. We have been clearly enough informed—and in good time, let it be said—about the ravages of the former and the fanatic state-worship that liberates humanity in concentration camps. But we may yet remind the latter, with their principled anti-statism, of some well-known facts which are enough to render their dream the other side of the same nightmare, and to make the "withering away of the state" a fearful slogan that has strictly nothing to do with a philosophy of resistance.

First of all, it is obvious that today, at the end of the twentieth century, we are living in the wake of a disaster probably without precedent, which can only be called the totalitarian revolution. I agree that this *successful* revolution—the only one for which the age will be known—remains largely unarticulated. But that it is like an obsessive fear, a barely cooled lava flow, which percolates through every form of power as soon as it can act absolutely, is indisputable. And that it covers the entire spectrum of politics, few systems escaping the contagion, is also very probable. All the same, this does not mean that we must grant the totalitarian revolution everything it asks for—namely, a complacent neutrality and an indifference to all values. Nor does it mean that, confronted with evil, we can do nothing but abandon any attempt at analysis and retreat bitterly to cheap solutions which, in the guise of "vigilance," in fact prohibit any authentic critique. And above all it does not mean that, like the cursed Ninevites of whom the Bible says that they could no longer distinguish right from left,[1] we must stop dividing the world according to the only valid criterion, murder and its madness. If it is true, in other words, that the struggle of our era is between fascism and anti-fascism, then the idea that one state is as good as any other is no doubt a fascist idea. If it is correct that, in this struggle, the primary consideration is the rights of man, then we must constantly repeat that the expression "rights of man" contains the word "rights," and that we also need states that speak of the Right. Hatred of the state depends on an abuse of language which, playing with words and the names of men's fate, trading on suffering and bargaining over its intensity, is clearly and literally a form of treason.

Moreover, such hatred of the state also depends on a dubious and dangerous philosophical naïveté that I have called elsewhere (but a number of misunderstandings require its repetition) the "naturalist illusion."[2] Describing power as a kind of shroud or mask that is supposed to have recently corrupted some imaginary human nature, it always drags in its wake the old reactionary fantasies of a return to the origins and wellsprings of the primeval world. Denying the reality of the prohibition which, the Freudians have taught us, condemns human desire to the inevitable constraint of Law, it always carries the banner of the revolutionary utopia—a radical new beginning and a mythological "new man." Imagining a historical end to power within a history that is, by definition, the history of power itself (or of the impossibility that makes power necessary), it is that very history which it in reality plans to abolish; and we know from Cambodia the atrocious consequences of that project.[3] Is it a matter of joining the state, as Eric Weill says? One doesn't join the state as one joins a tennis club; rather, the individual, in our sense of the word, would be completely inconceivable but for the state's record of his existence.[4] Can we strip off the state, like a badly fitting suit? No, because for once, clothes make the man, are intertwined with him, woven of the same cloth, a modern tunic of Nessus. A society without a state? In the universe of established and governing states, the slogan has no more meaning than idealist speculations about the reality of the world did in the past. The meaning of a paradox. At best, of a challenge or a wager; at worst, of a hypothesis. And nothing is worse than a hypothesis that is tested on the flesh of a living society, making that society its monstrous laboratory.

This was in fact the project of the founding fathers of the anarchist tradition. When will people stop celebrating the heroic virtues of those cutthroats who wandered through the Russia of the late nineteenth century, their heads filled with fantastic visions and murderous designs? Should we consider the ravings of Pisarev and Tkatchev insignificant? Tkatchev claimed he would liquidate every vestige and memory of the old world by exterminating all adults over twenty-five.[5] Is it possible to read without terror the statutes of the Society of the Ax, founded in St. Petersburg by Nechayev on Bakunin's orders, which contain the most staggering hymn to Holy Revolution conceived as a final solution and a perfect holocaust?[6] And when will we bring ourselves to read Bakunin himself, the man presented by a stubborn legend as the perennial opponent of authoritarian socialism while in reality, from the theory of surplus value to radical economism, from the work ethic to the attack on bourgeois freedoms, he shared most of its postulates and theoretical conclusions?[7] These outlaws of the anti-authoritarian struggle were also, it is too easily forgotten, fanatic anti-Semites; and it was Bakunin again who provided the first form of Hitler's notion of the triple international—"bourgeois," "clerical," and "Marxist"—woven together by the "Jewish plot."[8] It was from this ideology, far more than from the German philosophy of the triumphant nineteenth century, that Lenin soon drew the essentials of the theory of the Party, the militant, and the *coup d'état* that allowed him to lay the foundations for red totalitarianism.[9] It is therefore not very surprising that the Germany of the seventies was stunned to witness, in the ravings of the "Baader-Meinhof gang" (among the last consistent heirs of the old family) the resurrection, along with the darkest pages of the Stalinist family album, of the repressed specter of Auschwitz where, according to the "libertarian" Ulrike Meinhof, "Six million Jews were killed and thrown on the dungheap of Europe for what they were: Jews of money. . . . The Germans were anti-Semites, that is why they now support the Red Army Fraction. They have not yet recognized it because they have not yet been absolved of fascism and the murder of the Jews. And they have not yet been told that anti-Semitism was in reality hatred of capitalism."[10]

Suppose that that is the very kind of madness which the state blocks. Suppose the state—the hideous, abominable state—is also a mechanism for censoring such ravings. The assumption is not absurd. It was, for example, Thomas Hobbes's conviction. It provided the outline for the modern form of the state at the moment of its establishment. And I think that once again a genealogical detour is necessary to make certain points evident. In fact,

we can understand nothing about Hobbes's derivation of the
contract if we persist in looking, as is usually done, for a theory
of absolutism and (why not?) of totalitarianism. The texts say
exactly the opposite. They are based *theoretically* on the most
thoroughgoing individualism, and they lead *practically* to the
most advanced form of a liberalism that had hardly been born.[11]
They contain notably the explicit affirmation that the sovereign
could not possibly, without serious danger, interfere with the
consciousness, indoctrinate the minds, "correct the spirit"[12] of
dissidents against the established order. The key axiom of the
pact is that of a "natural law," which makes "right" and not
"duty" the basic moral reality over which the prince stands
guard—a majestic but constantly scrupulous watchman.[13] What
better protection could there be against the naturalist fallacy
than this strange "state of nature," about which Rousseau and
Montesquieu noted that it is in fact a "civil state," an *a priori*
form of the social bond and of an impossible harmony of immediate egotisms?[14] The first lines of *De Corpore politico* say:
"Very little strength is needed to take the life of a man."[15] Too
little strength, in other words, for an economy, a homeostasis of
murder, to be spontaneously possible. So little strength that an
exchange is enough to abolish it—the exchange of the power to
kill for the right to live. So many individual powers at the same
time, innumerable and dispersed, that nothing less than Leviathan is needed to oppose their blind operation with a pattern of
codes and illusions. Very little, too little, so little, and so many
powers: Hobbes's entire politics is perhaps nothing but the ar-
ticulation and connection of this play of forces. There is a physics of the state, a subtle and cunning mechanics that makes it
both necessary and a necessarily saving presence.

For what does this physics say? And what does this mechanics
mean? Strangely enough, they have a sacred and religious character. They can be understood, even if the word is not used, as
the economics of a mysterious and fundamental sacrifice. It is
said that in the past, herds of men and monsters periodically of-

fered a part of their wealth to cruel and terrible gods, from whom they hoped in return for forgiveness and clemency. In the same way—the philosopher seems to say—individuals, when they accept the contract, immolate a part of themselves to an omnipotent but now single god, also cruel and full of violence, from whom they expect in return peace for soul and body. This sacrificial portion which they give away is in this case a part of themselves, not of their wealth but of their desire. The element they sacrifice is that part of everyone which urges him to murder and exposes him in return to the danger of being murdered. This physics of sacrifice is therefore precisely the opposite of the chemistry of genocide invented by the moderns. The absolute that it establishes and projects into heaven is not the absolute of force but of form, which contradicts force and consumes its excess. Contrary to totalitarianism, the Hobbesian faith in the state is a worship whose incense does not so much celebrate crime as avert and exorcise it. And there is such a disturbing resemblance between the formulations of *Leviathan* and St. Anselm's proof of the existence of God because statism in its infancy was something better than a religion or a pagan sanctification of the political realm; it was, rather, a politics, probably the last, which made its essence depend on a transcendental order.[16] That state is clearly the absolute contrary of fascism; it is the profane version of the original "Thou shall not kill" of the most ancient commandments.[17]

Does the lesson seem futile, outdated, paradoxical? I am afraid that the paradox has more immediate relevance than one might think. And I can note one example, among many others: the question of the death penalty. What do its defenders say, from Robespierre to the present? Curiously, on the essential point, they say the same thing as its opponents, that the guillotine is the fixed point, the majestic or abject basis for the authority and dignity of the state; for Beccaria the abolitionist as for Hegel the supporter, a prince who executes is a leader who terrorizes. What would the Hobbes of *De Corpore politico* respond? Probably the opposite, equidistant from both sides: that the guillotine is not the triumph but the eclipse of law, the point at which it breaks down and rights retreat, the bloody failure of the state to ward off the call for blood. A prince who cuts off heads is a terrorized prince. Concretely? This is indeed what happens when a court decides to send a man to the scaffold. The maddened crowd howling for the death of the accused on the steps of the court has often made itself judge of the judges, assistant to the prosecutor, arbiter of the state. This is indeed what happens each time a statesman, on the strength of a "poll," shaken by the murmurs of his silent majority, rejects a prisoner's final appeal for his pardon. It is not law that has decided, but passion—and the "opinion" to which it has surrendered. State violence? The expression has no meaning unless one adds that the head does not roll on the altar of reason, but rather, reason of state on the altar of illegality. Legal murder? No doubt, provided one corrects the statement: the murder of legality, violence done to the law, by the "little strength needed to take the life of a man."

Is this an exceptional case? On the contrary, it is generalized every day in totalitarian societies. In General Videla's Argentina, I met men and women who went to bed every night with their minds trembling, eyes opened wide to the horror of the coming night, in terror of blind commandos, unofficial police and their mad assassins.[18] These men and women, confronted with the arbitrary and the reign of insanity, called for nothing but a state of legality, or a legal state. In the country of the Gulag, in the great necropolises where torture is carried on in the name of innumerable laws, in obscure quarries where every man who awakens is one who has escaped from the dangers of the night, in the giant slaughterhouses where law has given way to the lunacy of murder without rhyme or reason, what do those who still have voices say, what do they shout? That it is better to have any state than no state at all, better a class state than one that thinks it is so no longer; it is even better to have a pure tyrant than the prodigious "egocrat"[19] who dilates his own body to the size of a whole society. Formal freedoms? Ask those who, confronting oppression, have recourse only to the form, the *pure form* of freedom, what they think of them. Rejection of the state as such? Ask what that means to those who are locked up in the name of a state that is withering away. Attack organizations and institutions? Since Mao, we know that the first to be affected are particular men. For the dissidents of the entire world, the combat for the state, in this sense, has only just begun.

We must finally get used to the idea. It is perhaps an unfortunate habit which makes us link, as though it were a matter of course, the words "state" and "totalitarian." The expression is inappropriate to describe societies whose avowed dream is sometimes to do without a state; to designate states whose fantasy is always to disappear on the horizon of civil society; or to name despots who intend not so much to reign as to melt and dissolve, to blend body and soul with the bodies and souls of their martyred subjects. It is also a mistake to perceive the pinnacle of oppression in some indescribable munificence of a solar and sovereign state, majestically enthroned in the firmament of society, pronouncing its decrees as a god would deliver oracles. For the worst horror perhaps begins when that firmament collapses, when the distance that kept the shepherd separate from his flock is abolished, when the law vanishes, taking with it any referent for the power of the rulers and hence any recourse for the distress of the ruled. It is finally wrong to imagine thoroughgoing totalitarianism in the shape of a blocked society, for example, a compact and immobile bureaucracy. For that very compactness is frequently the *maquis* of the people's resistance; it is always what resists the rulers' desire for transparency; it is the useless light that obscures their dream and that they must constantly strive to dissipate. Every totalitarian prince realizes sooner or later that a ponderous mechanism is not the best means to propagate his power. Every totalitarian revolution periodically decides to destroy, to ruin the state itself, and the useless undergrowth of organizations that slows down and sometimes flows counter to the tide of its development.[20] If there is, as the political scientists would say, a totalitarian *model*, and if this model is not the same as that of despotism, the difference lies in that destruction, and not simply in an extreme of coercion that would hardly have been enough to inflame the fervor of the masses. To be a thoroughly consistent antifascist means to recognize that logic and to derive all the appropriate lessons from it, in spite of amnesiacs and their unrepentant teachers.

What did Stalin do in the middle of 1928, on the eve of an unspeakable and unprecedented reign of terror? He unleashed the masses on Red Square, in an assault against a party that had placed him in the minority and was momentarily delaying the procession of socialism.[21] What did Mao do forty years later, on the brink of a revolution that "aimed directly at man's soul," and dreamed, in other words, of making each man his own policeman?[22] He set his Red Guards against "headquarters" which, since they formed a kind of screen between the soul and itself, were beginning to become an obstacle to uninterrupted fascism. What did the victorious Khmers Rouges do after the fall of Phnom-Penh, at the outset of the great massacre for which they would soon be notorious? They too declared war on the state, that old bourgeois mechanism, above all the final vestige of an "oriental despotism" which they knew very well was "reactionary" and represented a serious obstacle to the creation of the "new world."[23] Of course, these are merely examples, but examples burdened with corpses, and each one a key stage in a hideous escalation. They say unanimously that, in its darkest hours, fascism is not only love of but also hatred for the institution. They teach us that a successful fascism is not only Leviathan at war with the People, but the People itself at war with Leviathan. They remind us of the old equation, proposed early by Lenin and inscribed in letters of blood on the flesh of so many martyrs: A power that is growing stronger can mean a state that is decaying, and a society without a state is a state of unlimited terror. I never granted much credence to the argument that Marx was the most fanatic of state-worshippers. I find it easier to believe in the profound coherence of those passages, scattered throughout his work, which speak of the necessary "withering away."[24] But I will simply say that the formulation of this withering away is one of the subtlest forms of legitimized murder. How many Cambodians, how many camps and mass graves, how many human wrecks and victims of torture will we need before we agree to understand that real totalitarianism proceeds from bottom to top as much as from top to bottom, and that the abolition of the state is a Nazi fantasy?

Yes, I said Nazi, and in this case I mean it literally. For, contrary to all expectations, the Hitlerites in power also dreamed in their way of making the state wither away. Despite the legend, they believed no more than their rivals in infamy in the myth of the "totalitarian state." And, whether we like it or not, that myth is precisely absent from both the theory and the practice of the apostles of the *Führerprinzip*. It is of course true that the idea, invented by Carl Schmitt, was briefly prominent in the early thirties.[25] It can be found here and there in the work of a few young thinkers associated with Ernst Jünger and the very marginal Hanseatische Verlagsanstalt of Hamburg;[26] two works, but only two—*Das Werdende Reich* by Gerhardt Gunther, and *Dertotale Staat* by Ernst Forsthoff—give it a central position in their theorizing.[27] But certain historical truths are always forgotten. In this case, the fact that as soon as they were published, these two works were disavowed by the leading lights of the NSDAP. That with one voice, as early as 1934, they banned the very term from the language and from the Nazi political arsenal. That they were unanimous in seeing it as a danger and a trap—the trap which, they said, would destroy Stalin and Mussolini. And that, in the year the "Thousand Year Reich" was established, the year in which the definitive orthodoxy of the régime seemed to be fixed, when Wagner the anti-statist made his ceremonial entrance into the vaulted chambers of official palaces,[28]

Carl Schmitt and his disciples were already renegades, Adolf Hitler's "Trotskyites," the supporters of a deviation the high priests of the *Volksgeist* had been able to avert in time.

Alfred Rosenberg opened the attack in a resounding article published in January 1934, in which he proposed against Ernst Forsthoff the idea of a "total party"—a party that would rule the state, absorb it, and reduce it to the role of a mere instrument.[29] Then Roland Freisler, a few days later, again in opposition to the "total state," advanced the notion of a *Totalvolk*, a *total völkische Idee*, in other words, a totalitarianism based on the mystique of People, Soil, and Race.[30] Some time later, Wilhelm Stuckart gave the concept its *coup de grâce*, saying that its only function was to adorn the inconsistent chatterings of the "Italians" and "Romanians," and to spread confusion and ambiguity in the ranks of the true and pure revolution.[31] Stuckart, Freisler, and Rosenberg, the all-powerful "minister of *Weltanschauung*": the stakes must have been substantial for these three ideologues to enter the arena at once. Their texts are very learned, mobilizing all the worthy resources of Wagnerism and romantic vitalism.[32] The assault was harsh enough and conducted briskly enough for the formula gradually to disappear from works of propaganda.[33] In 1937, when Ernst Rudolf Huber, a former disciple of Schmitt, began to publish his monumental *Verfassungsrecht des Grossdeutschen Reiches* which was to be an authoritative text in the new Germany, he chose purely and simply to dodge the question.[34] And, as though to make himself better understood, as though to make *us* understand him better, to support his position he quoted this strong statement from the Führer: "The point of departure of National Socialist doctrine lies not in the state but in the People."[35]

The People and not the state? The opposition is not unusual. It recurs constantly in Hitler's speeches and in his policies. It is even the leitmotif of his strange "statism."[36] This is perhaps why, from 1933 to 1945, no one took the trouble to endow the new state with a new constitution. One might say that the Weimar constitution, never officially abrogated, continued through all circumstances to fulfill its modest function. Hence, in *Mein Kampf,* the poverty, the platitude, the awkward and forced tone of the chapter on the state, so different from the fiery, fervent style of the passages devoted to party or race. The question evidently hardly stirred the author—it was indeed only a "question," almost an academic assignment.[37] Finally, and most significant of all, this position is the source of the merciless battle which the Reich constantly waged, down to the final disaster, against its own army. Decapitated, degraded, divided, by 1933 it had disappeared from the political stage.[38] The following year, on the occasion of a test of strength with the Prussian SS, it lost the substance of its power and its *raison d'être:* the monopoly of legitimate violence.[39] The political education of recruits and the organization of the military reserve were taken away from it in 1939, on the eve of the outbreak of war, and assigned to paramilitary groups indirectly connected to the state apparatus.[40] To its *esprit de corps,* its sense of hierarchy and discipline forged by continuous loyalty to the German state in the period of formation, there was opposed the Spenglerian notion of a corps of legionnaires personally bound to the Führer, the new Roman Caesar. As with Stalin, the Party ruled the guns. As in 1793, it was the nation in arms against the armed state.

Most important, against the nation-state there stood a nation tirelessly making war against the institutions of the state. It is always said that the Nazi Party was a monolithic, monumental organization. What is striking, on the contrary, what struck Rauschning, for example,[41] was the extraordinary flexibility, the fluidity of its apparatuses and structures. Never had there been such a proliferation of divisions, local representations of power with infinite ramifications, in a complex tissue of cells and micropowers. Never had there been such a vigorous struggle, from the rank and file to the top and back again, against dead spaces and the risks of paralysis, against pockets of inertia and the rigidities of the mechanism. Every authority was accompanied by a counterpart, a counterauthority. Every *Gauleiter,* every obscure drudge, constantly moved from one place to another in the apparatus. Every organ of decision had its counter-organ, its supervising body.[42] Was this a mania for seeing plots everywhere, a phobia for intrigues? I am afraid that it was rather Bormann and Rudolf Hess inventing "self-management." Was it a concern for efficiency and rapidity of action? Rauschning says that it was more probably a matter of keeping the masses under pressure, in a state of alert and permanent revolution.[43] "The new state," prophesied Jünger, "will have no constitution."[44] No juridical constitution, as we have seen; but also no substance, no density of being, either. As though it were necessary continually to deconstruct it; as though, before Mao's or Pol Pot's, Adolf Hitler's state were already something to go beyond.

It had to be, and in fact it was, at least symbolically, as much as in socialist societies. As proof, or at least as evidence of this, we can cite the very particular status of the SS within the Third Reich. For here was an "élite" body, a pagan "knighthood," adulated by the régime, armed like no other body in the country, and yet having the peculiar characteristic (unlike the SA, for example) of never having bid for power.[45] This countersociety, this diabolical laboratory, crucible of the "new man," fully realized model of the future society, remained and was determined to remain at the fringes of the state, in its powerless reservation. And yet these SS Death's-Heads, these Antichrists of the German hell, were at the same time assured of a wide range of privileges—great areas of permitted illegality where they reigned unchallenged, sovereigns in their kingdom like priests in their temple of horror.[46] Moreover, it was to these outcasts, who claimed to prefigure the "empire of the final days"[47] and who were supposed to be shaped according to "eugenic" rules of selection and education, that was offered the supreme honor of ruling over the holy of holies, the concentration camps. Why the SS and not the Gestapo? Why these "irregulars" and not the state police?[48] And especially why the camps, those summits of Nazi frenzy? Because Auschwitz, directed by the SS Hoess, was perhaps the *exemplary* situation of a "new man" at the outposts of the "new age." Because this particular abominable conjunction was necessary in order to bear witness, outside the old world, though still in the world, to the blessed shape of the landscapes of the world of the future. Because this was—already outside the state though still at its edge—the living and enticing image of the messianic kingdom of the last days, when there would no longer be any state at all.

Anti-statism is once again, and unmistakably, a reversal that preserves intact the shape of what it overturns. Like all atheisms, religious hatred of the state is nothing but an exacerbated form of the denied religion. And this is why we must finally bring ourselves to listen differently to some contemporary notions and themes. For me, and for all those who, like me, refuse to wash their hands of the flesh the century has consumed in ashes and smoke, no doubt is possible. The question of the state, of the historical end of the state, is, for the moment, a barbarous one.

The King in Check

But the question has yet another form, which is less ignoble of course, but perhaps more insidious. Since the state, it is said, is an unavoidable fact, why not accept this state of affairs and adjust it so that it is in close harmony with the social bond? If it is impossible to destroy the state and have done with its necessity, is it unthinkable to rebuild it, to begin to change it, and to reverse its evil form? If by rejecting the state we rush toward servitude, is it not possible, by accepting it, to march toward freedom, for which the state would become the cradle and the creator of happiness? This is the question of all those who, fantasizing a "good" power, can imagine it controlled, subject to its subjects. It is the position of those who, proposing a "new relationship" between the rulers and the ruled, dream of a pattern in which the state would be popular, the people would legislate, the legislator would be everyone, and everyone would therefore be in power. It is the concrete project, apparently very seductive, of an "anti-Jacobin" socialism that sings to us of liberation to the tune of "self-management," "autonomy," "worker's councils," and "popular control." For my part, unfortunately, I am afraid particularly of finding in it another form of surrender, another face of the same delusion which always leads to the same misfortune, and closes off just as effectively the paths of resistance.

The history of this blockage is indeed a long one. We must attempt a return to the eighteenth century, in this case, in order to understand its lesson; to a certain kind of Rousseauism in which, at the turning point of modern times, the pattern of its necessity was established. To the heart of a theoretical drama, an unprecedented tragedy, a shattering and singular experience which Rousseau himself no doubt lived through. And I maintain that he has bequeathed to us, in the *Contrat social*, the stigmata of its mystery and passion. In the beginning, there was the slip of the pen. The one, for example, which made him compose the text of the chapter on "civil religion"[1] on the reverse side of the manuscript pages devoted to the legislator, and then, at the last minute, as though he were seized by a final scruple, to transpose it obscurely to the end of the work in a less glorious and almost clandestine appendix. The slip which, in the same passage, led him to give a dual response to Bayle and Warburton: to the former that "a State was never established which did not have Religion as a basis"; to the latter that "Christian law is . . . more harmful than useful to a strong constitution for the State."[2] Then there are the retractions—the puzzling deletions scattered through a book they bore into with their anxiety—which constantly refer to a hypothetical "divinity," a "democracy" that suddenly becomes terribly problematic. "It would take Gods to give laws to men,"[3] and, "if there were a People of gods, it would govern itself democratically."[4] Should these slips be dismissed? Should the deletions not be mentioned? Should we write them off, as is usually done, as incidental to the argument? I think they are too insistent not to be eloquent. The withdrawal of the divine is repeated too often to be meaningless. And the author of the *Profession de foi du Vicaire savoyard* is also too pious to be saying nothing in this case. What he is saying is perhaps this: the terrifying discovery of a heaven slipping away and suddenly undoing the millennial embrace that had tied it to the earth. It is the profession of a religion that indicates at the origin a broken bond, *but one that has been reconstituted,* and whose thread—on which until then had been hung dubious, improbable, and too human hierarchies—is snapped for good. It is the inability to conceive of the founding Revelation—only one, at least one—without which, since Moses, the Law has never been thinkable, and in the absence of which, nevertheless, it is necessary to continue to think. In other words, for the first time in the Judeo-Christian tradition, a philosopher recognized that the heavens toward which his thoughts continued to gravitate were empty and hollow; that the text which had always sanctified the language of authority was illegible. For the first time in the history of monotheism, speculation about the state forced itself to forget its decline, to forget the absent being that ruined it, to forget the idea which it rejected but which was alone able to anoint it with legality. Act I of the drama, the prelude to the journey—for which Jean-Jacques paid dearly in his own lifetime, for having made the attempt and followed the path to the end—was, a century before Nietzsche, the consciousness of what must indeed be called the historical death of God.

In the body of the book, in any case, the effects were soon felt, and there is no major concept that does not come out of the test undermined, stumbling, tinged with an improbability that threatens and invalidates it at the very moment when Rousseau attempts to establish it. For example, is the "general will" the infallible guide which makes certain that a politics does not go astray and that it joins with the good? "By itself," says Book II, "the People always wishes for the good, but by itself it does not always see it."[5] Is the law, as he constantly asserts, the supreme figure of freedom? A régime that places the law above men is simply "undiscoverable," as he agrees "ingenuously" in a letter to the elder Mirabeau.[6] Is democracy the ideal whose realization he called for? It was precisely an "ideal," as illusory as it was necessary, since "taking the term in the strict sense, a true democracy never existed and it will never exist."[7] Is it not at least a *regulating* ideal, a category of reason, unattainable to be sure, but continually postulated? In the *Lettres écrites de la montagne,* the postulate is fixed and frozen in the bitter observation that "the best government is an aristocracy."[8] The entire *Contrat social,* in fact, can be read first of all as the chronicle of a disappointment and the history of a formidable defeat. Instead of the model of community and transparency which is glimpsed occasionally, it is a demonstration of their implacable and insurmountable vanity. Instead of the perfect compact, established on the basis of principle and reason, seen by so many commentators, we find unsteady reason, undiscoverable principles, a suspicious compact uncertain of itself. Far from the proof of the superiority of the democratic form of government which two centuries have looked for, we find the proof of its profound, radical, theological impossibility. Jean-Jacques does not provide grounds for the existence of Right; he shows that it is nonexistent, incapable of transforming itself, crystallizing into a Fact. He does not solidify the foundations of the constitution of the secular state; rather, he shows how and why, in the age of a theology that escaped from every theoretical grasp, that constitution was unutterable—by definition and almost by vocation. He did not establish a new politics, but gave voice first of all to the crisis of the political realm as such, idol of the twilight, dead and tarnished star gently dissolving in the blur of its solstice. For in the second act of the drama—and this is the mark of his greatness—he comes face to face with the certainty that the idea of a "good" power as such is without meaning, and that, in the void left by the withdrawing gods, the very category of legitimacy—the legitimacy on which Hobbes could still rely—was discredited at one stroke.

The text, unfortunately, does not stop with this certainty; it does not remain long with this skeptical recognition. And it can be read a third way, as the narrative of a reconquest and an exactly inverse effort to break out of the dead end. For, after all, what is the problem? God is dead? This was hardly a surprise for anyone who had read Pascal, Meister Eckhart, and especially Luther, where the statement is explicitly set out. The news

had been known, thoroughly known by everyone, in the air ever
since the Middle Ages in the chapter on Calvary and the Resurrection of the most insignificant catechisms.[9] The catastrophe is
not a catastrophe provided one knows enough to interpret it in
its classic and liturgical sense of recognition—beneath the corpse
and the incarnation—of the form of the New God. The obstacle
is not insuperable, nor is the precedent of Hobbes insurmountable, for anyone who can set against the politics of sacrifice a
politics of Calvary, a political calvary, a new religion, a religion
of Politics. And this is in fact what Rousseau attempted. He laid
the cornerstones for this new religion. Before Nietzsche and
Marx, he diverted the tradition and played on the ambiguity of
the Christian formula. And, in a parody of resurrection, in a reversal of unparalleled audacity, he invented the dialectic with
which we have been living down to the present.[10] There is no
longer a theology on which to establish a good contract? That
doesn't matter, he says now; you will be "like gods," like gods in
power, all-powerful theocrats on the scale of the human race.
There is no longer any divine stock on which to graft a democracy? I will simply transplant the divine roots, restore and fix them
in human soil. There is no more Paradise or Referent on which
to base the social bond? The Referent is no concern of mine, for
I have built the holiest of altars to society, on which arises the
naked and monumental Host of the general will.[11] This Jean-
Jacques is no longer a disenchanted mystic; he speaks of politics
in the language of mysticism, a rediscovered mysticism, which is
triumphant because it is immanent. He does not give up transcendence; he changes its direction and transforms it until it is no
longer a boundary that sanctifies the law but a form that makes
it sacred.[12] He invents not only the profane state but the state of
fetishes, of icons, and of idols, of the goddess Reason in Robespierre's sense.[13] The *Contrat social* is not an anti-*Leviathan*, but
something entirely different—the replacement of the old process
of sublimation with a procedure that has no better name than
paganism. In political terms, this state which no longer has the

right to the ancient and defunct title of "legitimacy" has constantly, in the course of the succeeding two centuries, called itself "sovereign."

What then is this all too possible "sovereignty" to which Rousseau retreats? Instead of transcendence and movement toward heaven, it is perhaps the flat immanence of a circle, or better a spiral which, emptying its circles one by one as it rotates, creates a space for the servitude of each concrete person. There is first of all the circle of the individual, sometimes a natural phenomenon, a basic and initial fact, sometimes a pure artifact which the pagan state creates with its establishment.[14] This is a diabolical trick, to attribute a subjection that has been decreed to nature and thereby to cut off any recourse for the subjected being. There is the circle of the law—the law which no longer oppresses because it expresses nothing, by definition, but the will of the oppressed, and because through it they are taught to be free.[15] This is a brilliant construction, closing off all resistance, which is considered inhuman, deviant, and outside the law. Then there is the circle of the people, the new master-signifier, which is sometimes named "sovereign" inasmuch as it makes the laws, sometimes "state" inasmuch as it is subject to them.[16] Here we have a homonymy which, playing with the names for a single reality, decreeing that the ruler and the one who submits are identical, makes the "assembled people" a simple counterpart of the prince, encircled by and as it were displayed within the orbit of his will.[17] And finally, there is the circle of the prince, what Rousseau calls the "government," which is also equivocal because in one place[18] it is a simple "minister," an insignificant "officer," the contingent instrument of the general will, and in another[19] an active agent, a principle of cohesion that "brings together," "sets in motion," and "does in the body politic what the union of body and soul does in man." The metaphor is clear and perfectly Cartesian, making a banal "minister" into an authentic "substance," which arbitrarily fuses together the "accidental being"[20] of the contractual society—still a new

God who seals a fantastic conjunction from the outside. Individual, law, people, prince: all terms that, spun on the wheel of sovereignty and woven by paganism, become principles of despotism.

The individual in power? He is indeed, without doubt or deceit. But it is a strange power, which commands him to accept, to submit, and endlessly to control the circle of his chains. The people as legislator? There is no doubt about that either; the people is the incontestable author and subject-king of the law. But it is an accursed royalty, which creates happy slaves, forbidden to revolt, having forever surrendered the passion of the great refusal. The state is sovereign? There is no way in which it could be more so or in a stricter sense. But it is a sovereignty that, no matter which way you take it, no longer means for men anything but a blocking of those escape routes and external recourses that other contracts in the past had been able to leave open. For there is here an extraordinary difference from medieval law, the law of Rufin, for example, which, preferring to make power a simple divine "mission," limited in theory the power of the rulers and provided a basis in practice for the resistance of the people.[21] A great distance has been traveled since Manegold and that other social pact on which Rousseau probably drew, but which not so much bound the people to its prince as it bound both of them to God, ordering obedience from the prince to the omnipotence of the Law, and from the people insurrection against the great weakness of laws.[22] What a regression—the word is not too strong—in comparison to Beaumanoir, Simon de Montfort, Abbon de Reims,[23] and many other precursors, theoreticians of a bond that released the individual, of a pact that excluded the people even if they pledged obedience to it, of a political authority that, because it owed nothing to the human will of its subjects, was in principle dismissible and in fact frequently dismissed.[24] This distance, this regression was, as we shall soon see, the beginning of the method by which the "sacred" returned and stepped over, as it were, the long interval of monotheism. In this respect, the name of Rousseau and the internal contradictions of his work are of little importance. The point is the great lesson he unknowingly delivers. In abolishing for the first time the distance which, separating the subjects from the rulers, also separated their fates and left open to the subjects the appeal to heaven and to revolt, the theory of sovereignty creates subject-rulers who are still oppressed but are already oppressors.

The concrete results are staring us in the face. We hear them constantly here in the West as well as in the countries of the East. To give just one example among many: the celebrated "self-management," which is generally considered the liberal alternative to despotic socialism, but which appears in reality, in the light of these analyses, as fundamentally totalitarian. What in fact is "self-management"? It is first of all a theory of the state, thought of as a usurpation, a monstrous prelibation, an extortion of surplus value—not of labor but of power—which dissociates the "producer" from the "legislator" he contains within himself.[25] It is a doctrine of freedom that returns to the sender his lost letter, to the citizen-worker his confiscated surplus power, to the enslaved individual his sacred right to govern.[26] It is a project for autonomy in which, if words have any meaning, the position of sovereign is claimed for everyone only to make each one a boss, a cop, a judge.[27] A self-managed state, in this case, is a state in fragments, a state in each head, a state relieved of its function by thousands, millions of households and henchmen. Generalized self-management is the generalization of vigilance, surveillance, self-control. The model, the only model of a self-managed people, would be a people of inquisitors and thus also of suspects, as we saw, for example, at the time of the Baader affair in a Germany enflamed by a delirium of denunciation, a formidable demand for a state-substitute, an unprecedented fragmentation of the form of the state in individual minds, against which a liberal government in the end had to resist.[28] There are well-informed observers—taught by experience[29]—who say that, horror for horror, it is easier to breathe in the U.S.S.R. of the camps than in the Yugoslavia of communes and workers' councils, where fascism comes from below, rises from the "masses," and allows nothing to escape from its prophylactic madness. Nor is the Chinese cultural revolution far off, with its "management committees" and its "red sentinels"[30] who, *with complete sovereignty,* as the pure guardians of an effervescent legality, did indeed "self-manage" the tasks of repression and illustrate this absolute rule: that when power is disseminated, violence wins and the death instinct reigns. The pattern is not very far from that of the "withering away" of the state. And there is perhaps no "self-managed sovereignty" that does not also conclude with a dream of apocalypse and, practically speaking, of terrorism.

Self-management is also, it will be said more prosaically, a theory of the factory and industrial labor. Indeed; but again, what does this theory mean concretely? To listen to union officials, the work place is a version, a declension of the state, that must be "democratized," as the political order was democratized in the past. A democratized work place is a unit of production, a cell of power, tied to neighboring units and cells, which "correct, confront, and mutually control one another."[31] The same words again, that speak of freedom in the language of war, discipline, and the police. To listen to the red technocrats, efficiency experts, and specialists in "productivity," it is a technique—a simple operational technique—which presupposes that there is in any particular business a "collective decision-making body." This collective body is itself the place where the rigor and the constraints of the "plan" and the anarchy of the rank-and-file workers' initiatives are combined. Always the same dialectic, fundamentally Rousseauist, in which, since everyone collaborates with the order to which he is subject, no one can, with complete rigor, call himself or be called oppressed.[32] Finally—if we are to believe the politicians, creators of the ideal and prophets of utopia—the project is based on a general eschatology and a veritable philosophy. It proposes, it aims for a "society transparent to reason," in which some day a "postulated unity will be reconstituted."[33] Thus it really functions only as it is attached to the old fantasy of a final solution and a classless society, without disagreement, without difference. Once again we have the eminently totalitarian notion of a harmony of egotisms, a politics diluted in the pure management of souls, a society against the state, which makes itself into and wishes to be the state, merging entirely with the dismembered body of the state. Unfortunately, those who are chiefly concerned, I mean the workers, do not think like politicians or technocrats, still less like union officials. Leaving the dreamers to their dreams, wise men to their wisdom, and delegates to their delegations, they scorn a system in which, since everyone is for himself both "subject" and "substance," order reigns over the machines in the lubricated silence of an entirely too comfortable consensus. Fearing a "sovereignty" they suspect will be paid for by a new kind of policing of labor, repelled by a "freedom" which means, to speak clearly, the perpetuation of their unhappiness, they prefer to bet on the liquidation of the condition of the worker as such. And in the meantime to struggle, to resist step by step the slow death of daily degradation.

Thus the very idea of that struggle and that resistance must perhaps be reestablished on the basis of these remarks. Currently there is talk, in the name of some libertarian loyalty, of a merciless struggle against the political order, of resistance to its organizations and a deconstruction of its institutions. I say, on the contrary, that the political order is *also* the mirror in which are crystallized the obscure depths in each man that give birth to the executioner; and further, that hatred of the executioner, the wager against murder, the libertarian "spirit" itself, rethought and thoroughly understood, strictly demands a struggle for the political, but as a separate area of public performance. I have heard it said in various places that the major battle of the end of the twentieth century will consist in broadening, "enriching" democracy, in adding "content" and a new concreteness to its bourgeois, formal, and abstract freedoms. We must dare to answer, on the strength of a century of fascisms, that there has never yet been and no doubt never will be any democracy except formal democracy, any concrete freedom except through respect for its abstract forms, any broadened democracy except an authoritarian and fascistic democracy. And it is against that fascism, too, that I call for resistance by all those who are weary of preachers of enlightenment dismembering humanity even as they promise it salvation. Being on the "left," in these times of confusion, apparently means dreaming of a novel relation between the leaders and the led, planning to break their millennial externality, imagining systems of dispersion, of sanctions, and of representation that will be able to "restore power" to those who are excluded from it. My "left," the left that is close to me, says exactly the opposite: It wants power to be as distant and foreign as possible; it fights for exile and maximum externality. Do I dare to rely on what I think I know about the wishes of "simple people"? Everyone knows, in any case, that sheltered by rights but separated from power, they carve out of the body of laws areas of *illegality* and pleasure in living. That only a state based on rights, accepted in principle but scrupulously kept at a distance, allows a little room to breathe and sometimes to carve out, here and now, little islands of freedom. And that, in this case, it is no longer the state at all that is to be resisted but, more profoundly, more painfully, the state in men's minds, minds filled with the state, the ideal of the state in one's flesh and brain.

This distinction between the "state" and its "ideal" is simple, but I think it is decisive. For example, it allows us to explain the strange mystery which now surrounds the strategy of the communist parties in western Europe. The mysterious logic of the French communists, who are deeply familiar with and trained in the theory of the seizure of power and yet, since the end of World War II, seem to have been organized and programmed precisely *not* to seize it. The mystery of the Italian Communist Party, a conquering organization which, beginning in the sixties, has occupied the provinces of the peninsula one by one, reigns almost unchallenged in the streets and in men's hearts and yet, curiously, on each occasion seems to delay further the moment of reaching the top. And the case of the mysterious Santiago Carrillo, who devoted an entire book to proving that the seizure of power is no longer on the agenda, but, in its place, the "reversal of ideological structures," the "democratization" of the university or the press, the sanctimonious co-optation of religious, patriotic, and monarchist feelings.[34] I say that herein lies an enigma—and one that the old fogies of classical political science have not yet penetrated. I say that this is a turning point, probably entirely novel, and that we can understand nothing about it if we see it solely as tactical maneuver and pure hypocrisy. "Have the communists changed?" Yes, of course they have changed; even more than one might think. Unfeignedly and definitively. And they are quietly on the road to an authentic revolution. For what is changing in fact is, more than tactics, the very conception of action. From this point on, they are acting on the foundation of things: first of all, control over the rank and file, domination over men's minds, cultural hegemony, and thus the dissemination of models of submission. What is changing is, more than action, the meaning and the object of the will to political power. There is no point in controlling the machinery of the state when it is possible to be the source from which it derives its ideal. An "historical compromise" is a division of labor, in which the responsibility devolves on some, impotent at the summit, to execute the laws while they think they are legislating, and on others, eagerly waiting in the wings, to occupy the new position of tutor and prompter while they pretend to temporize. Better still, the "new communists" are carrying out an agonizing reappraisal of the definition of power as such. And perhaps we will stop asking the inept question of their "real desire," their real or presumed "intentions," on the day we understand that they are no longer the last professionals of the conquest of the political realm but the first specialists of the management of social life, and that the other side of this management is the generalized diffusion of sanctions, the flattening of the political to civil society, the perfect marriage of the organization and everyday life, in short, the perfected form of spiritual terror.

Here then, for those who repeatedly criticize me for my "primary anticommunism," we can perhaps find the formulation of a secondary anticommunism. What in effect makes it possible to suspect and condemn—as the extreme left does in Rome, Paris, and Madrid—this new line? Anti-Stalinism? There is no longer any question of Stalinism, a "Stalinism" that as such never existed, being a pure invention of the Marxists, a simple name to make horror banal and familiar, a theoretical trick that names the brute reality of the misdeeds of socialism a "deviation."[35] Anti-Marxism? We are far from Marxism, a Marxism that has also long ceased to exist, being a too pure invention of the Stalinists, a simple name to disguise horror and make it a little more dignified, a political fiction that puts a veneer of "science" over the flat reality of the banal madness of a police state.[36] The anti-Sovietism of the traditional right? Aside from the fact that, from Tirana to Phnom-Penh, there is no lack of examples of radical anti-Sovietism which, leading to an excess of crime and totalitarianism, makes the argument irrelevant,[37] I am no longer quite sure that we should consider the protestations of independence and the sometimes very real gestures of emancipation from Moscow on the part of the European parties as insignificant.[38] The usual argument about their internal liberalization? It does indeed seem that the new line of control of the provinces, cultural hegemony, and unofficial supervision of the official holders of power was applied for the first time precisely by the most hardline and least liberal of communist parties, a party from which the entire French left tremblingly expected a storming of the Winter Palace, while it was concerned only to gain control of some cities and to efface itself prudently behind the armed forces. I am referring to the Portuguese Communist Party, which I already considered the real inventor of Eurocommunism at the time of the revolution of the carnations.[39] For this is indeed the problem: Eurocommunism exists. It exists as it says it does.

It is nothing but the Leninist version of the theory of the sovereign—the most dangerous form, at the moment, of the dream of broadened democracy. And it is for that reason, and that alone, that we must resist it.

I wonder, then, if we should not search out and uproot all these models of sovereignty much further back, far beyond Stalin, Marx, and even Rousseau. All the mechanisms of submission—which oppress all the better because, deceiving their victims with an illusion of mastery, they begin by putting them in the shoes of their executioner and knit misery so solidly that the sufferer is at the center of his spiral of servitude—cannot fail to recall an ideal that is more than two thousand years old and to which this century, curiously, seems to be leading us back. I am speaking of the Greek ideal and the Greek reality of the citizen-magistrate and the city of princes which Fustel de Coulanges, for example, at the nadir of the Christian era, subjected to attack while he anticipated their imminent return. I am thinking of the admirable chapter in which, emphasizing the error which long made us believe that, in the "ancient city," the individual enjoyed "full and undivided freedom," he concludes paradoxically that "having political rights, appointing magistrates, being eligible to be archon" was not and will never be anything but a subtle form of enslavement.[40] I am also thinking of another text of about the same period, which is strikingly similar, in which Benjamin Constant opposed to the same "ancients" who made the "individual," who was "sovereign in public affairs," a "slave in private relations," the modern dream of a subject who is no longer "sovereign except in appearance," because he is "free" now, perfectly free in his everyday life.[41] I shall return at length to the details of this Greek model, to the fundamental totalitarianism that is its corollary, and to the dubious nostalgias with which it periodically provides us. But what seems clear to me, for the moment, is this old liberal lesson: There is no better definition of freedom than that of the "private" man; and being "private" means first and foremost being deprived of all power.

3

Liberal-Libertarian

Such a conclusion, I imagine, will disappoint lovers of striking novelties and philosophical brilliance. They will be surprised that so many words and detours have led so quickly to a worthy but banal lesson of prudence and good sense. It will be argued above all, and unfortunately with some justification, that Constant can hardly stand up to Marx, and that the folds of the banner are so worn, the liabilities so great, that one can hardly make an inheritance out of it with impunity. I agree. But certain things should be made clear. I have not brought myself to adopt this prudence and good sense without reservations; I shall not recite the lesson I have called upon as it stands, without imbuing it with the colors of the present. What is a new liberalism, a rethought liberalism, today, and what can it be tomorrow? What meaning can the slogan have, following the thread of its tradition, when we once more make it an urgent concern at the end of the twentieth century? It is this question, the question of this renewal and reshaping, that now concerns me and is enough to occupy me.

The answer is simple, provided one accepts the preceding arguments. What have I said, in effect, by showing that the prince is necessary and necessarily distant, separate, public? By show-

ing that he is inevitable, but fearsome at the same time if he sets
his weapons and his insignia in the minds of the people? By recognizing his claims, all his claims to express the Right, but by
denying his claim, his right to sovereignty? I have taken the opposite tack from that of the men of the heights who, planting everywhere the trees of their political vision of the world, conceal
from the men below the *maquis* of their own resistance. I have
adopted a point of view opposite to that of the potentates of happiness, who make their celebrated "power" into the golden key
to the gates of paradise, or, for the moment, of hell. I have established, in a word, that real freedom, the freedom of real men, is
not an affair of state; that if it is considered in that way, it goes
astray and we lose all chance of thinking it through. This means,
if you prefer, that the state as such has neither the dignity nor
the ignominy granted to it by its zealous supporters or its pas-
sionate detractors. The question of power is now no longer the
central question for all those who are determined finally to think
about the concrete misery of concrete subjects. It is not even a
question for all those who are determined to escape once and for
all from the traps of Hegelianism and its unavoidable twists and
turns. So, here is the first article of a consistent liberalism: An
attitude that wagers on something other than the political; a procedure that chooses to reduce the political to its simplest expression; a morality that decrees that the problem is secondary, derived, unessential. Wagering, choosing, decreeing. We have here
a deliberate reversal, a conversion of soul and vision, which deserts the ontology of the prince with which, in most great systems, philosophical concern culminates.

In speaking of ontology I do not mean, of course, that we must
forever desert the political debate itself, but that we must put it
in its place, restore it to its proper sphere—that of a contingent
debate subject to "true opinions," to a plain "doxography" in the
Platonic sense. In saying conversion of vision, I do not mean
blindness, nor a total refusal to see, but simply a refusal to confuse directions and genres, to treat as a "rigorous science" what

is in fact no more than one of those "high practical interests" which Husserl made the concern of "good sense."[1] In calling it a secondary problem, I do not mean that it is a matter of indifference, still less that it is trivial, for the question of the concrete form of the state to which we are subject is crucial in a sense, but precisely in the sense of law and institution rather than metaphysics and its ceremonial displays of reason. I speak of reducing the problem to its "simple expression." This is not to discredit it, but rather to describe the qualifications of the jurists, for example, who will resolve it. In fact, I don't know whether the sages who once a year present us with their "new" theories of the state and of power are right or wrong. I simply think that this is an example of magical thinking which, celebrating its mystery because they cannot elucidate it, never moves one step along the road to freedom. I know that against their powerful and subtle "ontopolitics" it is necessary to set, much more modestly, a *Realphilosophie* concerned with the "probable" far more than with the "true." In other words, I am sure of this second article of the liberal attitude: Replace the question of the best possible state with the question of a good or a better constitution.

The question of a good constitution presupposes in turn another type of reversal, which is also decisive and full of consequences. The sanction of the "good state" was the relationship it maintained with the will of its subjects; this sanction must disappear, and along with it any pertinence of the dialectic of the prince and his people. "Ontopolitics" argued spontaneously in terms of content, the content of power, material delegations of interests and desires. *Realphilosophie* will mean first of all the rejection of this procedure, a break with any thought concerned with content or matter, freedom thought of in terms of pure formalism. There is thus one way and only one of judging constitutions, and weighing one against another: through the relationship of the leaders, no longer to those they govern but to the pure form of the law in whose name they rule. A régime is not primarily popular or élitist, faithful or unfaithful to the wishes of

its constituents; it either has or does not have a symbolic reference, which simultaneously establishes it and limits its arbitrariness. The problem is no longer—as it was for Plato and Aristotle
as well as for Marx or Carl Schmitt—to know who will exercise
the dictatorship, but rather to conceive institutions so that the
leaders, good or bad, do the least damage and commit the fewest
ravages possible. A democratic constitution is not, as we still believe, the opposite of an aristocratic or oligarchic constitution; it
is the opposite of caprice, of the state of arbitrary decisions; it is
the form of the universal against the anti-legalism of leaders and
the blind terrorism of crowds.[2] The best régime is not the most
sovereign one, it is the one that prefers the ideal of justice to the
ideal of sovereignty—just and *legal* recourse when depotism
threatens. The least evil of princes is not the one who, his eye
fixed on the presumed source of his power, carries on a permanent plebiscite, but the one who, on the contrary, before returning to his subjects' cave, makes a detour through the law as the
principle of all authority and the source of all vision. I have borrowed the formulation of this third liberal article, this resolute
formalism, from Moses: The king will always carry the text of
the Torah with him, and his daily meditation of it will prevent
him from raising himself above the hearts of his subjects.[3]

Should one conclude that I am arguing for and supporting a
theocratic system? That would be jumping to conclusions, and
would indicate ignorance of the tradition on which I am relying.
For if words have any meaning and if the notion designates a
state in which God alone governs, through the intermediary of
princes, and in which the princes in turn are nothing but scribes
bowing before his injunctions, then monarchy according to the
Bible was the exact opposite of a theocratic régime. Its priests
were not, as is still believed, emissaries from heaven to this vale
of tears, but rather ambassadors of earth to the heavenly man-
sion. A veritable tribute paid to the Almighty, the priest was an
offering, in a sense a sacrifice, according to Deuteronomy, chosen from among the first-born of each Levite family.[4] Nor were

its kings, as they were in the French Ancien Régime, for example, God's lieutenants deputized by Him on earth, but delegates of men, entrusted by them with the beyond; the prince was moreover a tithe, the group's sacrificial offering. He is, says Jeremiah, the portion "consecrated" to God, the "first fruits of its labor."[5] The Torah itself is not the representation of an ideal, the code of a secular law, the model of a society whose verbose insubstantiality must be literally embodied in the substance of things. It is simply a model; nothing but an abstract model, the infinite in the finite, without a temporal boundary, refractory to everything and particularly to any idolatry. This is the deep meaning of the incredible story in Samuel[6] of the investiture of Saul, who could in fact govern only because God, at the outset, *refused to prescribe his Law.*[7] For it must be said, against Renan and Spinoza, that the Mosaic state is one in which God reigns only because he does not govern; it is a state with a Law holier than any history, and at the same time with a history that is never sanctified by the Law. It must be said especially against all the modern supporters of totalitarianism that a good constitution is one which, expressing only the good, refrains from willing *all* of it, and which—fourth principle—venerates the Law so much only because it is known to be strictly inapplicable. Therein lies a paradox, essential to biblical consciousness, whose details and consequences we shall consider in a moment.

In fact, contrary to received opinion, real theocrats are always recruited elsewhere, from among the murderers of God rather than his worshippers. Saint-Just, for example, who killed the absent God, that is God himself, only in order to make the Supreme Being the omnipresent governor of his "republican institutions," was, in the strict sense, a theocrat.[8] Marx and Nietzsche, who executed Christ only in order to realize him more fully, to resurrect him everywhere, in the body of the new man, on the ruins of the end of history or those of the eternal return, were also theocrats.[9] The terrorists of Germany and Italy, who chant "Neither God nor master" only in the name of a holier

God, a more divine master, a superstitious law whose text they tattoo and machine-gun on the flesh of their victims, are also theocrats.[10] If we call "theocratic" the will to confuse, to embody God in the world, then a revolutionary politics is always theocratic in nature; and it always, in practice, leads to barbarism. If, following the Bible, we name "monotheist" the will to disconnect, to disembody God from the world, then monotheism is the foundation, perhaps the only foundation for a politics which, forever incomplete, believing only in a good that constantly eludes our grasp, is another name for resistance. "Monotheist resistance" against "theocratic revolution"? A Christian might say that the whole question of politics comes down to the debate engaged through the centuries between Augustine and Joachim of Flora. The former, distinguishing between the City of God and the city of men, created contemplatives, never barbaric angels; the latter, confusing the two in a great messianic dream, caused thousands of men and women to be burned in his name on the stakes of the Apocalypse. A Jew would say, rather, that a Messiah is always, by definition, a false messiah, that is, an assassin; and that what is politically urgent is to distinguish between the Law understood as the motive force of history, and the law considered simply as the judge of its meanderings. In both cases, we have a fifth principle: Distinguish the rule of the "virtuator"[11] from the rule of the state based on rights; scrupulously disentangle the infinite demands of the Law from the finite prescriptions of murderous legality.

Hence a sixth principle, which will no doubt be surprising but which is rigorously derived from the preceding principles: A good constitution is one which, because it is concerned with rights, is totally indifferent to morality. I have heard, from various sources, that the distress of our age stems from the fact that the shepherds no longer offer their flocks a "social plan" or a great "mobilizing" project. Yet I fear nothing so much as a state which mobilizes, inflames the hearts of its subjects, dispenses them from the trouble of thinking, and then one fine day leads them like sleepwalkers along the paths of glory and concentration camps. It is commonly said that, if "the young" rebel and sometimes prefer a P-38 to the vote, this is the fault of the rulers who have failed to provide them with a "meaning to life" (that cliché). How is it possible not to see on the contrary that the rebels of old Europe are attacking an excess of meaning and values, and that an "alienated" life is not one which has a shortage but a surplus of ideals? We have to cease mouthing the absurd litany of the "crisis of civilization" and of those "ideals" that are supposed to have suddenly deserted an exhausted West. There has never been so much moralizing as in the century of Stalin and Hitler, the age of fanatics who, in the name of a morality of race, nation, or proletariat, treat men like dogs and carry on politics by committing murder. We must therefore give up the fashionable dream of finally reconciling politics and morality. For a moral politics, a political morality certainly exists; it exists everywhere in the world, and it is called "fascism" or, with more banality, "moral order." My ideal of the state, in other words, is a state without an ideal.[12] The least evil of régimes is the one which admits that it is totally incompetent with respect to those "fundamental values" in which despots always take such pride. And if, for example, I rejected the union of the left in France in 1978, it was neither from hatred for the "left" nor love for the "right," but from disgust with a politics which claimed to "change" a life that belongs only to me.

Once again, what does this really mean? The worst abuse of power is that of states which, in the name of their ideal, promise us delight. The greatest delusion is that of the new princes who, not satisfied with promising, sometimes offer peace and serenity. Contemporary barbarism no longer simply provides peace through suffering but offers us peace through happiness, and often prefers that path. Yes, happiness, slavery through happiness. It goes as far back as Saint-Just, this new idea of a happy, luxurious, and accepted servitude. Comte was saying nothing different when he reserved for his "servants of humanity" the dizziness of knowledge and the intoxication of suffering.[13] We all remember the terrible pronouncements of the Grand Inquisitor in *The Brothers Karamazov* and of Pyotr Stepanovitch at the end of *The Possessed:* "In Chigalevism, there will be no more desire. We will keep desire and suffering for ourselves. The slaves will have Chigalevism."[14] And there is Alexander Zinoviev to remind us once again that the model is flourishing in Soviet Russia, in which the sovietized masses find satisfaction in oppression and in the big sleep of the soul that is its corollary.[15] In fact, the entire modern age has probably done nothing but reiterate the lesson of this pleasant slavery: Give up your soul, surrender your desire, that useless burden, that luxury which is ruining you, and you will have in exchange pleasure through the institution. The entire West has probably dreamed the same dream from the very beginning, as the famous passage from the *Nichomachean Ethics* indicated: To the question of discovering what is the science and the architectonics of happiness, Aristotle answered, at the end of the inquiry, that it could only be politics.[16] Which gives us yet another reason for establishing, against this infamous exchange, a seventh and final principle: A state without an ideal is first of all one that has given up the ideal of beatitude, and the best constitution is the one that decrees that happiness is a totalitarian idea.

It is clear that the formulation is simultaneously very close to and very distant from those of Constant and Fustel. Very close because of the constant concern to *minimize the political;* the democratic state is a minimal state, the state which is the least state possible. It is also very distant, with the appearance—along with the refusal to weld morality and politics and the mistrust of organizations that think through our heads—of the sign of a tradition I would call "libertarian" if the word did not have what appear to me to be distressing connotations. Liberal or libertarian? I have attempted nothing in this chapter but to join together two traditions which everything separates except etymology. "Liberal-libertarian"—this is the name we should give to a poltical approach that excludes politics from the essential and reduces it, as Gorky said,[17] to an insignificant "emotion," which "resembles base physical necessities, with the disagreeable difference that political necessities are unavoidably accomplished in public." For we know now that the only state worth anything is the one which, firmly maintaining its monopoly of *law*, abandons to its subjects the responsibility for *meaning*. The only democracy that can stand is one which, inflexible on the laws, permits values to flow from ordinary people. The only philosophy that can stand and is worth anything is one which, drawing all the conclusions from this ebb, will bring tiself to make one more wager, to accept a final conversion of vision that will make the intellectual from now on a man of the depths, an "underground thinker," changing his point of view, adopting other perspectives—those of the individual and his singular conception of the world. Which can be said in another way, parodying the famous expression: Limit politics to make room for ethics.

Resist the Plebs

Yet we must agree on the definition of this underground. There is another cliché, in fact—perhaps the most persistent of all—which makes the "People" the correct name for those below and the blessed source of all legitimacy. It is enough, it seems, to have the grace of a "mass" movement, for all values to collapse and the worst barbarism suddenly to take on an aura of sanctity.[1] We are even told of the divine "plebs," real or imaginary, who crystallize in their glory all the ruined attributes of the defunct proletariat and bring them to the incandescence of a just "rebellion." But I say that that too is a final deception and another master-signifier; the pivot of political idolatry, perhaps, of its closing off of ethics and the principles of freedom; and the surest way, paradoxically, of avoiding, of walling off the underground of the will where different forms of resistance are feeling their way and thinking themselves through. And I wonder, in that case, whether the first right from below, the first right of man, is not to resist that people too, that mass, those plebs whom the century has praised so much.

Sacrilege? But listen to the masters of the earth and the paeans they sing in honor of their good *People*. Hear how they insistently, on the right as well as the left, praise the plebeian coronation which, they say, made them kings. Notice the efforts they make, however deadly they may be, to call on the name of the People while the victims scream in the torture chambers. Isn't it strange that they are so intent on assuring us that all those massacres and infamies were perpetrated in front of the "masses" and for their greatest "good"? Is it enough to answer that they are lying, these assassins, when they all act with the same zeal to assert their deception and sometimes even (why not?) to deceive themselves? No, this is a symptom which has to be treated as such, for it is too consistent not to be eloquent. Here we are touching on a law which, unwritten though it may be, is nevertheless exemplary and characteristic of the modern era. This law seems to say that the People, as such, is the source and the principle, the referent and the horizon of every power worthy of existing and worthy of being believed. That a state, any state, before being democratic, oligarchic, or totalitarian, is always and first of all, necessarily and by definition, a "popular" state, which draws the justification for its eminence from the People and the People alone. That this People is not therefore a crude reality antedating its use, but the title and the coat of arms of leaders who can no more refuse its baptism than their ancestors could in the past avoid divine anointment.[2] Suppose the People, in that case, rather than Leviathan, were the God of the twentieth century. And suppose the People, rather than the Marxist Party, were the undiscoverable "modern prince." What is certain is that its blessed name, chanted in every language, hammered out in every war, echoing from hecatomb to hecatomb, is like a talisman over which the great family of executioners struggles savagely, and that this is a disturbing sign, a very real problem, which we cannot claim to sidestep as a simple effect of deception or "ideology."

The problem is all the more real because it is not only implicit. Intellectual historians know that it was in fact written about in the past, at the dawn of modernity, by the handful of thinkers in the seventeenth and eighteenth centuries who attempted to think about the puzzle of human power. We can find it explicitly in Hobbes, for example, in the fragment of *De cive* in which he declares that "the People is what I call the Sovereign," that it is therefore nothing but a "name," an arbitrary decree, an artifice or artifact invented by the theoretician to characterize the social bond.[3] It can also be found in Grotius, Marsilius of Padua, and Jurieu,[4] all three of whom were unanimous in repeating the mysterious tautology that "the sovereignty of the People is exercised by the Sovereign,"[5] that the former makes the latter, and in turn the latter makes the former, in an unending circle within which a single gesture, a dual and simultaneous release, establishes the "Master" and, along with him, the "assembled multitude." We find it again in Rousseau, when it takes on its full brilliance with the doctrine of "sovereignty," of which the "general will" is not, as we have seen, the necessary condition but the corollary—less a part, a member, or an organ of the real social body than the body in person, the body in majesty, provided it is looked at from the viewpoint of its cohesion and harmony. What appears in each case, if we raise ourselves above the political philosophy of which, whether we like it or not, we are the unreflecting heirs, is the unprecedented concept of a "People" suddenly arising in history in the place long occupied by "God," "King," or even the "simple folk." But it has the curious and decisive particularity of not being, as they are, empirically identifiable and identified. Of existing, in fact, only by convention or arbitrarily. Of being literally, as a consequence, a pure institution.

What purpose can be served by this far from banal institution? Without dwelling on the details of texts or labyrinths of theories, it is possible to observe the same sophism in all of them, which provides their real unifying thread. From the fact that the People is first of all "what one calls the Sovereign," it follows mechanically that it has to be granted a "body"—and this is what is meant by the famous frontispiece of the first edition of Hobbes's *Leviathan*. From the fact that it is a "body," we must next conclude that it is endowed with "will," that this "will" is "single," that it moves the body with a single movement—and this is the meaning, of course, of the most famous metaphors of Rousseau's *Contrat social*. From this single will is derived in turn the demand, indeed the necessity, for an "officer" who is no longer distinct from the "will" he administers but forms one body with the body in which he is incarnated—and this is the reason why the entire eighteenth century, in its despotic as much as in its democratic side, never stopped dreaming of a "power" residing in, inhabiting its "sovereign." From this residence, finally, from this substantial joining together, it follows that the People is nothing but another name for the prince, the torso and the head of the king, the real and dilated image of his body and his soul, on whom it confers by this token, and in this case with complete rigor, the evident attribute of omnipotent excellence. A miraculous answer to the perennial puzzle of politics, the People realizes the dream of the leaders to govern their subjects with their tacit consent, if not their enthusiasm. A final solution to the insoluble equation, it is what allows the shepherd to say: I, who lead them to pasture, am identical to my flock. Free or enslaved? A pure mirror of the state, a simple mechanism of power, the People was born first of all as the fantastic principle of order, which dissolves all resistance in the heavy silence of the human herd.

On this basis, we could reread John Locke's *Second Treatise,* which a stubborn tradition has presented for two centuries as the charter and the Bible for the rights of man in the modern sense. Does he speak of a "law of nature" in which these rights can be rooted and on which their legitimacy can be based? That law never finds its expression and its appropriate location in the individual but in the community.[6] Does he sketch the portrait of a "reasonable" creature, capable of "judgment," instead of the submission fostered by dictatorship? This is more the portrait of the "majority"[7] than of the men who make it up and who have, once and for all, surrendered their powers to it.[8] Does he evoke the possibility of a supreme "arbitration," an "appeal" to the justice of "heaven," a resistance against the powerful when they betray the "trust"[9] they have been given? This concerns the community again, *always* the community, for it alone has the duty to decide and, sometimes, to rebel.[10] Is the situation different for the inalienable right to life, to integrity of the body, or even the right of "property," in which it is customary to see, whether it is praised or deplored, the sign of a "possessive individualism"?[11] Here again passages abound in which this right is not attributed to the individual as such but paradoxically to the "group,"[12] the only representative, once again, of the Eternal Law.[13] What then of the "private person" when injustice strikes him and when, in a "religious struggle," for example, he has "lost his wealth"?[14] He should hesitate for a long time, the philosopher recommends, before rebelling, for the ignorant individual must know that a misfortune is of no importance unless it "moves the People," and that the "People" in its wisdom is hardly troubled by private calamities.[15] If he nevertheless persists in demanding what is his and proclaiming abroad his vain and noisy suffering, he should not be surprised if, threatened in its vital interests, the "greatest number" represses him, dominates his insignificant rebellion, and even uses "Force" to overcome his sedition.[16] John Locke, it is clear, may very well be the thinker of habeas corpus, but he really only recognizes a "body" in the "community." He grants the dignity of subject only to the abstract "majority," in which "ambition," "pride," and "turbulence" disappear.[17] As a child of his century and of a philosophy of the "People," he could see in the individual man only a semi-creature, a zero degree of humanity, despatched without warning to the fringes of illegality where, along with beggars and vagabonds, all the rejects of the society of Reason swarm.[18]

The fact remains, of course, that the *Treatise* as a whole cannot be reduced to this coercive pattern. It also contains the very precious rudiments of a theory of the rights of man. Like all the philosophers of the following century, Locke was unconsciously torn by a basic ambiguity in which the salvation of the subject is probably at stake. Far from denying this and condemning the "Enlightenment" in toto, I am now arguing for a new judgment and a critical inventory. But an inventory and a development of the legacy that go directly contrary to the tradition and to received opinion. Against the experts of the philosophical police who distinguish, for example, the "good" Rousseau of the *Contrat social* from the "bad" Rousseau of the *Rêveries*, I choose the latter because, peremptorily asserting the suffering and the odyssey of a soul, he seems to me closer, more attentive to the mute voices of the rabble. Contrary to the classic interpretation, which praises the Enlightenment for having permanently established a doctrine of the "Sovereign" on which politics can stand, I see this rather as its most subtle curse, by which, behind the mask of freedom, perennial existence is assured for the millennial slavery of the humble, heads bowed before the altar of the atheist state. Far from seeing in their ethics or their "religion"—in Voltaire's "tolerance" or Diderot's diffuse religiosity, in Montesquieu's *Carnets* or Locke's "appeal to heaven"—remnants, echoes, anachronistic fragments of the old world, I see these as the essence of what they contributed to us, the essence of what is left to us who are so defenseless in the face of the triumphs of barbarism. To the question of what must be kept and what must be discarded in "possessive" and "bourgeois" individualism, the only answer that stands, and stands in the face of the horror, is the opposite of what is always said: Yes to everything that saves, that allows a body to be spared; No to everything that preserves and guarantees the body of the People; Yes to everything that protects and conserves the consciousness of the subject; No to everything that combats and reduces the egotism of a soul. Where are the "progressives"? Where the "reactionaries"? If words have any meaning, what made for progress in the eighteenth century was precisely its bourgeois element, including the notorious and infamous "right to property" which is, as we shall see, the only possible prop for an inner life. And the century is reactionary precisely in what is usually praised and glorified: that "popular will" which, from 1793 to Stalin, dictators have adored.

"What does the people want?" This was the very question Hérault asked Hanriot during the night of June 2, 1793, on the eve of the arrest and assassination of the Girondins. "The people," answered Hanriot, "wants to be handed twenty-two guilty men." And the guilty were handed over, sacrificed to the divine will, under the threat of guns but also in the shadow of the assurances of the philosophy of the sovereign.[19] And yet, Isnard had argued, doesn't "Reason" demand more moderation, more respect perhaps, if not for the Assembly, at least for the life of its members? The Assembly, concluded Hérault,[20] knows that "the force of Reason and the force of the People are the same thing," and that it suffices that the People speak, that it "ask for a magistrate," for the "representatives of the people" to comply, to *execute* the guilty, and offer them to the popular "thirst." It is no longer enough in this instance to say that real fascism operates from below as much as from above and that it never tires of urging the masses to assault institutions. We must specify that its power is so absolutely murderous only because, in the minds of the participants, there is no longer either "above" or "below" at all, and because the summits of "Reason"—Isnard's poor "Reason"—have suddenly collapsed into the abyss of plebeian "force." Laurent Dispot has admirably described the pattern of this "machine of terror," born with the Montagne, in which the energy drawn from below is continuously changed into terrorist heat at the summit.[21] We should perhaps add that the mechanism would not work so well if the source and the estuary were not confused, if those who go in and those who go out were not, as Hérault said, "the same thing"; if the masses, in a word, were not themselves the machine, the whole machine, nothing but the machine, the bloody and monstrous crucible of totalitarian alchemy. As for Stalin, fabricating an "opposition" which was the negative image of his proletariat, and for Hitler, too, unceasingly creating the "Jew" as the inverse image of his *Volk*,[22] the clogged body of the "People" according to Hérault and Hanriot is no longer satisfied with repressing, with blocking resistance. It strives instead to create division, to generate factions, to exhibit still more monsters which it immediately, in the same movement, hastens to hurl into the darkness of counterrevolutionary hell. In this respect it is the first model of the great barbaric universals which have continued, ever since, to torment the world.

An extreme case? Yes indeed. Then here is another one, closer and more anodyne. There are two UN treaties which codify human rights on the international level. One concerns "civil and political" rights; the other, "economic, social, and cultural" rights. Curiously, both begin with the same article: "All peoples have the right of self-determination."[23] Practically speaking, what does that mean? What is implied by this *first* right, "in virtue of which," we are told, all those that follow have validity? Why this order, this priority, and is it without meaning? What it says, in reality, is that there is no "civil," "social," or "political" freedom that does not pale before the brilliance of the "Freedom" and the "Autonomy" of the "People as a whole." What this conceals is that this autonomy itself, which the diplomats call "independence" and which parenthetically always presupposes a strengthening of the power of the state, has become the condition, the unconditioned foundation for the satisfaction of ordinary people. And what this posits, without really admitting it, is the frightening axiom that freedom *of* the social body—with all that that implies of blind nationalism, political infantilism, and military or police vigilance—precedes, logically as well as chronologically, freedom *in* the social body, the very freedom which nevertheless affects real individuals in the depths of their being. And the conclusion of all this, quite naturally, is that hunger, poverty, torture, and the infamy of everyday life are of little importance when the victims come together as a People that is struggling "heroically" for "free self-determination." It is easy to recognize here the argument of the red czars who have reigned since Lenin over the slaughterhouses of the new Russia; the practice of the Chinese "helmsmen" whose famous slogan about

"the states that want independence, the nations that want freedom, the peoples that want revolution" forgets to evoke only the
will of concrete men and women; the alibi of innumerable post-
colonial dictators who, because the People finds it so difficult to
liberate itself from such long-lasting dependence, always put off
until tomorrow, a tomorrow that never comes, the granting of
real "privileges" to those men and women. The strange standard, finally, which allows our experts on the "left" to weigh—
to "relativize" as they say—the violations of human rights in
Vietnam or Cambodia, where everyone should know, for heav-
en's sake, that history forms a pattern whose stages are established in the fixed order that moves from the People to its subjects.[24] It is always, in fact, the old murderous sophism, adopted
from the Enlightenment, barely modified for present taste,
which thus accedes to the ultimate consecration of international
law.

Besides, do our specialists in progressivism know that their
"right of peoples to self-determination" has still another pedigree, an even more shameful one, if that were possible? Do they
know that it was also, for at least seven years, the basis of Nazi
foreign policy, which has too often been reduced to the banality
of a search for *Lebensraum?* [25] Why don't they read Haushofer,[26]
for example, the Führer's tutor in the subject, who, not satisfied
with proclaiming the principle, went on to theorize it with a proliferation of subtleties which, I am sure, would turn them pale
with admiration? They would find, first of all,[27] a strong geopo-
litical conception of the world, divided, as is only proper, between "cells of revolution" (Germany, Italy) and "fragmentary
spaces" (central and eastern Europe). They would learn that the
least important "People," however backward it might be, however impoverished, has an "inalienable right" to determine its
own fate. They would nevertheless hear the voice of wisdom explain that "right" is not "power," and that each people unfortunately does not have an "equal capacity" to realize its preroga-
tive. They would understand, then, why the Transylvanians, for

example, can, in virtue of their "right," escape from Romanian rule but must, because of their "incapacity," be attached to Hungary. Why, in the name of the same subtle dialectic the Crimeans or the Czechs of Bohemia are entitled to secede, but also, with the same necessity, should join the German nation. How, again, the perennial problem of the Ukraine, that "skeleton in the closet," will finally be solved on the day when it is subjected to the formula dear to the German Sering[28]—but also (by accident?) to the Georgian Stalin—of a federation of peoples gravitating around a single kernel, which will sovereignly guarantee the "independence'" of the "small nations." We could go on forever enumerating examples and being enraptured by such wonders. There is not a problem of the planet to which Haushofer, on the basis of his simple principles, did not have an immediate answer. There is no disorder in the absurd puzzle of the world which is not ordered and arranged when the magic wand strikes. Everything, absolutely everything, falls into order when we are among ourselves, that is, among peoples, and when we have expelled from the stage those perpetual troublemakers, men of flesh and blood. Chamberlain and Daladier allowed themselves to be taken in, one morning in the summer of 1938 in Munich, when they met a Hitler who was very sure of himself and who claimed for the Sudeten "people" the inalienable right to "self-determination."

It would have been in bad taste, in any case, for them to have appeared surprised, since it was already so clear that the man they were confronting was effectively an unmatched leader of peoples. These "pacifists" knew very well that at the moment when they were coming to terms with the rising barbarism, this barbarism was another name for a formidable popular fervor that had inflamed millions in the service of their Führer. Everyone knew that this Führer was serving not so much the interests of a state which had been mortified by iniquitous treaties as the passion of a *Volk*—made of blood and soil, of space and memory—which, thanks to him, was attaining to its mystical truth after so many "romantics" had sung its useless glory. Churchill himself, the "old lion," the future symbol of resistance, recognized this in the incredible open letter he addressed to Hitler in the *Sunday Times*, in which he wrote, in August 1937, that "if England were to experience a misfortune similar to that of Germany in 1918, I would pray God that He send us a man with a strength of will and spirit equal to yours."[29] It was not so very much earlier that the National Socialist leaders had been in the vanguard of the regenerated workers' movement, tough, pure spearheads of the great Berlin strikes they supported so ardently that they momentarily lost the backing of the bourgeoisie, terrified by these "Girondins" who were incapable of controlling the mass movement from below.[30] Everyone remembered their attitude toward the peasant insurrections of the west coast of Schleswig-Holstein, when they joined ranks with the hordes of rebels marching on the cities, flourishing the black flag with its red sword and white cart as a coat of arms, behind Claus Heim, their charismatic leader.[31] How could we forget that it was to support the peasants that the NSDAP established its first major regional newspaper, the only one at the time?[32] How can we consider it insignificant that, in the committee established in 1930 for the liberation of Heim, Nazis were shoulder to shoulder with the communists?[33] How is it possible not to think of a Hitlerite version of Engels's *Peasant War in Germany* when we read the epic narrative of the whole adventure presented by Ernst von Salomon in *Der Stadt?*[34] The fact is that when Helmut Plaas speaks of "converting" popular energy to the "service of the nation" while fearing that this "conversion" might "cripple" it,[35] we are still very close to Saint-Just's "machine of terror" and his "the revolution is frozen." And we must at least admit that the Nazis too, for our sins, undertook the terrible and deadly experiment of great popular uprisings and government of the People, by the People, and for the People.

In the face of this experience and its implacable lessons, one

can only be overcome, and it becomes urgent to rectify a few slogans. Is it certain, for example, that "the eye of the masses sees
clearly" and that truth always comes from their vision? What is
certain is that this was the opinion of Niekisch, who saw in the
plebs a "new imperial figure," and the opinion of Hitler himself
in his closing speech at the Parteistag in 1935, when he "recognized in the people what lasts and what is."[36] Can we continue,
as though nothing had happened, to proclaim that "service of the
People" is the aim and the standard of all politics? This was
again the Führer's conviction in the "secret memorandum" addressed to Goering in 1936, and it was shared by Goebbels, the
Strasser brothers, and Rosenberg, who all swore by the *Volk-
stum* of Hölderlin, Schlegel, and Wagner.[37] Could it be that this
Volk was an evil people, born good but everywhere in error,
after diabolical leaders had turned it away from its vocation? It
would be very difficult to find a "better" one, in those strange
years when the Communist Party had nothing better to do than
to fight with the Nazis for the same voters, the same mass base,
in the same factory movements, and on the same picket lines—[38]
in November 1932, a "unity of action" that was so close it led, in
action, to an authentic *popular front!*[39] Should we assume, then,
that in every case we are dealing with disarmed masses, already
broken by repression, whose fighting spirit had already been
ruined by the decline of Marxism? This is easily said, far too
easily, when we know that on the contrary it was almost always
under the influence of Strasser's gang leaders that the German
workers' movement, dismembered by the failure of Spartakism,
regained its radicalism, militant preparation, and training for
armed struggle, which had been refused to it by the communist
bosses and the great social democratic organizations.[40] It is
enough to read the first pages of Goebbels's *Kampf um Berlin*[41]
to understand how, with their "extremely proletarian character," their "constant revolutionary élan," and their strange madness as well, in which were mingled workerism, nationalism,

and class struggle, the SA of Prussia so quickly removed the political "superego," the heavy Marxist chains that had for long forbidden the masses to rebel.

But are they not, as they say, "always right" to rebel? In fact, I am afraid not, for the unleashed crowds which, from Silesia to Württemberg, acclaimed the swastika were indeed rebelling, and from the progress of this rebellion, "preached ceaselessly, hatefully, systematically, pitilessly," as Jünger wished,[42] came nothing but convoys of the dying and piles of gassed flesh. It is beginning to be admitted today that Hitler in his youth was secretly subjugated by a "scientific" Marxism whose traces can be found in his entire conception of society;[43] that between the two families the border was so fuzzy, so permeable, that it is impossible to count the number of communists who moved discreetly to the SA, or of SA who moved noisily to the KPD, not to mention the waverers endlessly drifting in both directions;[44] that, finally, these crossings, these back and forth movements gave rise to strange bridges, political monsters with baroque but eloquent names: "national communists," "conservative revolutionaries," "national bolsheviks," grouped around minuscule journals, youth organizations, or agitation committees.[45] What is less well known is that these were not colorful and marginal grouplets but the vital source, the matrix of the movement. It was in fact in these obscure circles, in which, as early as the twenties, former members of the Freikorps foretold the German-Soviet pact,[46] that most of the future leading lights underwent the greater part of their political and ideological apprenticeship.[47] Contrary to legend, Hitler himself did not build his own party; this was done by "complete Marxists," as he once said,[48] by "heartfelt Bolsheviks," as they proclaimed themselves,[49] Otto and Gregor Strasser, unrepentant Leninists, admirers of the U.S.S.R., expelled only in 1932 after they had irrevocably drawn toward the Nazi machine the great rumbling of the streets.[50] The strict truth obliges us to agree, in other words, that National Socialism was born red and on the left, like most of the fascisms of this century.

Once again accepted opinion, which claims that it disguised real management of capital under the colors of socialism, is false; the German liberal press in the thirties was closer to the truth when it deplored, on the contrary, the fact that a thin nationalist veneer covered the tidal wave of a triumphant mass movement.[51] And we can no longer repeat that Marx was wrong to foresee revolution in Germany. He wasn't wrong at all, since the revolution in fact took place there and it changed, as Goebbels said, "the relations of men to each other, and the relations of men to the state and to the question of existence."[52] He was so little wrong that it succeeded as well nowhere else, it never inflamed hearts so much, never so galvanized a people in rebellion; he simply forgot to tell us that this people in rebellion would bring death to the world and put Europe to fire and the sword.

We should therefore not be surprised that, beyond Marxism and Stalinism, in which it never ceased to see its implacable rival, Hitlerism went further, deeper still into the memory of peoples to find the source and the model for its unprecedented revolution. Referring to the little known episode of the Shleswig-Holstein riots, I said that with *Der Stadt* Ernst von Salomon had given the movement its *Peasant War*. I might have said in reality, and not at all metaphorically, that there is in Rosenberg's *Der Mythus des 20. Jahrhunderts* an insistent echo of the "peasant war" itself, the war of the vagabonds whose memory has been immortalized by Marx, Engels, and their followers. It contains an entire chapter, in effect, in which the minister of *Weltanschauung* extols the Beghards and Béguines, the "brothers of the free spirit," the Rheno-Flemish mystics, and Thomas Münzer in particular: yes, Münzer in person, the Anabaptist rebel decapitated in 1525 for having simultaneously confronted civil and religious power.[53] The book contains, as in Chamberlain and Hitler, many references to the apocalyptic tradition that inflamed all of medieval Europe for four centuries, at the time when humble brigands rebelled against the powerful in the name of the Heavenly City and its imminent coming, in the

name also of an ardent egalitarianism very close to the communist dream. How can we not think of those medieval insurrections and the traces they left in the German collective memory
when we see the Hitler youth, whose role in the adventure we
know to have been decisive, christening themselves "migrant
birds," "white knights," "free German spirits," "pathfinders,"
or "league of vagabonds"?[54] Didn't anti-Semitism itself have solid roots in the annals of the Crusades when, as the chroniclers
relate, one never left for the Holy Land without first taking the
head of a Jew in Mainz, Hanover, or Berlin?[55] Who invented
the pogroms if not these vagabonds, these rebels, whom I am
perfectly willing to accept as heroes on the condition that we not
forget that their wild wandering, their senseless nomadism, was
punctuated by the burning of synagogues? In fact, and at the
risk of shocking, I believe that we could reread all of Nazi propaganda in the light of those "terrors" whose splendid and popular legend we are sometimes asked to admire.

Thus, for example, when Hitler made his hatred of the Jew
into the "Lord's own battle,"[56] and Goering, in parallel fashion,
saw in the children of the Bible the "figure of Antichrist,"[57] they
were not thinking of Gobineau, nor even only of Richard Wagner, but also, beyond him, of the millenarian tradition whose vocabulary they adopted. In the trials of Catholic priests convicted
for "immorality" or "illicit currency dealings," we can certainly
hear an echo of the Moscow trials, but also, more probably, an
echo of the "flagellants" of the twelfth century accusing the cler-
gy, already, of lucre and simony, the two weapons of the plot to
delay the coming of the "Emperor of the Last Days."[58] The image of this "emperor," of this "just and pious" king whom all of
heretical Christendom awaited with such fervor,[59] returned to
haunt the diseased mind of Chamberlain when he claimed, as
early as 1924, to recognize in Hitler the new messiah appointed
by fate, like the *novus rex* of the past, to take up again the fallen
scepter of Frederick and William.[60] In Rosenberg's writings,
Hitler became a leader of war and faith who would be able to

restore the brilliance of ancient Teutonic culture,[61] and this is, almost word for word, the description given in the *Book of a Hundred Chapters*—a fourteenth-century work attributed by legend to a mysterious "revolutionary of the upper Rhine."[62] In the *Book with a Hundred Chapters* one can read, along the way, a demonstration of the "election" of the German people, of the German nationality of Adam, and of the late appearance, after Babel, of the Hebrew language—all themes whose future existence on the fringes of the death camps is only too well known. The very name of the Third Reich and its promise of the "millennium" could not fail to evoke, for a moderately educated German, the prophecy of the "three ages of the world" and the *evengilium aeternium,* the idea of which the Franciscan monks took from Joachim of Flora to disseminate through the rebellious countryside.[63] We will understand nothing—as Europe, in fact, understood nothing—about the mad expansion of the Reich if we persist in diagnosing it as a classic nationalistic paranoia that made Hitler a natural child of Bismarck, while, beyond Bismarck, he was dreaming of the Holy Roman and Germanic Empire which was still, and had been for so long, the supposed end of messianic expectation.[64] When, after the *Anschluss,* he insisted on having the Empire's emblems presented to him, he knew perfectly well what archaisms he was resurrecting, to what authentically plebeian utopias he was enjoining his real People to come for nourishment.

We can see, at this point of madness and horror, the distance that has been covered since modernity in its beginnings discovered the glories of the collective. In fact, this totalitarian People, having moved imperceptibly from the history of ideas to an idea in history, is no longer what theoreticians presupposed in order to give their discourse meaning, but what leaders endow themselves with to serve as an object for their will. It is no longer satisfied, as in the Rousseau of the *Contrat social,* with denying Man in man, that is, that in each man which makes resistance possible; rather, it exalts the inhuman in the human, that is, that

in the subject which makes him capable of killing. It is no longer, as in Grotius and Jurieu, a pure institution, that is, finally a
form, but form pushed to its truth, to the extremity of its dissolution, to the amorphous and the indeterminate; it is less mirror
than substance, informed by the definitions of barbarism. It no
longer aims for peace, the dream of civil peace which after all inspired Hobbes; but, on the contrary, for war, the war of all
against all, the war of the People against itself, that critical and
extreme state in which death, striking by chance and breaking
all social bonds, reduces humanity to the fundamental indeter-
minacy that has become its horizon. It is no longer a question of
life—of "preserving" it, of "saving" it—but rather of death, of
the great final *Viva la muerte!* intoned by Hitler in his bunker,
condemning his people to death before immolating himself, rather as Robespierre condemned himself to the guillotine after he
had doomed all of France to it. What are the "masses," after
that? "Mass" is the name the baker gives to unformed dough. It
is the name the metalworker gives to the boiling liquid he is
about to pour into the mold. It is the term in physics which designates what in bodies has no quality and is nothing but simple
density. Humanity reduced to its "mass" is nothing, in this
sense, but society reduced to the totalitarian body of the prince,
itself monstrously dilated to the dimensions of the body of men.
The plebs *and* the state—this is still the state *in* men, one and
the same reality seen in one case from the viewpoint of its matter, in the other from that of its form.

It is easier to understand now why the idea of "listening" to
the "speech of the masses" no longer has the slightest meaning.
Reduced to such a state of apathy, how could they be heard,
since they no longer speak at all, or their "speech," says the Bible, is "madness"?[65] Materials and tools for the will to power of
the leaders, their speech is at best only that of participation,
communion, prayer. A pure corollary of the idol-state, which
speak in oracles and commands, their language is dissolved in
ritual and trance; in political terms, the appropriate language of

the plebs is always the plebiscite. In the same way, it is absurd to pretend to put oneself "to school" to the people, as so many enlightened enlighteners teeming in the ranks of the totalitarian left wish to do. What do they have to teach us, in effect, those aphasic crowds whose "mouth," says Isaiah, utters infamy?[66] If culture is first of all what distinguishes and discriminates, must we not agree that undifferentiated humanity does not even have a culture? If the plebs exist only in the mirror relation to their promised and desired death, what can they tell us but this message of death? Mass culture, in this respect, is what in modern terms is called "propaganda." "Plebiscite" and "propaganda." In confronting these two modes of discourse which, besides the shadow of Goebbels and Hitler, bear the indelible mark of the only Montagnard who succeeded, Bonaparte, and besides Bonaparte, of the man who Babeuf already called "Emperor Robespierre," in confronting these, I repeat, the only ethics that can stand will be one which, against the People too, will be able to support the muffled voice of ordinary people, that is, of pure subjects, in their invincible and irreducible singularity. And the only tradition in which I can perhaps succeed in recognizing myself is precisely that of men *alone,* who were not afraid to rebuke the peoples when the peoples went astray, who did not hesitate to identify them with the state when they bowed to the state, who had the remarkable audacity to think of the Good and the True without ever subordinating them to the number of those they won over. Those heralds, those solitaries, those men of little repute about whom the texts say that they are also ordinary men, if only ordinary men think with their heads, that is, with the Law—these are the men whom the Bible calls "Prophets"; and we shall see what an irreplaceable model they bequeathed to the world, a model of resistance thought though outside the paths of idolatry.

What is certain, for the moment, is that many things shift on this basis, and first of all the brilliant landscapes through which the experts move and in which the noonday light abolishes all shade. Seen from this rediscovered underground, the essential thing is no longer to "interpret," still less to "change" the world. Having left its orbit, philosophy is now only an attentive and modest ear listening to the small noise men make when they protest against unhappiness. Freedom, from this point of view, no longer has the glorious definition which, from Plato to Hegel, promised its wonderful and popular mirages to every man; whipped by the wind of the galleys, battered by countless trials, it is renamed resistance, strictly resistance, and does nothing but react, gain a little territory from the cancer which the religion of politics fosters in our heads. With this reaction as a test, right and left take on real meaning: on the right, what kills, what mineralizes a man and recognizes his roots only in the divine body of the prince or his substitutes; on the left, what preserves him, keeps him from being mutilated, and leaves him enough solitude so that from it he can draw sufficient strength to touch the solitude of other men. One value and only one, finally, for the operation of rights from below; one criterion and only one, to whose discipline we must from now on patiently adhere: that of the "individual" as such, a splendid and useless ruin whose voice has been lost but still pursues us like a silent reproach. I see the empty eyes of the dead rising from the depths of darkness to remind us of some of our mistakes in calculation.

PART TWO:

ATHENS OR JERUSALEM?

What is the "individual"? Does the word still mean anything in this age of vast suspicion? Does this pure subject, which I have taken as a basis for resistance, even exist? Isn't he a chimera, a unicorn, another delusion, this ruin about which I know nothing except that he demands my attention? It is clear that these questions are no longer academic forty years after André Malraux proclaimed the imminence of the "death of Man."[1] Indeed, they are more urgent than ever, in a time of intellectual schizophrenia in which men claim to defend in practice the rights of a "Man" whose demise in theory they constantly assert. This is surely the fundamental problem for an ethics concerned about its status and its truth. And it seems clear that, for the moment, in the great modern uproar, we can spell it out no more forcibly than in the form of internal divisions and contradictions.

Hence the obligation, the imperious duty, to resume the debate and recast its terms. This explains the urgency of a genealogy which, more attentive to vestiges than to arguments, will attempt to determine what, here in the West, once made possible the emergence and then the decline of this paradoxical figure, who is, after all, unique in the history of civilizations. The necessity for a work of memory that will account for what we must continue to remember and also for what we must force ourselves to forget, if we are to continue to will ourselves to be free today within the terms of our humanity. The following four chapters should be read as stages and stopping places along the path of an odyssey whose most familiar perspectives are perhaps the most unexpected. And its trajectory lies between the two sides of a millennial conflict that is nevertheless more topical than one might think: the conflict between paganism and monotheism.

5

The Pagan Mausoleum

How could this ancient conflict be outdated? Can we believe that, by decree or agreement, we can erase immemorial vestiges from the memory of men? Aren't they evident everywhere, universally resurgent, in the era of genocide and concentration camps? Should we, for example, consider the notorious "war of the gods"[1] of which Hitler spoke to Rauschning insignificant? Isn't the strange fanaticism with which all totalitarianisms attempt to liquidate the legacy and the tradition of monotheism symptomatic?[2] Wasn't the dream of a "new religion" already at the heart of romanticism, from the Athenaum to the pre-Nazi ideologues?[3] Can our own Pétainist revolution be understood without the insistent reference to a "return to origins," to those old "maternal" principles in which some have recognized the very matrix of fascism?[4] Have we forgotten that the French right, the right of Auguste Comte, Charles Maurras, and countless others, was also—first of all perhaps—a militant paganism, which claimed to reestablish connections with an archaic "polytheism" that had been closed off by the biblical message?[5] Again today, as I write these lines, the same refrain has returned in the ranks of a new right, which has found no better banner than that of neo-paganism. Under the dubious colors of a rediscovered

"Celtitude," "Germanness," or "Aryanism," the war against "Judeo-Christianity," and sometimes simply against Judaism, has quietly reappeared.[6] Illiterate buffoons tell us the fable of an "Indo-European" culture in which the exhausted West—which has lost, so they say, the sense of "energy," of "sacrifice," of "heroism," or of "force"[7]—will be able to recover its strength.

I shall return to all of this, of course. To this reversion to the sacred in which I am inclined to see one of the greatest dangers of the time. To this "political spirituality," which might well be the source, once again, of the most terrible regressions. To this "question" of the religious, finally, which will perhaps be the key question of the late twentieth century.[8] But let us proceed according to the order of our inquiry by turning, first, directly to the most difficult matter, to the preeminent pagan model and tradition; the only one, in fact, which calls for and can withstand analysis. To the greatest—and also the hardest to circumvent— of all the pantheons; a landscape of true, high civilization in which there is no doubt that we are steeped; the crucible of a philosophy there can be no question of dismissing with a stroke of the pen, capriciously; the cradle of a culture and a literature that are, of course, comparable to those of the monotheist universe; and the relay station by which was transmitted, filtered through its language, the biblical heritage. In a word, Greece— the Greece of Plato, Pericles, and Antigone. The Greece of what we have lost and of all our nostalgia. The Greece of "democracy" and the "Greek miracle." But a Greece of which I nevertheless say that we must exorcise its glories. A democracy that I think fostered none of the values to which I believe I must hold. An origin which we must, no doubt with difficulty, perhaps against all reason and logic, attempt if not to repress, then at least to demystify. Forget Athens? Heed its message, at least, which says practically nothing of what its contemporary apostles claim they read there.

What in fact is an "individual" for an Athenian of the classical age? Does he have a "consciousness," for example, in the sense we give to the word today? The *syneidesis* of the philosophers, which the Romans did in fact translate as "*conscientia*," is attested in this sense only around the Christian era, in Diodorus, Dionysius of Halicarnassus,[9] the Septuagint,[10] and the New Testament[11]—late, then, very late, after the God of Abraham and of Jesus had begun to win over declining Roman civilization. Is he an introspective subject, listening within himself to the voice of his particularity? It takes all our contemporary blindness not to see that the famous "Know yourself" means exactly the opposite—an appeal to propriety, to fusion with things, to externalization of the self, to the assumption of a place in the motionless order of the world. Does he enjoy a "freedom," a substantial "autonomy," which makes him an "originator," sovereign over himself and others? The texts, read in their context, once again say the opposite; they designate by *autonomia* not the character of an act, which has its source in the self, but the capacity to bend, to adhere to the laws of a Fate that is only distantly, secondarily human. Does he even have a "will" as distinct from "reason" and able to direct it? The hypothesis is ruled out by precisely those who are always credited with having been the first to advance it—I mean the Stoics who, from Epictetus to Sextus Empiricus, constantly belied, in their books and in their lives, their latter-day reputation as teachers of energy, contention, and resolution of soul.[12] We could go on multiplying and scattering references. From the strict viewpoint of the simplest philology, there is nothing in the Greek lexicon that expresses the capacity to be oneself or to have a self to which can be related the elements of what, since the Scriptures, we have called a "psychology."[13]

Take Euripides. An extreme case, to be sure; but the one who is considered, since Nietzsche, as the wordiest, most dialectical, most "psychological" of the three great tragedians. Yet where is the "psychology" in *Hippolytus,* for example, when no one for a single moment doubts Phaedra's innocence, beginning with the gods and even Artemis herself?[14] Where are there "states of mind" when the heroine escapes from the dizzying experience of a "confession" that Oenone makes in her place; Racine's Phèdre, on the other hand, savors its delight and torment.[15] Where is the "dialectic," since everything is decided in advance, from incestuous love[16] to inevitable death[17] through the "revelation" that leads Theseus to curse his own son?[18] Is there even *time* for dialectic, psychology, states of mind, since hardly has the action begun when Phaedra says to the Chorus: "Silence, we are lost,"[19] and halfway through she poisons herself and leaves the stage?[20] In truth, she debates only once when, at the hour of death, she wonders about the nature, almost pharmaceutical—"potion" or simple "ointment"—of the drink she iş about to swallow.[21] With this single and trivial exception, there is not a trace of the slightest internal drama in the entire play. The action is set in motion precisely from the outside, by chance and contingency, because of a slip by Oenone, a simple blunder.[22] Without this bad luck, this unforeseeable imprudence, nothing (as Phaedra herself says to the Chorus) would ever have happened, and there would have been no one to "reveal her sorrow."[23] For "silence," she says again, would have been enough to hide such a "dreadful secret."[24] A crime is only a secret, without weight or density, as long as it remains "private." The private, in other terms, is nothing; literally nothing, the absolute non-being of feeling. And this is why, contrary to the Christian tragedy which baptized the ancient model two thousand years later, Phaedra does not appear as the subject of any possible "ethics."

Besides, what could an ethics be for a Greek in Euripides's time? There is not a word, not a concept, in Demosthenes or Plato, in Aeschylus or Isocrates, to express, for example, "guilt," "obligation," "responsibility"—all those recent notions that weave a personal, subjective bond between a moral agent and an act that might be attributed to him. All Greek tragedy is built around the mystery of inherited sin, of guilt without crime, of a crime separated from its criminal, which condemned heroes pass on from father to son like a family jewel—"the race is wedded to

sorrow," says the Chorus in *Agamemnon*.[25] When the Chorus of
the *Women of Trachis* tries to suggest that for an "involuntary
sin," this sorrow is "governed by less anger," the accursed heroine retorts bitterly that these are the words of "someone whose
home is free of any evil," someone, consequently, who does not
understand that sin is not a matter of will nor the penalty a matter of merit or value.[26] Although there are occasional manuals or
treatises of morality written by "theoreticians," these are never
déductions from principles, nor even prescriptions, but catalogues of portraits, successions of pictures outlining an ideal of
good sense, an aesthetics of charm, in which conduct is distinguished less according to rights and duties than to what is worthy or unworthy of "praise."[27] Although Greek jurists and philosophers speak of good and evil, vice and virtue, justice and
injustice, these terms are inductive rather than imperative, and
the only law that regulates them is the law of habit, of custom, of
nature—the law of the eternal order of the cosmos, the mute,
servile, almost mechanical contemplation of which suffices to
regulate a life with as much precision and rigor as the revolution
of a star.[28] An "ethos" is not an ethics; it is not even mores. It is
rather stasis, the condition of being at home and rooted in the
matrix of a *physis*—which is the final word, and also the proper
name, of the master for a pagan.

We can go further. The very idea of "singularity" is, *by nature,* absent from the imaginary and visible world of the Greeks.
It is still believed that Aristotle, with his *to deti,* his principle of
particularity and specific identity, succeeded in thinking about
the distinct and separate individual.[29] But it is forgotten that he
roots this principle in "matter," and that matter, according to
the *Metaphysics,*[30] is the image of the unthinkable, pure and
empty "potentiality," not susceptible to any knowledge or any
apprehension. And no one bothers to explain why, in the *Politics,* when he undertakes to present the genealogy of the state,
Aristotle stops with the "family," and goes no further back, as
though he had suddenly and irremediably come up against the

unnameable "idiocy" of the monadic subject.[31] It is also known that, on this precise point, the Stoics broke the old system. We can delight in showing how, against Aristotelian logic, they established a nominalist logic, which recognized being only in the individual and concrete quality of a real and given object, defined by an inventory of its differences.[32] But it is less well known that such nominalism is of no value, because it is finally content with replacing the thesis, "There is no science except of the general," by the proposition, "There is no science except of the necessary," that is, of objects that are dissolved, once again, in the "system" of an omnipresent physics.[33] There are finally some passages in which, refining his theory of "man as actor," Epictetus says of the wise man that he is more than all his roles, that he establishes their repertory, that he exhausts himself in none of them, that he keeps within himself a "voice," a "person" full of "persona," a sort of substantial availability, even when he has removed his actor's "buskins" and "mask."[34] But that still proves nothing, when the same fragments add that this voice is only an echo, the shadow of a superior *pneuma* common to all men, which places each one thereby in the strange and paradoxical situation of owing his singularity less to what is irreplaceable in him than to what joins and blends him with others.[35] There is no more individualism through form than through matter. Strictly speaking, there is no such thing as a Greek "soul."

For what does a culture require in order to succeed in thinking about what we call in the present age a soul? First of all, there must be a belief in a personal principle, a sort of proper name, attached to each subject, a veritable identity which stays with him until death and possibly beyond. And this idea remained incongruous in a universe which, from the Academy to the Stoa, thought of the *psyche* only as filled with the *daimon*, and destined to return to it in an undifferentiated state of confusion. The idea is literally absurd when a mythology speaks of an "impersonal" immortality, which perpetuates less the individual than the clan and the lineage, and which makes the soul of a dead man a dead and nameless soul—*nonumnoi,* as Hesiod says.[36] Did Plato intuit the possibility of something else, of a personal immortality? He would still have had to succeed in endowing it with a founding, positive, architectonic function, in the constitution of an ethics, for example. But he managed to write all of Book Ten of the *Republic,* his entire deduction of the Good, of happiness, and justice, while referring to it only at the end, once the demonstration had been concluded, in a useless and insignificant appendix.[37] Does the *Phaedo* go further, with its theme of the "body as tomb" in which there appears, according to the commentators, the first theory of the separation of substances and the autonomy of the soul?[38] Another misunderstanding. For this body is not matter, a biological materiality, the physico-chemical part of the self, but a relationship, a simple tropism, the principle in the self which makes the tangible attractive. Nor is the "tomb" a real place in which the spirit is trapped before it frees itself. It is a perversion, nothing but a modality of desire, even all desire, insofar as it turns toward the multiple and toward appearance. Is the soul which is "in prison," finally, enclosed within another substance foreign to its essence? It is a prisoner only of itself, of the relationship to its desire, of the evil use that it makes of its own appetites.[39] Nothing is more foreign to Platonism than the asceticism so often tacked onto it by Christianizing readings. There is nothing that allows us really to distinguish, as two heterogeneous realities, a body made of matter and a psyche made of spirit.

Nor is this all. For even if we could overcome all these obstacles, there would still be one more that is absolutely impossible to circumvent: the incapacity of the Greeks to think about or represent time, and thus to think about the personal history, the particular fate, of a man. The subject of the Stoics, for example, is not a subject, since he has no standpoint but the present, recognizes being only in the moment, and conceives of acts and desires only as accomplished in the conviction that they could be, that they should be, that they *are* in fact the last ones.[40] How is it possible to think that the Platonic soul has the slightest depth, when the *Phaedo* says that "concern for the future" is the motive of a "vulgar" man,[41] and the *Laches* refuses to define courage as "knowledge of things to be feared or hoped for"?[42] What can we think of a static and immobile wisdom, without progression and without a future, which is related to men only insofar as they are failed gods? Wedded to the transience of the interval, the Greek lived in a sempiternal present, without memory or future. Enclosed within the ghetto of a time without duration or passage, he experienced history only in the form of a blemish. If he had written biography, it would have been nothing but a succession of moments, or rather a set of simultaneous pictures, whose contemporaneity would be set out in absurd dispersion only because of the requirements of narrative. When he did in fact write biographies, as in the case of Plutarch or Diogenes Laertius, they presented strange figures with no depth or surprises, crystallized and petrified in a ritualized rigidity. Much later, at the dawn of the Christian era, when Porphyry presented a portrait of Plotinus, or Damascius a portrait of Proclus, their narratives still lacked the dimension of life, the evolution of feeling invented by the moderns after St. Augustine. Like the sculptors of the classical period, who discovered in the volumes and gestures of living forms the law of astral revolutions, oceanic movements, or the shapes of the earth, these early biographers were cosmic augurs who found, in the speech that sprang from the open bodies of their models, once more nothing but the pattern of the great orders of life. They described situations, positions in the order of things; but they quite simply forgot the *human condition*.

Again, this eclipse is demonstrated most clearly in the tragedians. What was Aeschylus's theater, in fact, if not the theater of a world that was not quite a world, of a human universe not fully torn away from the other universe, of an inhuman comedy that did not for a moment move toward a separate existence? It contains beings made of lacunae, who seem to come from a divine dream, and who, in their slightest gesture, are secretly hounded, assaulted from behind, by Hera, Apollo, or the Erynnies: Prometheus, for example, whose immortal agony would be inexplicable if, in his very secession, he did not remain bound to, entirely filled with Zeus, like a meteorite fallen from the height of Oympus;[43] and Clytemnestra who, we sense clearly, does not lie because of her own inclination or in her own voice, still less by virtue of a necessity or a twist of the plot, but because a playful god gave the "demon" of lying the power to seize her and to speak through her voice—a poor borrowed voice which does not bear a human form.[44] With Sophocles, on the other hand, could it not be said that the vise began to loosen? There are now speakers, kinds of human animals, bellowing their perdition in the brutal silence created by the unspeaking gods. One even glimpses shadows, half-real forms still enveloped in darkness, riveted to their solitude and their dereliction. But it amounts to little to say that they are alone, since they are, in fact, rejected, cast out, abandoned to their wandering. Yet the soil is too harsh and the suffering too horrible, and its leaden color makes Ajax and Oedipus a-physical, utopic, atypical beings, not only violated but themselves living violence, of the order of nature; and the heroes expire again, walled up, for example, or simply blinded, at the very moment of the *fiat* that called them out of limbo. It is perhaps with Euripides that the grip really begins to relax: Hippolytus, at last, can rise up against Aphrodite when he refuses to acknowledge her at the gates of the palace.[45] Is there not in this case something like a suggestion of humanity, an authorized speech, in the words addressed to Artemis, holy and good protector whom he does not hesitate to call his "personal friend"?[46] Yes, of course. But barely a suggestion, for the demigod also dies, and he dies, as Theseus says, because by carrying on a dialogue with heaven, he has been guilty of arrogance, *askesis, Autosebein,*[47] an unpardonable crime in the earthly city. He disappears in silence, without even a glance upward; for, by making himself a subject, he has sunk into a *hubris* that condemns him to exile. Unthinkable in Aeschylus, impossible in Sophocles, the human condition has now become unlivable and *criminal*.

It is on this basis, on the basis of this unlivable crime, that we should reread *Antigone* and perhaps dissipate some of the absurdities with which modern interpretations have afflicted it. There is, first, the misunderstanding which consists in seeing a "conflict" in a drama that unfolds entirely without the shadow of a debate. Antigone and Creon are barely protagonists, they never confront one another, and they hardly attempt to persuade one another. Each one speaking for himself, in the other's profuse silence, their speeches cross but do not succeed in establishing an exchange. We should rather speak of two human declines, separate and parallel, equally lamentable, with one following the other like its inverse image. And besides, it is Creon who has the last word, lamenting that he "cannot unbind what he himself has bound."[48] There is a second misunderstanding, which is to see in Antigone a kind of "martyr," an ecstatic witness to an "unwritten law" that speaks only to her "conscience." For she says, she never stops saying, precisely that she is inhabited by no ecstasy, that no *ecstasis* inspires her, that no foreign voice possesses or constrains her. We must listen to her when, incredibly weary and gloomy, she agrees that no transcendent justice has inspired her with its wisdom, not that of Zeus of course, nor even that of *dike* which she has betrayed just as much.[49] Like a living candle burning in vain, she undergoes the harsh, arid, and almost wordless experience of the radical impossibility of any law of the heart that might provide support for a will to rebellion. "What is the good," she asks, "of lifting one's eyes toward heaven?"[50]

For it is a third misunderstanding to see in Creon the simple representative of a cold reason of state against which Antigone resists—all the more so because he in fact constantly refers to the gods and calls on their protection. His piety goes so far as to be concerned, in the very midst of his madness, to leave in the cave "the food prescribed by the rites."[51] His indignation is not assumed when he replies peremptorily to the Chorus, who suspect a divine hand or a divine intention behind the sacrilege, that the very idea is "revolting."[52] And the truth is that this prince is also and primarily a priest, one of the two in the play, occupying by himself the entire field of the sacred as it was conceivable in a city like Athens in the late fifth century B.C.—not "law" against "faith," but one joined to the other in the "law of faith" which was literally Greek religion.[53] There is a fourth misunderstanding, finally, which sees a hymn to Antigone in a drama that is written entirely from Creon's point of view, if not indeed to glorify him. It has not often been noted, in fact, that the Chorus gives Antigone the *coup de grâce,* and that the Chorus in the tragedies always expresses the opinion of the poet and of common sense. There are four strophes in which it condemns, irrevocably, the absurd "blindness," the mad "aberration," the excessive "violence" of this "girl" who, "taking evil for good," has contravened that sovereign justice which the entire text emphasizes has indeed the universality of an intangible and absolute principle.[54] Such is the order of the Greek cosmos that Antigone's sin is a metaphysical sin, which places her unquestionably not only outside the law but outside the order of the world. "For my misfortune," she recognizes, "not a tear, not a friendly sigh."[55]

Of course, this is too schematic. But the lesson is nonetheless clear; and it will soon be understood. Where is "reason of state"—the notorious "reason of state" because of which the heroine supposedly perishes—when Antigone confesses to Creon that she "knew very well" that she would die, that it was "inevitable" and "even without his edict"?[56] On which side is the "unwritten law," when she thus admits that it was not a royal decree, a human and written law that she has violated by her action, but a principle which, in fact, goes beyond any writing and any law? Where is the "insurgent conscience," when the entire drama expresses its failure, its necessary defeat, beginning with Ismene, the faithful Ismene, who warns at the outset that the undertaking is "madness," its success "improbable," because it aims for the "impossible"?[57] The "impossible": the word that is the true subject of the tragedy is spoken early. The impossible conscience, which we see less being constructed than dissolving and disintegrating. The impossible personal will of a soul who rebels less in glory than in shipwreck, collapse, and the ultimate degree of torment. The great mistake would be to read some pre-Christian edification in the implacable demonstration that, without the gods of Ismene, the Chorus, and Creon, there is only ruin and silence: only a half-voice, arising in the darkness, without origin and without a listener, quickly doomed to expire in the frightful spectacle of its own movement toward nothingness.

This movement toward nothingness is again illustrated, in the savage beauty of the myth, by the choice of punishment, the final torment. Why walled up, in effect, and not condemned to hemlock, *barathron,* or flagellation, like countless criminals in the real Greece of the time? Because Antigone is precisely not a criminal who has imprudently infringed a human and banal prohibition. Her crime is so high that it is not enough to punish her with a memorable sentence; her very trace, the scar she has made on the earth of men, must be effaced. It is less a matter of repressing her than of annihilating her, less of making her pay than of removing her, less of executing a deviant than of cutting off an excess being, who no longer has the slightest place in the hierarchical order of the cosmos. Dead, alive? "Neither living nor a corpse," she must have a cave which is like a non-place for the non-being she has become. Descend to Hades? "Rejected by the living and the dead,"[58] she is released from the realm of life without however joining the kingdom of the dead. Like Niobe dying, who continued to shed tears while her body turned to stone, she must become a being of nowhere, of nothingness, in suspension. The individual is the one without a home. To make oneself into a self is to disappear. A soul is, once again, one soul too many.

Yes, once again, as with Aeschylus and Plato, Aristotle and Epictetus. But with a new element, all the same, which now allows us to clarify the reasons for the phenomenon. Finally, what does the legend say if we recapitulate its outline? That Creon derives his power from the fact that as archon he speaks as a priest, and as priest he speaks as a magistrate. Antigone's weakness comes from the fact that her sin is a sacrilege as well as a civil crime. The Chorus's conviction comes from the fact that it conceives of no religion outside political categories, and in return no politics that is not filled with religion. In other words, what prohibits the heroine's insurrection is, first of all, this strange circle, which moves back and forth from one sphere to another in an endless series of mirrors. If her defeat is inevitable, this is because there is no heaven that has not fallen to earth and been mingled with earth in a perverse confusion. If her despair is limitless, this is because Thebes, like every "city," is a closed world with no outside, in which the orbit of the sacred is blended and inextricably woven with the thread of the social bond. The entire affair depends on a corruption of the divine, brought down and repatriated to the surface of the human world, which itself no longer finds in the divine the foliation of its disorders. Anti-individualism is a horizontality, an ontological flattening out that is the very bedrock of Greek civilization from whatever direction one approaches it. Just as Aristotle reduced the subject to his political animality, just as Epictetus made ethics a version of physics, so Sophocles confines all consciousness within the enclosure of social existence. The rejection of the personal will always has the same face—the face of a religion thought of within the horizon of a general cosmology.

This also means that we must stop seeing the springs of Greek tragedy in some undefined, terrible, and blinding confrontation between gods and humans. If Antigone loses the battle, this is precisely because she lacks the knowledge and the capacity to look at the gods face to face. If her insurrection fails, this is because she has failed to establish with heaven the bond of protection, filiation, submission to which, I agree, she aspires, but which is metaphysically prohibited to her. If the self is impossible in Thebes, this is because there is lacking a transcendence that, even though burdensome and constraining, would grant the subject another dimension, rooted in another place—the only thing, in fact, that could save him from his cosmological flatness. Omnipresent in the world, Greek religion is absent from human beings, almost too familiar to speak to consciousness in the direct, personal, individuating contact invented by the Hebrews. Is it not characteristic, in this respect, that the only form of spirituality that ever escaped from this pattern was Dionysianism? For the specific trait of Dionysianism was to be reserved for barbarians, slaves, and women, that is, for those who were excluded from the natural order. And the sole religion of confrontation—of trance and enthusiasm—was fitting, therefore, only for lesser beings who did not fully deserve the dignity of being human. We should not forget that Antigone is also a woman. Creon does not forget, and he constantly repeats that while he "lives," a "woman will never make the laws." For this is what she has to be shown: that only a god of trances could establish a consciousness; but since this god is good only for barbarians, the status of person is itself a zero degree of humanity. Or alternatively, and this amounts to the same thing: that since the religion of the city is an exoteric religion, it is enough to banish all forms of inwardness, and that it establishes subjects only in their social and ritual relation of externality.

This means, finally, that the notion of *fatum*, at least as it is usually understood, is rigorously absent from the ancient universe, and that nothing is more foreign to Sophocles and Euripides than the idea of a "fate," unique and implacable, sovereign and absolute, dictating to men a Law without recourse and without appeal. Let us return, at this point, to Hippolytus's fall. What is the reason for this horrible death, in solitude and dereliction? Far from the *fatum* that has been claimed, he is the victim of a dubious battle between Artemis and Aphrodite, of a divided heaven, then, riven by uncertain struggles of which he is the plaything. Why does the arrogant consciousness which he has triumphantly forged sink to the nothingness of an inglorious evanescence? Nothing is written in advance; on the contrary, everything is improbable in this feudal Olympus where gods with living eyes quarrel over possessions, fiefs, privileges. The problem, in other words, is not in fate but in the contingency of the divine. It has less to do with the authority of the sacred word than with the debility of a heaven humming with contradictory speeches and undertakings. What blocks the subject and prevents him from standing on his own feet is not absolute power but the relativity of the gods' power, their power relative, in each case, to the network, the system of power, of opposing gods. What breaks down and reduces any tendency toward the personal will is, in the last analysis, the fact that the Greeks knew, in the realm of the divine, only powers and principles, which, although they had an identity and even a civic status, were nevertheless not free agents eternally regulating the necessity of the world's course. Instead of a personal God, creating in His image subordinates who are persons, there was a surplus of gods, that is, polytheism.

Thus the circle is closed in this mournful apotheosis called the "Greek miracle." So ends the course of this sinister twilight in which one can perceive a dawn only by forgetting on what an omission, with what a formidable void, it is constructed and flourishes. Such in any case is the ideal and reconstructed order of an age that was able so easily to reject consciousness, ethics, psychology, singularity, time, and the human condition, only because it was based on a cosmological, exoteric, polytheist—in a word, pagan—religion. Is it necessary to repeat that I am not drawing up an indictment of Greece as such, dragged before an imaginary tribunal of some completed history? I am well aware of the dangers of those backward movements which, reading the past in the reflected light of the present, hunt down in the truth of the past the unthinkable shadows of the truth of the present. I have no doubt, if you prefer, that, read in a direct manner, and in consideration of its context, the Greek world of Plato and Antigone has a particular genius with which it is *always the time* to engage in a fruitful dialogue, as the entire monotheist tradition has constantly done. But I am simply asserting that when a monument becomes an argument, when a stele becomes a banner which, from Voltaire at least as far as Nietzsche, Maurras, and beyond, provides food for very concrete philosophical or political slogans, then it is important to know exactly what we are talking about. That, at a time when we hear songs of praise for the virtues of a "new Greece" and a return to the sources supposed to be the image of our future, it is no longer a matter of indifference to examine the tight silence of the texts and the unspoken lacuna with which we are invited to identify. Moreover, if the historians who write after the event are pitiful prophets, then those who are nostalgic for origins are reactionaries who, testing the truth of today against their fantasies of the day before yesterday, transmit, as we shall see, the most fearsome archaizing passions. If we agree today, in the age of these recurrences and this insistent nostalgia, on calling "totalitarian" any thought that blocks and reduces the individual, then we will perhaps have to admit that the first definition of totalitarianism, the only one which includes more than its merely political dimension, is quite simply pagan regression.

6

The Genius of Christianity

Consequently, as you may already have guessed, there is a second surprise in this genealogical outline. A surprise at least for those—and they are many—who see the shift from paganism to Christianity as the beginning of a long night, a Middle Ages of the soul in the course of which the subject was defeated, wounded, shattered to his depths. A paradox for the mockers, yesterday's free spirits and today's Voltaireans, who see the individual as the fruit of a long struggle to be free from the dominance of the God of confession and submission. A scandal even for contemporary banality, which endlessly drones on that Man is a recent idea, one that has recently appeared on the surface of knowledge—a scar, a simple fold of the landscape after the earthquake of the death of God and the great atheist, secular, and scientific Revolution. For we must say the opposite, if we consent to listen to what the Greeks whisper from the depths of their necropolis: It was not secularism but rather antipaganism, not atheism but in fact monotheism, which alone was capable of making room for something resembling our free subject.

It is difficult to imagine the extraordinary explosion of joy and fervor that set the world ablaze in the early days of the Revelation. The astonishment of Origen before this incredible God who, creating "all men in his image," "shaped them one by one," in a face to face encounter with each one.[1] The exhilaration of Clement of Alexandria or Maximus the Confessor hailing the decline of all the stars of misfortune that had for millennia regulated men's lives according to the rhythm of their implacable and unchanging courses. The gentle, mad intoxication of Gregory of Nyssa, John Damascene, or Andrew of Crete upon seeing the instantaneous crumbling of the whole horde of powers, spirits, demons that had enclosed the fate of the soul within the anti-fate of natural, physical, and cosmological revolutions.[2] A whole people, along with them, took to the roads to proclaim to heaven the scandal of the unprecedented News. Masses of believers, suddenly disoriented, intoned the same paean of a humanity released from its ontological and immemorial slavery. A world ringing with heroic freedom was abruptly established and spread the word of the glorious and astounding prophecy to the ends of the earth. If God exists, everything is permitted, and first of all establishing oneself, a creature of flesh and misery but also one who has an aura of spirituality, in the center of the universe and its fateful laws.

The frescoes of the catacombs have preserved for us the memory of those great astonished figures who then emerged, pupils dilated by ecstasy, from the depths of pagan darkness. In these representational and perfectly realistic scenes, there is, however, little reference to reality, to the concrete and literal materiality of the world. The figures are presented in bloodless settings, strangely uniform and abstract, against which they stand out alone, though still ill-assured, in the lustral dignity of their new status as creatures. They form compositions that are no longer situated in the space or time of beings, but in a shimmering of lights, a halo of implicit symbols in which the order of the cosmos seems to give way to subtle and impalpable spiritual hierarchies. It was there no doubt, in the silence of those underground grottoes, that the embrace of earth and the soul began to come undone. It was there that Christian consciousness ceased to be a microcosm, a simple effect of the world, and overflowed, went beyond all effects of the world. It had been a cog; it became a totality. It had been contained; now it contained and encompassed all of nature. It had been something infinitely small, keeping its place and its role in the order of the infinitely large; it became the imperceptible glimmer, buried in the shadows of the night, which held and raised up the chains of creation. *"In parvo magnus,"* said Origen, followed by St. Thomas and Bossuet. For the first time the subject, *each* subject, was of more value than any object and any material being.[3] *Psyche,* finally, was divorced from *physis.*

For what was wonderful—I might almost say miraculous—in this new embrace was that, in wresting man away from matter and from himself insofar as he was matter, in separating out a part of his desire, which it refined and attached to the vault of heaven, it endowed him with a freedom that was thenceforth the corollary of his capacity for escape, exile, and elevation. A creature, he was endowed with the attributes of the creator. The product of an absent cause, he too was thereby a producer and a creator of effects. If it were properly carried out, said St. Thomas, he received from this divine touch the "dignity of a cause."[4] Perfectly heteronomous, it was in this heteronomy alone that he would find the source of and nourishment for his complete autonomy. The Greek god had said: My will be done and not yours; the new God answered: Let your will draw sustenance for its power from mine. The ancient City had wanted an enchained will, trapped in the dark waters of immanence; the City of God proposed a transcendence which, far from swallowing up that will, represented the living spring, the clear water of its strength. A strange dialectic, which the Jews called *Devekhut,* whose literal sense of a "conformity to divine intention" should not conceal that, unlike Stoicism, it represents an area of disengagement and retreat that alone permits of a judgment, a rejection of the course of the world.[5] An enigmatic embrace, which Christians celebrate with the name of grace, and whose unavoidable rigor (sometimes its surrender to misfortune) should not make us forget that it designates a creature wedded to freedom.

Of course, the Christian soul traded an archaic submission for another, more modern one, which would produce all its effects later when it passed through the network of the institution. But we should also understand what this uprising of the subject in the monotheist other world assumes and implies about the capacity to rebel. Everyone knows that Augustine's *City of God* opens with the narrative of the tragic day of August 24, A.D. 410, when, breaking through the Salarian Gate to sack Rome, the barbarian hordes cut through with one stroke the bond that tied man permanently to his city and thereby established his subjection. But it is perhaps less well known that the entire text of the *City of God* is nothing but the theory of that break—the gates of the city still further broken through, the liberating devastation forever repeated through a new covenant which, releasing the subject from his human vows, authorizes him to judge, to disturb, to cut through the political order in the name of a celestial ethics. Will it be admitted that, in this very orthodox separation in theory of the two kingdoms, the kingdom of God and the kingdom of men, in the practical possibility always of appealing to one against the dictates of the other when misfortune is too harsh or when princes fail in their sacred trust, there lies the origin (perhaps the only origin) of what must be called a revolt or a resistance, whose principle of transcendence, we remember, was unavailable to Antigone? Comte was not mistaken when he deplored in Christianity, and particularly in Augustinianism, a whiff of "anarchy," of "social disintegration" which, because it binds the believer to God, releases him "from his neighbor and from his social duties."[6]

Can we say, then, that the Christian, with his eyes fixed in awe or devotion on those infinite spaces, thereby loses contact with the pure finiteness of his inner being? Here again, we must assert the opposite, and this is what Augustine never stops saying throughout that admirable odyssey of his illumination, the

Confessions. It is true that they contain no accidents or incidents of life which do not assume the insinuating action of an occult and omnipresent God. It is also true that there is not a feeling, a sin, a lie, that is not a secondary cause through which a Being who flows through his entire being attempts to bring the soul back from its wandering to his truth. But at the same time there is such subtlety in the description and analysis of those insinuations. There is such lyric power to delineate the invasion of the self by the flesh or the struggle of the angel against the beast. And there is a sumptuous picture, at this early date, of the misery and the grandeur of an "I" doomed to instability and ambivalence. It was the first time, in any case, that a philosopher, a writer, had dwelled at such length, so indulgently, on the aftereffects of action or the hesitations before choice, on the swings of desire or the specious charms of the moment. On a level with the great modern novels of introspection, but in a relentless hand to hand struggle between grace and freedom, in a disorderly array of dubious figures all bristling with holiness, in a psalm of the flesh in which the body may speak only against a background of silence which places it on the rack of its anticipation of the divine, the *Confessions* mark quite simply the appearance of "psychology"—and, in its wake, a hint of eternity.[7]

It may be objected further that this dual vision, within and outside the self, is accompanied by a dogmatism whose principle of authority undermines the rights of consciousness at the same time that it recognizes them. This would imply leaving out of account the extraordinary critical efflorescence represented for centuries by scholasticism, so badly named and so often reduced to a banal caricature. It would imply forgetting that, two centuries before the Enlightenment, it was generations of priests, scholars, and clerics who invented the "examination of the conscience," even "free examination," which they made a duty for the *liberum arbitrium* and a weapon against the popes. It was the Franciscan Vitrier—a fervent preacher and subtle reader of Origen—who made the "heart of man," the intimacy of its contemplation, the seat of all life, and all religious truth.[8] And it was Erasmus himself who, as early as 1504, in his *Christian Soldier,* opposed "true piety," again that of the heart and soul, to the "mere ceremonies" by which ventriloquists profane, while reciting their lessons, "the books in which the heavenly word still lives and breathes."[9] Once again Comte was right—and the whole nineteenth century as well—when he saw the essence of Christianity in "individual examination of biblical beliefs," and thus "personal examination" set up against "social judgment."[10] The school of feeling, individualism, and personal thought, this Christianity did not wait for Voltaire and Fontenelle to make, with Calvin, each believer a theologian and each man the measure of his relationship to the world and the divine.

This was all the more true because Christianity also had at its disposal, from the thirteenth century on, that extraordinary nursery of consciousness represented in western Europe by the monastic ideal. We lack a general history of this unparalleled enclosure which invented, among other things, the figure of the intellectual, and in which men and women who wished to be consecrated to God devoted themselves to the dizzying and delicious experiences of the inner life. From the *riches heures* of the Company of Jesus, there remain the *Principles and Commandments,* which are one of the finest examples of moral, intellectual, and psychological taxonomy ever imagined, and include along the way a portrait of the General of the Jesuits, for example, which Marx and Schumpeter would have only to copy to represent their "Entrepreneur."[11] The ashes of Jansenist monasticism were soon dispersed by the winds of ecclesiastical argument and rising atheism; but we still have the *Pensées* or Arnauld's *Communion* which, in the shadow of the cloister, in the silence of pure contemplation, already had more to say about the mysteries of the "human heart" than all the "hateful self" of all the secular revolutions.[12] Of the first Trappists, I will simply quote Chateaubriand's sublime remark on Rancé: his devotion, his asceticism, his movement out of himself, his body and his flesh, left him "alone in the face of his passions."[13] Yes, he says, "his passions," his poor mortified passions, made more painful by solitude, and which were, according to Chateaubriand, only more endemic, completely exposed, and self-conscious. Yes, he says, "alone," as though in this dialogue with the Saviour there were a silent soliloquy, a false game of mirrors, which orders the subject into exile only to condemn him more completely to retrace his own path.

A paradox? No doubt; but one found far beyond the cloister and its particular form of enclosure. It is a paradox that haunts, for example, the prodigious creative force of the *Mémoires d'outre-tombe,* or even *Le Temps retrouvé,* in which two great secular writers, two profane sentinels of memory, can reconstruct the chronicle of their existence only by immobilizing it, opening like an abyss onto the fallen world, backed against the confines of the void that swallows it up, under the gaze of an impossible but necessary eternity. And Verlaine in his cell in Mons, suddenly struck down by a "revelation," saw a phantasmagorical saraband reconstruct all the "logical categories," the "compartments" of his mind; the "reasons which used to flit like dragonflies," the thousand shattered fragments of fine "crystal" of a self that faith and faith alone could restore to its identity.[14] Then there is Rousseau above all who, at the end of his life, opened his *Confessions* with the famous apostrophe in which he calls on the "eternal Being" to "gather around him the immense crowd of his fellows," and makes Him the silent Witness, the necessary corollary, the single authority that can support and fix his existence;[15] once again the principle of heteronomy in which a consciousness, which he has constantly proclaimed inalienable and autonomous, must be alienated. I know few great classical writers, in fact, who, at the moment of truth, the moment of *their* truth, at the decisive moment when the derisive routine of ephemeral existence is shattered, have not relied on such a detour, such a paradox, such a reminiscence perhaps, to shape out of the shifting sands of time the hard atom of a self.[16]

I am not saying, of course, that Verlaine, Rousseau, and Cha-teaubriand were unconscious Trappists, nor that the cork-lined room in which Proust chose to isolate himself one fine day was a secular Port-Royal. I am simply claiming that all of them could discover the model for this atom of the self, this atomism of the subject, neither in the *Encyclopédie* nor in bourgeois law nor even in the Romantics; but, without their being aware of it, no doubt, in obscure monks, forgotten clerics who—arguing for centuries about "freedom," "grace," or "universals"—established, whether we like it or not, the first and perhaps the only theory of a consistent individualism. We would have to relate how, well before the Copernican revolution, theologians of the thirteenth century like Robert Grosseteste[17] or Guillaume d'Auvergne[18] had already destroyed Aristotelian physics at its weakest link, its conception of "quiddity."[19] We would also have to show why it was the Augustinian Duns Scotus who, a little later, by inventing the *cogito,* freedom of the will, and, against St. Anselm, the Cartesian proof of the existence of God, forged the concept of a "person" defined in terms—which might be called pre-Lacanian—of a "limit," a "powerlessness," the non-relation of two substances incapable of joining together.[20] Finally, above all, we should dwell on the figure of William of Occam, the English Franciscan of the early fourteenth century who, setting up a radical nominalism against the logic of "genera," the evidence of the "particular" against the science of the "general," the pure "insularity of the existent" against Thomist "finality," imagined society as a myriad of absolutely dispersed islands which are each, as it were, absolute, naturally "autonomous," and subject to "natural law."[21] This "natural law" is already Locke's "Right." This "insular existent" is already the "perfect and solitary whole" of Rousseau. This myriad of subjects is already the principle of liberalism. This critique of teleology is already the future basis of democracy. It is difficult to go further in the praise of dispersion or in the isolation of the pure human monad. And it is so little remembered today because the great shadow of the Enlightenment quickly decreed obscure what it strove so hard to darken.

It is clear, on the other hand, that the early fourteenth century, in the shadow of the cathedrals and their stone missals, saw a return of painting on canvas and the extinction of great Gothic art, which devoted its dying energies to individualizing the figures of its saints, virgins, and martyrs. This was the age when Giotto, on the monumental frescoes of the basilica at Assisi, under columns humming with the murmur of divinity, drew the anxious profiles of the beings of flesh who were henceforth to sum up all of Christian dramaturgy. This was the age when, in the sobriety of the gestures of St. Francis "struck by the Seraph," in the outspread arms and the head resting on the two joined hands of the *Descent from the Cross,* Italy discovered, with mingled delight and awe, the human, too human tragedy of those figures who were so familiar because they were so perfectly *personified.* Never before, and perhaps never since, had there been seen so much sorrow in a mouth, so much gentleness in eyes under the tense arc of brows that seem to sink into, to be sculpted out of a space apparently made of stone, labile and trembling. On these faces ennobled by meditation or drawn with suffering, in these bodies illuminated by a hidden inner glow but nevertheless abandoned to the horror of nature, it is the human condition itself that bursts into pictorial representation. In the center of the canvas, forever separated from God but forever bound to Him, definitively abandoned but still stretched toward Him, we see already the *uomo singolare* who will be for a long time the subject of all Italian painting.

This *uomo singolare* was above all the subject—we should say, the hero—of great Christian literature, and particularly of tragedy, in which he completed the shaping of his glorious and equivocal form. Take, for example, what Racine made of Euripides' Phaedra, in whom we saw so clearly the Greek inability to think of subjectivity. In Euripides, there is a dance of puppets without density or depth, performing a ballet directed by the uncertain duel of two rival goddesses. In Racine, we have a human tragedy, in which characters of flesh and blood occupy the entire

tragedy, in which characters of flesh and blood occupy the entire stage with their madness, their laments, and the tortures they inflict on one another. In one case, the heroine dies halfway through without affecting in the slightest the pattern of the plot; in the other, she is the central, the single figure, who eclipses the others to the status of walk-on players, who seem to be present only to echo her confession. The Greek model presents a humanity of innocents, among whom Phaedra herself is excused by Oenone, Hippolytus, and Theseus. In Racine, on the contrary, we see only the guilty, a humanity of sinners, from Phèdre rebuked by her fellow creatures to Hippolyte, to whom the poet was so determined to "attribute some weakness,"[22] and including Thésée himself, to whom he ascribes a curious bad conscience entirely absent from the proud figure in Euripides. In this human tragedy that presents only criminals, in this inferno of the soul that knows only moral consciousness, one does not die of consumption but of shame and repentance.

But this is because one lives first of all—and here is the essential difference—in a halo of wonder, an aura of mystery and miracle that is paradoxically absent from the divine drama of the Greeks. The Athenian never calls his Phaedra *"la fille de Minos et de Pasiphaé."* She never speaks to Venus and the sun as her natural audience, alone worthy of her suffering. In addressing them, she never adopts the vocabulary of prayer and supplication which gives Racine's monologues their beauty. It is in the Christian drama that *fatum* weighs—the dreadful fate forbidden, we remember, by the contingence of the pagan notion of the divine. It is in the human, ethical, psychological tragedy that the real dialogue, censored in the model, between the believer and the divine takes place. It is Racine, the poet of freedom, who chains his free will to a reverse grace, a perverse predestination which, by itself, binds the heroine to the wheel of her bad conscience.[23] It is as though his poem could sing of the soul of a pure individual only because that soul had come first from heaven, abandoned by heaven but still consecrated to it by a mystic plea.

One might believe that he could dramatize a self—an authentic person and her tissue of contradictions, torments, and duels—only by locating the duel less between Phèdre and herself than between Phèdre and the gods, or her conscience and God in her. A strange subjectivity, said Sainte-Beuve, which "acts against its desire, desires against its will, wills despite itself."[24] This is because, as for Giotto, Occam, or Pascal, there had to be a transcendence and the call of an elevation for the subject to be able to stand and speak its own language. And it was there perhaps, on that stage and on that ground, that the monotheist embrace reached its completion, in the pitiless double game of presence and absence, of distance and speech, of the absolute separation between the creator and his creature, and yet of their perennially renewed connection.

Altar or stake, Hell or Paradise? The die is cast, in any case, and it continues to roll today, making the modern individual a monotheist Oedipus who everywhere proclaims his freedom and submits to necessity. For, as Berdayev says, "where there is no longer a God, there is no man either."[25]

The Death of God

It is therefore easier to understand the meaning and the scenario of that formidable hammerblow which rang throughout the West when its catastrophe had reached its peak, and which is called the death of God.

It was first of all, we must say, like a new Annunciation. We seem to see, two millennia later, the same crowds of heretics brandishing the same torch of a soul restored to itself. We seem to be dreaming when we hear the joyful songs and explosion of jubilation that appear to have arisen from the beginning of the world. Since Christianity, there had never been such wild enthusiasm, blowing like a wind over heads that rose again, and echoing to the ends of creation. Here were new Fathers, wandering in new deserts, with the radiant colors of freedom. Companions of the free spirit, tolling the knell for the dead ideal with the same fervor that Origen had had to celebrate its divine baptism. Cohorts of iconoclasts, dancing joyfully on the ashes, to the sound of forgotten orchestras, in murderous jubilation. There was Feuerbach, for example, apostle of *"homo homini deus,"* creature without creator, god without the help of God, man humanized by Man alone. There was Nietzsche the Antichrist, exposing to future condemnation the false Eternal who, diverting from the earth the attributes of its dignity, had made them a diadem that could now fall from his unmasked head. There was Marx, of course, howling his hatred for an old world that had so long infected humanity with its "opium" of alienation. Everywhere there was talk only of the opening onto nothingness from which, in the heart of each individual, had flowed the divine principle. God was nothing but a hemorrhage of the soul, and this soul urgently needed a tourniquet.

And then, suddenly, the dream capsized and turned into a nightmare. Strange eclipses from time to time covered the light of history; the shadows came closer and the new brightness thickened. There was the same breath of happiness, but it seemed to come from beyond the grave; the same frenzied crowds, but they acclaimed the swastika; the same fervor too around the giant portraits of Stalin; and the red guillotine, already, celebrated in the Place de Grève. For do we know what Saint-Just would have been if, in addition to being a regicide, he had not also been the first deicide of contemporary history, establishing his politics of crime explicitly on the murder of God?[1] Why is there a museum of atheism in Moscow where they solemnly celebrate the march toward socialism and the Jewish and Christian martyrs who line the road? Has it ever been asked why the SS called Christ "that pig of a Jew," and why Hitler was still telling Bormann at Stalingrad that the greatest crime of the Jews was the invention of Christianity?[2] The fact is that, from Eckart to Rosenberg, Nazi irrationalism was also defiance and hatred of monotheism as such. From Robespierre to Mao, there is no totalitarianism without this insistent, pathological, obsessive reference to slaying the one and sovereign God. By one of those devilish twists which history has a habit of producing, the death of God in politics seems indeed to be an Annunciation that turns into confusion, and a dream of liberation that becomes the agony of hope. In the beginning was light. Beneath the light, the ignoble. And finally, graveyards, slaughterhouses, crematoria, infernos without paradise where the masters lead their peoples.

Why? What on earth happened? What had those at the source of the death of God touched on? "That man," says Kirilov to Pyotr Stepanovitch, "was the most sublime man on earth. He gave it a reason for existing. The whole planet, without him, is nothing but madness."[3] The passage is admirable, and it could serve as an epigraph for the whole great shipwreck. It says in fact that the assassinated God was, from the very darkness of the past, an impossibility of assassinating. That this demystified absolute was what made me, confronting the world's aggressions, a kind of absolute. That this violated sanctuary was the living spring which nourished, for everyone, the reasons for his inviolability. God was not in God but the aspect of universality in man. He was "the most sublime" because he made a human being in the full sense out of a vagabond. With his death, everything is not permitted, but everything is a matter of indifference—good and evil, the noble and the ignoble, life, death, and murder. And everything is therefore nothing but "madness," on this great unmasted vessel drifting without a chart on the currents of nihilism. There are no more "reasons for existing" in this twilight of the idols, which makes all values into useless and insignificant icons. And they sound hollow, so hollow, under the hammer of the free spirit, those high values of Justice, Right, and Truth, which no longer have a source for the sap of their intransigence.[4] "What can one do with a soul," Malraux echoes, "if there is neither God nor Christ?" What can a subject do if, released from the absolute, he is abandoned to the chance movements of the meaningless? Nothing, answers the century. He is nothing but matter, the very relative matter of the great work of history. He can do nothing, with a flower in his gun, but fall to the bottom of the abyss.

The question itself is vertiginous; it opens on the abyss. Every time it comes to the lips of a hero, notes Gide in his *Dostoevsky*, "we can be certain that soon thereafter we will witness his defeat."[5] Every time Ivan, Raskolnikov, or Stavrogin takes up the challenge, they can only stand by, pale and powerless, in the face of a nameless disaster that leads them to the brink of suicide. For Dostoevsky, followed by all modern literature, made this discovery: If there is no more sin, the soul itself is a crime. If there is no more redemption, life is an expiation. If God is no longer the Master, then death always wins. Deliverance? Imprisonment rather, more insupportable than ever. Are the heavens without God empty? They are full, so full of his absence, that great silent absence, more demanding than any presence. Is the atheist liberated? We have never been less free since we ceased to believe. "What is going to happen when men notice that there is no longer a sun?" asked Nerval in a passage of *Aurélia* when, leaving Notre-Dame-de-Lorette, he saw a red globe over the Tuileries.[6] Kafka answered in *The Trial* and *The Metamorphosis*: lighting the flames of their remorse in a drunken heaven, meditating a guilt without object until the end of time, men have lost all track of themselves.

We are far from Racine's Phèdre and her tormented self, but a self that was nevertheless cultivated in the depths of her torment. The contemporary theater presents chance figures, void of all psychology and reduced to a mechanical condition. This is not, as has been said too often, the drama of "incommunicability," a play of noise and meaning in which men struggle, willing but unable to understand one another. It is rather the unprecedented phenomenon of a total *noncommunication* between beings with no insides, deprived of all inwardness, literally absent from themselves and consequently from others. Beckett's lifeless heads with the glazed eyes of dead fish, like the young Hitlerites in Ödön von Horváth's *Youth Without God*.[7] Ionesco's unseeing characters, not only in search of an author but above all in search of a creator, pure empty points in the sands of a henceforth infinite space. As with Giacometti, there are indeed masks, but there is nothing beneath the mask, nothing but a shrinking head that continues to wither, never reaching the end of its exhaustion, its truth destroyed by theatrical and fleshly torment. As with Malraux, in the sharp duels between Tcheng Dai and Garine, Ferral and Kyo, there are no more individuals except as they are contained in their effigies and the unheard monologues they pretend to exchange. Where are the blessed days when we were still interested in the emotions of Mme Bovary, the inconstancies of Corinne and Adolphe, the moral dilemmas of Bourget's *Disciple?* One might say that, along with eternity, time itself has flown, and along with divine belief, human introspection. There remains the dry and colorless voice of men—Antigone's revenge—already drowned by the noise of boots and cannon.

If we had to set a date, a literary landmark at least, for this brutal decomposition, I would be tempted to locate it somewhere between Bourget and Proust. Bourget represents the end of the novel of the soul, its substantial atomism, its persistent essence, in a word, its transcendence—the transcendence whose implicit lineage made it unnecessary to establish, or even to doubt, the perennial identity of the subject. With Proust, a narrator of genius and an incomparable artist, on the contrary, begins a hallucinatory descent into the waters of a liquid, dismembered, scattered self, in which consciousness is nothing but a thin and fragile film floating like a "waterlily" in the current of the "Vivonne" or simply dust at the mercy of the winds of chance. Less noisily than Dada, but more clearly than Morand or Barrès,[8] the author of *La Recherche* excels in detecting the intermittences of the heart, the chiaroscuro of passion, the "coral reef" of strange images that make of everyone "a series of juxtaposed but distinct selves,"[9] the "hourly procession"[10] of the thousand and one actors in the theater of shadows which the self has become. *Swann* and *La Prisonnière* are not, as is sometimes said, novels of analysis or subtle psychology, but the sad irony of an impossible analysis, of an undiscoverable psychology whose very object has been dissolved in uncertain areas of confused afterimages and dis-

turbed echoes in which, midway between the nothingness of
sleep and the certainties of waking, the hard kernel of the monotheist subject wavers. In the room already lined like a tomb
where he decided to exile himself to carry out his project, the
narrator-author discovered the truth that the century would proclaim, that would arise from the trenches of the Great War: a
shattered man, torn from his bases, veritably dissipated in the
absurd saraband of his impulses. It was therefore no accident
that it was not until after the drama that a work published amid
general indifference took on its value of demonstration and
prophecy. It was perhaps necessary to hear the silence of the
guns and see arising from the fog the tottering figure of the
wounded and bloody man in order to understand the prophetic
meaning of this grandiose deconstruction.

And yet Proust still believed in the virtues of a memory that
stands against entropy and opposes to its drift something like a
simulacrum of eternity. In contrast, there is nothing of the kind
in all his postwar successors, who reveled in this new *mal du siècle* and in the nothingness of the soul displayed against the background of a meaningless world. It was the time when *"enfants
terribles,"*[11] *"fugitives,"*[12] the *"uncertain,"*[13] cultivating the li-
quidity of a self dissolved in an ocean of philistinism, gave their
novels such eloquent titles as *Le Feu follet,*[14] *L'Enfant inquiet,*[15]
Corps et biens,[16] or *L'Homme pressé.*[17] It was the moment when
Drieu described, in *Gilles,*[18] a "worn-out race," which could see
in "the individual will" only a "myth of another age." When
Gide, having definitively recovered from the Christianity of *La
Porte étroite,* noted that he believed "more and more that the
idea of freedom is nothing but a delusion."[19] When the aging
Rolland presented, in *L'Annonciatrice,* lost heroes wandering
through what was now nothing but "the desert of individualism."[20] When Montherlant, the musketeer frustrated by peace,
the Stoic filled with terror by the spectacle of human passions,
depicted, in the chapter of *Aux Fontaines du désir* which he
dedicated precisely to Rolland, the "thirst" that drove him to

"deny himself," to "destroy himself," to "bite his own neck," in short, to "reject himself" as he would reject "women."[21] When Crevel, as an echo, evoked in *Les Détours* an "abominably free" consciousness, which "looks for what it likes," and finally loses itself by its involvement with the miasmas of a society wallowing in its "imbecility."[22] The result of all this was perhaps a generation of intellectuals literally without consciousness, who knowingly abjured an individualism that was guilty of all the sins of the century. Penitents in red or brown shirts who struggled with the same ardor to break within themselves the springs of personal will and thought. Fellow travelers, as they are called, who had no other recourse but to surrender completely to the dual fascination which effectively dispensed them from being: fascism and Stalinism.

For, in the end, what happened—and beyond literature, in this case—in the mind of an André Gide, whose "honesty of spirit" had always prevented him from adhering to Catholicism but who nevertheless suspended "all the arguments of his reason," all the scruples of his conscience, and then all his repugnance in the face of the camps, the trials, the terror, in order to no longer "hold himself back" on the "slope of communism"?[23] By what extraordinary perversion of the spirit could a Rolland, who was for a long time the model of the intellectual above the fray[24] and who, in *L'Annonciatrice* itself, presented the communist with the hardly attractive features of a brutal and unscrupulous barbarian, bring himself to write of Assia, his heroine, that she "felt freer under the hard thighs of dictatorship than set in the enclosures of a pseudo-democracy"?[25] What is the mystery of the sudden conversions that led an Aragon, for example, almost without transition, as though touched by grace, from "senile Moscow"[26] to the notorious *Hourra l'Oural*,[27] and made Barbusse the humanist the dismally famous author of countless hymns to Soviet terror or the infinite "liberality of comrade Stalin"?[28] How did it happen, in a word, that "despite the disgust, despite the horror, despite the ferocious mistakes and the crimes," as Rolland, again, said,[29] there were so many—they were almost unanimous—who silenced their rebellion and their reservations, and that there were so few who chose to defend, or even thought of defending, against Stalin and Hitler, the simple values of freedom, democracy, and human rights? This represents a formidable surrender, which cannot fail to evoke the perfectly symmetrical surrender of the men of the right who, like a Brasillach, saw in Hitler "the mad dog of Europe,"[30] but who were nevertheless unable to refrain from following in his wake. This is a choice, an acceptance of the inevitable, we would say today a "politics of the worst," for which another fascist, Maurice Bardèche, provided a perfect expression when he proposed to "expel the enemy at any price," to pay "a just price," and for that purpose to "accept the inevitable, even communism."[31] It is a strange resignation, exactly like that of Maurras who, seeing "evil" less in "communism" than in "democracy," adhered to Nazism for want of anything better, because he conceived of it, in Gide's sense, not as an ideal but as *the only possible solution.*[32] Left, right? On the left as on the right there was the same pattern of decreeing that the horror was necessary, of claiming to hate it while adoring the face of its twin. On the one side, as on the other, there was a sacrifice; or better, a pure and simple forgetting of freedom and consciousness, so inconceivable did it seem that there was in the individual the slightest recourse against the dangers of the hour. Eternal fellow travelers on the two roads, they all agreed that they adhered against their will; but they adhered all the same, since the values of the will suddenly seemed to them to be outmoded.

What is more, they shared another common point—or rather a commonplace, in which their parallel abdications were rooted and which explains them. Who wrote in 1939 that "individuals of a good race are not at all grateful if we spare them, and they have more respect for leaders who call on them to sacrifice themselves"? It was neither Bardèche nor Doriot; it was Rolland again, in his *Robespierre.*[33] Who said to the new man whose silhouette was visible on the horizon, "Stand naked, valiant, break your bonds; to grow straight you no longer need anything but the vigor of your sap and the call of the sun"? It sounds like Brasillach praising "the young fascist proud of his vigorous body" glimpsed one fine morning in the sunlight of Nuremberg.[34] But this is in fact Gide speaking, in *Les Nouvelles Nourritures*, in which the Nathanaël of the past has become "comrade" without losing any of the vitalism, the diffuse Nietzscheanism in which he was steeped thirty years before.[35] Yes, vitalism, the mixture of naïve progressivism and the cult of energy. This was the constant of the period between the wars born in the shame of the trenches of 1917 and in the shadow of the "call of the soil" sung by Barrès, Henry Bordeaux, and so many others.[36] Yes, Nietzscheanism. This was, beyond ideological quarrels, the common and unmentioned source for those who saw in the new Germany "the poetry of the future"[37] and for the tired Clérambaults who restored their wavering faith with Marc the "young wolf," Assia the "young cat," and the robust pirates, the hard-hearted barbarians endowed with admirable animal strength who are the communists of Barbusse and Rolland.[38] Moscow the red? Berlin the brown? It was always the same city of light, in which mandarins with clean hands expiated their bankruptcy as intellectuals by enrolling in the school of life. Socialism? National Socialism? In both places they admired the same fascinating spectacle of an organic community populated with young titans, mounting joyfully and under the benevolent rule of Dionysian leaders the steps of the promised land.[39] Did some of them recover, return from the U.S.S.R. or Germany? What is striking in Gide's book,[40] for example, is less the discovery of a terror he had accepted in advance than the revelation of a society of mediocre people, bureaucrats and petty bourgeois, so far from the imagined ideal of a community of enthusiasm, ardor, and fervor. At the end, then, as at the outset of the adventure, there was still the same mythology of "élan," the same hatred of "decadence," the same desire for a "new man" against the anemia of the old world and the old man. From one end of the spectrum to the other, there was the same philosophy of life: all of life, nothing but life, even frenetic and raging, provided only that it "resist sickness" (Drieu)[41] or the "rot of death" (Rolland).[42] On the left as on the right, there was an identical romanticism, which seems to be the last recourse after the death of God and the dissipation of the self. Théophile Gautier had already exclaimed: "Barbarism rather than boredom."[43]

Better than a romanticism, a mysticism. And it is not the least significant paradox of these atheist socialists that they were involved with a strange spirituality, without God or transcendence, whose dangers none of them succeeded in averting. It is always forgotten, for example, that Barbusse was not only the author of an unpardonable biography of Stalin; he also committed, almost simultaneously, a stupefying *Vie de Jésus,* depicted as an Antichrist of pity and forgiveness, a socialist Christ so close to men and their suffering that he has forgotten to believe in God.[44] Nor was Rolland a humanist lost, for obscure tactical reasons, in a classical dilemma of ends and means. His blind faith, his will to penitence, his unreserved adhesion, could come only from a believer, devoted to an immanent religion which was sometimes— as in *Jean-Christophe*—that of an irrepressible life struggling against nothingness, and sometimes—as in the *Journal des années de guerre*—Gandhi's and Ramakrishna's Hinduism.[45] Nor can one understand anything about Gide's career if one does not see in his conversion the brief moment of conjunction, which he had so long sought, between the two terms of the dilemma in which he had always been caught: the Christian aspiration whose dead end was described in *La Porte étroite,* and the orgiastic religiosity of *Les Nourritures terrestres.*

I am not saying that all three—Barbusse, Rolland, and Gide—were not also sincere adherents, but that their communism, even their socialism, and certainly their Marxism, were only a thin veneer on the surface of a fundamentally religious drama that each one experienced in his own way. It is no longer enough, at this point, to speak of Nietzscheanism. For, in this immolation of the personal will on the altar of history and the state, how is it possible not to see the return of a forgotten sacredness, an archaic mentality, an age-old superstition? Here, too, the right was not outdone, with Châteaubriant, for example, the old Nazi *chouan*, who died in exile in Kitzbühel because he had wanted to reconcile an impossible Christianity with the attraction of the secrets and nocturnal forces (that modern Wotan tinged by the Breton peat-marshes) in which he saw the sanctification of Hitlerian madness.[46] For, in the last analysis, this is the key to those dark years and to the "totalitarian temptation" whose lineaments they captured and which has not failed, I hope, to recall more recent memories: the resurgence, on both sides, of what must be called a new paganism.

Yes, paganism. For if there is a lesson to be drawn from this example, it is probably that. The twentieth century, whose mad barbarism is illustrated but unfortunately not exhausted by the thirties, is not an atheist century. It is quite the opposite of flat materialism in the usual sense of that word, which it sometimes, blandly, attempts to accredit.[47] It is a religious age, no doubt more religious than any other, but with a pagan religion, whose gods, the "idols of stone and wood," are called State, Nature, Camps, or Party. Party? What do the Cambodians say today to name the unnameable fact of an individual death in which they go, not to the Eternal, but to the "supreme Organization,"[48] to the God of bronze and machines invented by the French Revolution, whose "thirst," as they say, seems decidedly unquenchable. The camps? In the face of the narratives of the survivors of Auschwitz or Kolyma, it is impossible not to think of secular versions, and therefore terribly real ones, of ancient representations of Hell, in which we seem to find, scattered on the surface of the earth, a minute reproduction of the details of the old iconography. The Gulag has no perennial name, and the only way to keep it from banality is to accept that it is not the divine but the "Diabolical Comedy" of our time.[49] Nature? We have heard

enough lamentations over matter deflowered, eviscerated, desanctified by technical rationalism; it has never been so full of
gods, so brimming with sacredness, so weighted with superstitions as in the new temples which the century has ceaselessly
erected to the Earth, the Race, the Blood, the People, to Man
himself—that Man whom a Rosenberg claimed to liberate from
his subjection to the "stars" the better to integrate him, "with an
imperious humility, into the great laws of the universe."[50] Finally, as for the State, it has taken all the foolishness of the Don
Quixotes of anti-technocracy to make us forget, behind so-called
Jacobinism, the very real survival of ancient idolatries. Such ideologies—henceforth rooted in the earth—flourish in organizations claiming to be secular. And secularism is first of all, at the
end of the long struggle that opposed states to churches, at the
end of a relentless battle—settled early in the East, more recently in the West—a fantasy of a temporal papacy, a dream of a
secular pontificate in which every spiritual rebuke becomes a
weapon brandished by the political order.

It is strange how things come full circle. How connections between earth and heaven are formed and dissolved. How history
suddenly stammers to the rhythm of an invisible and silent pendulum. For what is this paganism but a return of the repressed,
thought to have been crushed by the Jewish and Christian arch-
angel, but nevertheless present again: a paradoxical archaism at
the confines of the future? How can we fail to recognize in these
secular papacies the shadow of the law of *Antigone,* in this desanctified nature the echo of Stoic physics, in this earthly hell the
hell of Aristotle's cosmology, in these collectivized deaths a memory of impersonal death as Plato conceived it? How can we not
also be surprised that after two thousand years of progress and
enlightenment time thus turns back, erases its own tracks, and
seems to return, as though after a blessed pause, to an ordinary
barbarism, which had perhaps never ceased secretly to inhabit
it? Yes, Greece has returned; built around different frameworks,
but faithful to its ignorance of the one God and his creatures, the

latest potion of nihilism and the ultimate stage, for the moment, of the odyssey of the death of God. Polytheism has returned, exactly as Comte foresaw in his *Catéchisme positiviste,* so badly received in its time and still surrounded today by a silence that deepens as its "extravagant" prophecies are unfortunately verified.[51] One might almost believe that the normal state of humanity is indeed, as Comte said, an etymological "catholicism"—a religiosity reduced to its function of social bond, in which "organization," "constitution," "systematization," "discipline," in short, the Institution, is alone capable of enforcing submission on the body of the people.[52] One might almost believe that the monotheism which for so long attempted to oppose to this religiosity its "evangelical anarchism" was nothing but a "transition," a "late and ephemeral phase," a parenthesis destined to close as certainly as it had one day opened.[53] Suppose he were right, this visionary who promised himself that he would preach his doctrine in Notre-Dame. Suppose he saw correctly when he proclaimed to the "Conservatives" the marriage of "fetishism" and the science of "order."[54] Suppose we are in the process of stepping over, as he wished, the simple interval of the biblical era. In that case, the jubilant hordes in which I thought I recognized the crowds of heretics of the beginnings of Christianity would be closer to the troop of conspirators who, four centuries earlier, condemned Socrates to death.

Is this only a hypothesis, a fiction? The hypothesis and the fiction can be verified if you simply connect them to the primal scene of this pitiful adventure. The *"ci-devant* Capet," through whom the French Revolution attacked the person of God, was certainly not Socrates. Saint-Just, on the other hand, in that memorable indictment in which Camus boldly saw the first act of modernity,[55] in those icy syllogisms falling like heads from the guillotine, was, if not an Anytos, at least a prosecutor of fourth-century B.C. Athens. When he establishes an equation between the "state" and the "public welfare," how can we not think of Sophocles equating justice with the city? When he invokes "vir-

 board notation: ᢖ 11 5ᢖ

tue," is he doing anything but paying homage, often implicit, to the morality without ethics whose formulation was provided to him by the ancients? When he speaks, a little later, of the "force of circumstances," we seem to hear the voice of Epictetus and the "order of the world" of Marcus Aurelius or Seneca. And when he proclaims before the world, finally, that "happiness is a new idea in Europe," he simply forgets to add that this new idea—totalitarian, as we have seen—was above all a Greek idea. We always look for the intellectual origins of the Terror in the Enlightenment. In fact, we have to go back much further. It was ancient morality that haunted the conclaves of the Convention and the two Committees. Maximilien Robespierre dreamed of having Cato and Cicero sitting on them one day, not Rousseau or Diderot.[56] He had the Greek ideal of a citizen in mind again when he spoke, in a famous phrase, of "making man free and happy through the laws."[57] And when he bestowed the signal honor on a philosophical system of placing it on the list of festivals of the *Décadi,* he thought of the "Stoics,"—the Stoics alone and no other ideology, not even a contemporary one. In the depths of their cells, Mme Roland and Choderlos de Laclos restored their failing courage with the memory of Plutarch, Tacitus, and Cato the Elder:[58] Antiquity, always Antiquity, in minds which, even on the threshold of death, replaced the imperative of resistance with a senseless nostalgia for the legendary *amor fati.*

Indeed, we hardly know to what point, even before 1789, the entire Enlightenment was steeped in a climate of Hellenism, and particularly of Stoicism. It was in 1774 that Lagrange and Naigeon produced for Diderot their monumental translation of the *Oeuvres de Sénèque le Philosophe.*[59] Throughout the century, there were no fewer than thirty-seven editions and translations of Epictetus alone.[60] This was the century when Frederick the Great was called the "Marcus Aurelius of his age." Everyone was aware of the lunatic theories of Buffon and Bernardin de Saint-Pierre about the function of the elephant's trunk or the insect's claws,[61] literally copied from the Stoa's scientific treatises.

The Stoa was there too, as a physics and a general cosmology, when Shaftesbury noted that all the ills of the century came from the ruinous "war" that had been "declared against the universe."[62] A closer approach to Stoic morality and politics had never been made than with Locke himself, when he drew from Cicero his definitions of the body, of "uneasiness," and of "civil religion."[63] An ideological revolution? A revolution certainly, but in the etymological sense of a planet returning to its point of departure. Individualism? In a sense, yes, of course, but the author of the *Second Treatise* had no more words than Chrysippus to express the principle which individuates a subject.[64] In a way like Aristotle, coming up against the family molecule in his genealogy of the state, he too stopped with an individual who, already socialized in the very heart of the state of nature, nowhere appears in his atomism and his dispersion. In a way like Sophocles, incapable of thinking of the subject outside the network of a civil religion that exhausts and prohibits him, he created the concept of a man "capable of laws" who was nothing but the servant of legal bonds and relationships.[65] Finally, like all of Greece, crushing the personal will within the space of a literally totalitarian city, modernity in its wake made its *de jure* subject a simple accident in nascent secularism, the inverse of ancient sacredness. This was a new religion, then, which was thenceforth endlessly celebrated even, as I have said, in the supreme fantasy of its withering away: the religion of the state.

It will be objected that the philosophy of the Enlightenment was the only one that gave birth to a "Declaration of Rights" with which we are still living and which is, it goes without saying, of infinite value. Hesitating precisely between attributing those rights to "man," that is, to the Christian soul, or to the "citizen," that is, the Greek archon, this declaration was an element in a system which, dispossessing the subject of his will and attaching him to the wheel of a sovereign general will, quickly changed "right" into "duty," "freedom" into a "necessity," and made the "Terror" another name for "virtue." Is it not true that the modern state is the first one which included in its definition the postulate of a free individual who was author of the laws? This individual was precisely a postulate, a limit and a fiction which, owing his eminence to nothing outside himself, was nothing but a social fact—an induced and created difference, an artifact without inwardness or real autonomy, whose resistance is blocked at the very moment that it is assumed. Is there not finally a contradiction in the fact that the concept of "human nature" dates from this very point? The contradiction is only apparent because—again in an imitation of Athens, establishing the swarming crowd of its dungeons and gynaecea in a "barbaric" imaginary structure—the eighteenth century made its "state of nature" an ideal boundary, a fantastic fringe populated by the poor, the vagabonds, the deviants, all those hordes of the excluded who were, in Nature, the accursed negative image of the radiant society of Reason. For that is secularism too, that mixture of statism and naturalism, which creates citizens at best—a low-water mark of humanity—animals at worst—a zero degree of humanity. If we owe to it democracy and certainly tolerance, it has also bequeathed to us, down to Stalin and beyond, the figure of a bloodless individual, rarefied in the extreme, who, forgetful of his dispersion according to Occam, is once again impossible, at the limit of all thought, ontologically undiscoverable in the great neo-pagan desert.

8

Critique of Political Paganism

We shall encounter the landscape of this neo-pagan desert throughout the second half of this book. For the moment, it will suffice to point out very briefly a few privileged sites.

It is clear, for example, that Nazism was a militant paganism—and not only, as legend would have it, because of the "Nordic" folklore it attempted to glorify.[1] We can understand nothing about its racial theories, its cult of blood, race, and the fatherland, without the insistent reference to old "maternal" principles that made the Führer the faithful servant of a "humanity according to Nature."[2] We would miss the essential point of *Mein Kampf*—the book that was intended as an authentic pagan Bible—if we neglected its mad will to abolish three thousand years of rationality, affirmation of the Law, "paternal" mediation, and, in effect, monotheism.[3] Whatever the twists and occasional inconsistencies of the Reich's policies toward the churches, there remains the thread that ran through them of a dream of a new "Church," a "national Church of the Reich," for which Rosenberg composed the founding "thirty articles."[4] Nor was the choice of swastika as emblem for the régime insignificant; it represented both a scathing challenge to the theology of the "crucified one" and a return in force of that "Indo-European" archaism whose dark mysteries the unemployed corporal had discovered in the twenties.[5] Even the holocaust—that unparalleled and strictly unprecedented extermination—owed its particularity to the ravings of a diseased brain, which saw the Jews as the irreducible obstacle to the "election" of the "Germanic" people. To place it on the same level as the murder of the Poles, the communists, or the "asocial" is thus not only a moral outrage but an historical error, which neglects the capital difference between physical liquidation and the *metaphysical* hatred whose goal was to erase even the memory of the people of the Bible.[6] No, National Socialism was not an atheism, nor was it a politics. It was a war of religion. It was a religion of war. And the French fascists of the time, our gentle national fascists, understood this very well when, like Montherlant in *Le Solstice de juin,* they hailed the victory of pagan Germany over a decadent Christian France.[7] Or, like Drieu La Rochelle, they once more chose their camp: "I am probably, to the extent that I allow myself to consider the matter, of the religion of Plato and not of St. Paul."[8]

It is also clear that, much earlier, the Romantic movement[9] was a paganism, not of the same order, of course, but with strangely similar notions. In this case, too, it takes a good deal of blindness to see an individualism, a cult of the self and the particular, in a *Naturphilosophie* that, from Baader to Schelling, speaks of nothing but an immense physics in which everything exalts the subject only to invite him to annihilate himself, and in which consciousness never arises except to become more fully identified with the darkness of things. If the Athenaum was the first avant-garde movement in the history of literature, it was above all a fantastic regression which—claiming again that it circumvented the monotheist edifice and the commandments of its law—rediscovered the monism of the theosophists, the alchemists, and the visionaries of the Middle Ages.[10] These "moderns" were first of all "archaic," and they too dreamed of a "new Greece," an ideal Athens with the colors of the Black Forest, which was already the exact opposite of biblical Jerusalem and its insistent witness.[11] Again the same mimetic rivalry in cloudy, but significant, projects of a "regenerated" church, in which Friedrich Schlegel was to be St. Paul, Novalis Christ, and Tieck and Schleiermacher secular apostles.[12] Was Hitler a romantic? It is certain, in any case, that Möller van den Bruck, Spengler, and Keyserling were, and that this "neo-romanticism"—the only consistent new romanticism in modernity—was not far removed from Nazi paganism.[13] Another romantic was Jünger who, "beyond the painful reality of the battlefield," seemed to see floating over the carnage "the smiling face of a divinity"[14] restoring the soldier, "as in Homeric battles,"[15] to contact with an "earth" represented in the form of a fruitful and cruel "mother."[16] Again, it was the Schlegels who bequeathed to Rosenberg their praise of the "few great patriotic discoverers" who, building the "archetype of Germanness," only made the mistake of forgetting that "that Germanness is not behind but before us."[17] Nor can I see any misunderstanding or betrayal when the National Socialists called upon Wagner, who had written that the Jews were "the incarnate and triumphant demon of the degeneration of humanity,"[18] and that it "was necessary simply that they fear for their lives and that they believe that they see before them the people armed with clubs and whips."[19] And finally, for those who are nostalgic and ill-informed, I would point out that, at the moment when the Catholic Church seemed, provisionally at least, to have softened its anti-Semitic propaganda, it was the Romantics again, the Romantic family as a whole, which, from one end of Europe to the other, maintained the sacred flame.[20]

We could go still further and show how this neo-pagan motif can be found, although in a different form, even in Marxism. Marx liked to say that he was not the first "Marxist"; he would have been surprised, however, to learn that he was one of the last representatives of the Stoic tradition. How can we not be struck, in fact, by the strange homology between these two materialisms and their structures? How can we not see, in a philosophy of history that makes the subject merely a minor player on the stage of the "dialectic," the counterpart to the "system" that was already entirely built around theatrical metaphors?[21] How can we not hear, in the progressives' threnody assuring us that happiness is the reward for a consistent *amor fati*, the echo of the "fate" of which Chrysippus, among others, said that it was another name for providence?[22] What is "class consciousness"— that strange science of misfortune which allows us to live happily, because we know, in our chains—but the unexpressed return of the old "exegesis" that assured us that we free ourselves from pain by penetrating the secret of its law?[23] And what is the meaning of the imperative of being "in the direction of history," but the decision to submit to the "order of things," about which Seneca already maintained that it left the choice only between "following willingly" or "being dragged by force"?[24] Do everything within your power to bring about what does not depend on you, Marcus Aurelius commanded in substance;[25] adjust your free practice, Marxism orders in turn, to the revealed truths of theory. The highest good, said Cicero, is to live according to "the science of what happens";[26] the Revolution, says Lenin, going one step further, is a science which simply demands of its actors that they make their "objective interest" sufficient for their desires. "Live in conformity to nature," advised Zeno the sage; history, answers the young Marx, is a "second nature," the "natural science of humanity."[27] The details of the parallel are hardly important under the circumstances. The essential thing is that here too, quietly and discreetly, the return has been consummated. History, that "second nature," occupies the same place as the primary nature of the Stoa. Placed, as Kant had foreseen,[28] at the intersection of physics and theology, it has itself become a theology and a physics. Taking up the cosmological aims of each one, it has itself become a general cosmology. An implacable system of total knowledge, it calculates suffering, weighs the dead, draws the lines and the spaces between good and bad corpses, and assigns to each living being his rank in the new order of the world. Marxism is a historicism, but this historicism is structured like a Stoicism. And it is probably this Stoic paganism, to which I shall return, that forms the link with other modern varieties of totalitarian thought.[29]

In any case, this Stoicism is explicitly bound up with the wind of fanatical anti-Semitism that blows through the thought of the whole century. The documents of the case are well known. The famous formula of *The Jewish Question* according to which "the social emancipation of the Jews" depends on "the emancipation of society from Judaism."[30] The clever riddles of a brilliant polemicist: "What is the secular basis of Judaism? *Practical* need, self-interest. What is the secular cult of the Jew? *Haggling.* What is his secular God? Money."[31] The admirable theoretical intelligence of *Capital* in which we learn that all commodities, "however tattered they may look, or however badly they may smell, are in faith and truth money, are by nature circumcised Jews."[32] The outbursts in his correspondence: "the Jew with the honeyed smile," "the cursed Viennese Jew," "the Jewish pig," "the Paris synagogue-stock exchange," "Lassalle, the Yid from Poland."[33] And also the formidable posterity of this "theoretical" anti-Judaism, whose authority is invoked in the U.S.S.R., for example, every time an academician takes it into his head to denounce "Jewish capital" and the "Zionist plot."[34] Even the Nazis sometimes brandished the Marxian precedent as a basis for scientific analysis of the origins of "Jewish wealth,"[35] or to provide the gas chambers with a rational pedigree.[36] And finally, even today, there persists in the ranks of the communist left a "reasoned," "reasonable" anti-Semitism, strictly based on just hatred for "monopoly capitalism"—monopolized, as everyone knows, by "cosmopolitan tribes" (Benoît Frachon)[37] or by worshippers of the "golden calf" (Maurice Thorez).[38] All that is known—or ought to be, at least, even if it is sometimes urgently necessary to refresh people's memories.

What is less well known is that madness of this caliber was not based only on the anticapitalism necessary for the workers' movement. Or, more exactly, that it also derived from an entirely different passion, arising among the socialists and shared by the overwhelming majority of the intelligentsia of the time, which was quite simply the hatred of monotheism. This was the position, for example, of Wilhelm Marr, the probable inventor of the word "anti-Semitism," who, in 1862, published *The Mirror of the Jews* in which he analyzes, "from a non-religious point of view," as the subtitle says, "the victory of Judaism over Germanism."[39] It was the position of Eugen Dühring, who saw in Christianity "the shame of millennia," an obstacle to the anti-Semitic struggle, and an obscurantist mechanism created by the contemptible Jews.[40] Bruno Bauer also denounced "Jewish Christianity" and undertook the composition of a *Christianity Unmasked*—unmasked as "Jewish," of course—quickly confiscated and pulped by the authorities.[41] And Georg Daumer, fanatic of the atheist crusade, in *The Secrets of the Christian Soul* made Jesus the head of a Jewish cannibal sect; he was widely read and discussed in revolutionary circles, and soon thereafter in the entourage of Richard Wagner.[42] In short, the entire Hegelian left, the vast movement of criticism of religion, all the theoreticians of atheist humanism and the emancipation of humanity, provided a terrain, concepts, and a complex of problems for the Marxist phantasmagoria. Anticlerical as much as it was antibourgeois, anticlerical even *before* being antibourgeois, this new anti-Semitism saw Judaism as the source rather than the contrary of Catholicism. Exactly as with National Socialism, it was the "deiphoros" people and not, as in the past, the "deicides," that the socialists of the nineteenth century hated and dragged before the court of history. And this was a decisive reversal with incalculable consequences, whose concrete effects on the Russian Jews of today, for example, have not yet come to an end.

The reversal, in fact, was less novel than it may seem. It took place much earlier, and we must look for its origin further back in time—at the dawn of modernity, that is, once again, with the philosophy of the Enlightenment. It was then, in effect, that the

Jews of France began to discover, with what stupefaction one may imagine, that they were in the process of being transformed from the murderers of God into his cursed inventors. *L'Encyclopédie* clearly expressed the spirit of the age when, in the words of the neo-Stoic Naigeon, it presented Jesus as "an obscure and fanatical Jew" and the Jews themselves as the hated fathers of that child of misfortune.[43] Even better was the "Petition of the Tradesmen and Merchants of Paris Against the Admission of Jews," published in 1765, which mentioned all the traditional accusations except one, curiously: the murder of Christ.[44] Jean-Baptiste de Mirabaud, permanent secretary of the Académie Française, published in 1769 a collection, *Opinion des Anciens sur les Juifs*, whose central argument was that Mosaic Law, because it was at the source of Islam and Christianity, was the most dangerous and most superstitious of all superstitions.[45] The esteemed Baron d'Holbach, an attacker of superstitions if there ever was one, confirmed the diagnosis by seeing Christianity as a "schismatic sect" of Judaism, and Judaism itself as a practice of "cowardly and degraded Asiatics," which "gradually infected the whole Empire."[46] Finally, Voltaire probably went the furthest, at least in verbal violence, since, among the 118 articles of his *Dictionnaire philosophique* there are no fewer than thirty that, always in the name of the struggle against *l'Infâme*, heap the worst insults on "the most abominable people on earth."[47] I know very well that the author of the *Dictionnaire* is also the author of a *Traité sur la tolérance à l'occasion de la mort de Jean Calas;* but I also know that, even in this *Traité,* in the midst of an indictment of fanaticism, there persists the murderous distraction of the prosecutor.[48] I can very well believe, as his French communist editor[49] advises us to, that d'Holbach's anti-Semitism was "progressive for the time," and that it has nothing to do with "the barbaric racism of the late twentieth century."[50] But we are in the late twentieth century, and his works are regularly reprinted in the Soviet Union, one of the few countries—it can never be repeated often enough—in which "racist barbarism" has been elevated to the status of a state religion.

Nor is this all. If we consider the case of Voltaire a little more closely, we observe that he did not stop here. He was not satisfied with insult or obsessive references to Jewish "penises," "glans," and "foreskins," which seemed to disturb his distracted mind so greatly. He did not even confine himself to criticism of the superstitions, the intolerance, and the abuses of established religions. For this deist also had an ideal religion; this "gentleman of the King's chamber," as he wrote pompously to Isaac Pinto,[51] also had a country dear to his heart. And this country was, as though by chance, Greco-Roman Antiquity. Thus, in an imaginary dialogue with Cicero, he evokes the congenital "fanaticism"—congenital like "blond hair" in the "Germans"—of a people that might very well, he says, become a "mortal" danger for mankind.[52] His favorite argument against this "stupid" people was that it borrowed the greater part of its culture from the ancients and that it would take a great deal of "ignorance" to dare to imagine the opposite.[53] In *Dieu et les hommes*, he presented them as the cleverest and most skillful plagiarists, whose holy books were literally copied from Homer and whose entire religion was inspired by the religion of Hercules and Eurydice. He referred to "the Israelites without foreskins who sell old rags to the savages,"[54] only to contrast their immemorial barbarism to the sublime humanity of the "citizens of the Roman Empire." If he ran out of arguments or felt the force of his anger weakening, he strengthened it with Philostratos, Tacitus, or Juvenal, in whom he found nourishment for his inextinguishable rage.[55] When he found himself moved by the eloquence of the Book of Maccabees, he concluded—after a torrent of sophisms, intellectual acrobatics, and moral impostures—in *La Bible enfin expliquée* that this eloquence was too "human," precisely, to belong to the corpus of the Old Testament and that its presumed source must be the Greeks.[56] The knight of tolerance, in other words, not only hated the Jew as Jew; he hated him for not being Greek—others would soon say Aryan or Indo-European. And

this was not one stage among others in the history of the old phobia. It was the decisive stage, which removed it from Christian
territory and rooted it in Antiquity. Voltaire was not an ordinary
anti-Semite but the inventor, in this sense, of modern anti-Semitism.

We can now perhaps recognize the thread that connects this
original act to more secret phenomena. And we can see that it set
in motion an infernal machine whose unpredictable effects have
continued down to the present. The Middle Ages were certainly
not very merciful to the Jews, and no Auschwitz could ever erase
or make banal the pogroms of Hanover and Mainz. But the fact
remains that, in breaking off at one stroke the dialogue the Jews
of Christendom had continuously carried on with their opponents even in the ghetto, Voltairean anti-Semitism attained a
new dimension. On the ruins of the coexistence—full of conflict,
of course, and sometimes downright murderous—between the
Church and the Synagogue (which has left its traces in the motifs of the portals of countless cathedrals), there suddenly appeared a cold, brutal, and irrevocable hatred. Instead of the an-
tagonism of the past, in which the "chosen people" remained,
even in humiliation, in the depths of degradation, a kind of emblem, a "living monument," said St. Bernard, "necessary to the
glory of the Eternal," added Pascal,[57] the Jew became the absolute other, the one who was radically excluded, the material witness who must be eliminated at any price from the consciousness
and the unconscious of men. The Jew had been "different" from
the Christian; and that very difference was an admission of identity and of a common divine descent. He was the child of a
"race," the "new Greek" now said; and that "race" no longer
had a place in the sun with "regenerated" humanity. The idea of
extermination, whether we like it or not, was literally unthinkable, indeed sacrilegious, in a monotheist universe in which the
new covenant succeeded to the old. It became possible, thinkable,
reasonable, scientific perhaps, in the de-Christianized world
condemned to great pagan regressions. I am not saying that Vol-

taire and Diderot were the precursors of the death camps, but that after *L'Encyclopédie* and the unprecedented reversal which it provoked in the collective imagination, one could kill the Jew from behind and, for the first time, without speaking.

It is easier to understand, as well, the meaning of the alternative which, from my deconstruction of the Greek model on, has governed these reflections as a whole. It was not from a taste for provocation that I raised the question "Athens or Jerusalem?" but because the dilemma is present, monumental, unavoidable, imposed by the century and provoked by it. Nor is it an accident that I felt obliged to pay homage to the "genius of Christianity." This homage is only just since, at the end of a long (far too long) spiritual night, a Catholic pope has proclaimed to the world, "spiritually we are Semites." Nor is there any nostalgia in my recognition of the historical death of God, but precisely a recognition, an inventory of the disaster, an invitation to rethink, to escape from the dead end perhaps, to resist in any case the effects of barbarism to which we are condemned by events. And this is why, finally, hardly caring, at bottom, to "choose" between the Enlightenment and Romanticism, Marxism and Nietzscheanism, Hegelians of the right and the left—why not Hitler and Stalin?—I believe it is urgent simply to hear again today, against all forms of "reaction," the extreme modernity of the monotheist Book.

PART THREE:
THE MIRACLE OF THE NAME

The attempt will be difficult, and the road is a hard one. For it is not as simple as I have said to get rid of paganism. Not everyone can dwell in the house of the Book whose spine touches a heaven I know to be empty and without God. Should we forget one thing or remember another? I shall proceed very cautiously at first; self-consciously, and in a state of constant alert; a methodic vagabond moving systematically along the path traced by my name. It only remains to me to hope that the route has preserved enough memory to defeat or hold back the seductions of sacredness.

Hence these four tests, these four meditations, which I would like to have resemble circles or great hoops of steel. A set of fences, dikes, walls of stone and paper, in whose shelter there can arise the clamor of resistance. What must a man be in order not to be the victim of a concentration camp? How must he think of himself in order not to be himself an assassin? From these questions—the only ones that count—there follows a deduction that shapes the heart of the matter: at the crossroads of a Law, *a* wager on the universal, *a demand for* singularity, *and a retreat to* inwardness.

9

The Name of the Law

For how could I accept this silence of God and of man? Even if paganism were to triumph everywhere, I do not believe it would convince me. Even if it had reason and all the arguments on its side, a confused unreason would continue to deny it. Even if I were at the nadir of doubt, an age-old certainty would still keep me alert. I am, in fact, in doubt, certain of my nothingness and of the ruins of my concept; and yet something tells me that my head is not so empty for all that. Perhaps it is an obscure fact, a series of tenacious facts that I remember when, in the very midst of the débâcle, something in me stiffens, protests, and rebels. No doubt it is a truth which is truer than all the truths of ontology, a truth to which all the consciousnesses of the century hold so stubbornly from the moment they reject the temptation to surrender. I shall begin by attempting to exhume this truth.

So, let me start again. First of all, it remains true that of all animals I am the only one who dies, and of all living things I am particularly the only one who suffers. This suffering is sometimes so intense, so great is the burden it imposes on me, that I find it hard not to believe that it is aimed at me, that it concerns and pursues me in person. It is so insistent, so terribly insistent, that I can hardly imagine that it affects me as a thing, as a stone among stones, as a mass of nerves and bone, pure suffering matter comparable to all other matter. It presses me too closely, embraces me with too much patience, for me not to be obliged to presume that it has it in for my self, that it wishes a self that can bear it, and that it wants to become incrusted in a self shaped according to its requirements, as though for the express purpose of receiving it. That is indeed what I feel when, in the silence of anguish, I see myself stand forth, massive and suddenly so clear, the dazzling master of ceremonies of my nights of anxiety. That is the lesson I draw when, dreaming of melting, dissolving, disappearing, I am brutally called to order, the order of my name, a name re-marked by the sorrow without origin whose painful and singular torment Job was the first to experience—for himself and for all succeeding humanity.[1] There must indeed be something human, something of Man must survive in man, for there to be so much evil assaulting him, an evil whose savagery no meaning can ever mitigate. God or no God, in other words, this is a first proof, negative and by the absurd (slender and still very fragile) of my being as a subject: I exist because there is evil, because that evil is radical, and because, without the hypothesis of that existence, there would no longer be a basis on which the radical nature of evil could be thought.[2]

But it is also true that however much harm this evil may do me, nothing forces me or ever will force me to submit to it. It can pursue me, leave me no peace; yet nothing in the world will prevent me from disrupting, upsetting, sabotaging the patterns of the world. The world itself can be closed, enclosed by the law of a master; one man, a single man, who rises up, indicates by himself that something is functioning in the enclosure, that the enclosure has failed. Isn't the subject a pure effect on the social bond? The simple fact that I rebel proves that the bond is interrupted, that it has failed to take, and that a movement, coming from who knows where, is enough from time to time to break the thread. Can I prove this interruption, deduce it philosophically? Even if I could I would not want to, so refractory does it seem to me, once it has occurred, to any ontology or anthropology—a pure fact of coming into being, absolute evidence of freedom. Could I root this evidence in a self as one would root an accident or an effect in its basic substance? The procedure would be pointless, proving that which proves, deriving what is a source, referring to an origin this paradoxical consequence—primeval resistance. "If one doubts," said Maine de Biran, "that I am master of the application of my mind, I will answer that I am, and that is enough for me."[3] If one asks a rebel whether he is master of his rebellion and on what authority it is based, he will answer with another rebellion, exhibiting less its authority than the grace of his example. Not he is, therefore he rebels; but he rebels, therefore he must be. Not there is insurrection because there is a self first; but there must be a self for me to have been able thus to rebel. Therein lies, parodying Descartes, a second *a priori* proof, a second *cogito* of the soul—the *cogito* by means of a resistance which, through its power and pure immediacy, goes beyond all the truths of pessimism and the sanctions of empirical experience.

This is all the more so—and here is the third fact—because there are proofs that do not depend for their validity on the validity of their method of deduction. The existence of the individual is among these: not a piece of knowledge, a thesis, a concept, but rather a choice, an existential choice. This choice is not a matter of ontology but of ethics, of option, and pure postulation—absolutely necessary even if it is rigorously not supported. It is less a matter of identifying a substance than of placing a wager, *the* wager without which there would be no more reason to respect a body than to treat it like a thing, a dog, cannon fodder. When Vitoria and Las Casas said, for example, that the Indians were "men"—and not "savages" or "animals"—they were not speaking in the name of truth but in the name of the good and of morality.[4] When Nietzsche asserts, on the contrary, that I am nothing but a "meeting point" of currents, forces, and natures, I don't know whether he is right or wrong, for I know that, *before everything,* he has chosen barbarism and the sacrifice of what I am on the altar of what I will be.[5] When I say, in opposition, that I cannot be reduced to that nature, the problem is not even the value of my wager, but what I want—I who make the wager, thereby rejecting sacrifice and refusing to bring death to those around me. Even if this choice were barely probable, I would hold it for certain. Even if it were perfectly dubious, I would hang on to it all the more. Even if it were completely absurd, I would see in its very absurdity a motive for affirming it. And even if all the wise men in the world knew that it was undecidable, I would say that it was decisive in order to choose among values. Personally convinced that, in the order of Being, the individual is worth nothing, I would nevertheless repeat that, in the order of the imperative, nothing is as valuable as an individual. Although it is true that my pessimism whispers to me that the individual has no place in this world, the century which everywhere shows him degraded, debased, martyred, demands that I posit him, and posit him in the Absolute. There is no ontology, in other words, which does not pale before this *cogito,* reduced to its simplest expression, of a pure refusal of murder: I think myself, therefore I am; I wish to be, therefore I will be. The subject and his belief are one and the same reality.

One and the same reality? Logically, that means that this being identified with his belief is no longer a reality at all; that I can believe in him so strongly only by definitively making him a pure philosophical fiction; that this fiction is finally demonstrable only if I first presume that it is, in the usual sense of the word, deprived of all existence; that I can guarantee it against being denied by things only by separating it radically from the order and the law of things. This is virtually what the gnostics say, for example, when they reveal that my roots—my "stock"— do not lie here. My *cogito* is thus far removed from the solid assurances of Descartes and his *poêle;* the fortunate man was illuminated by the brightness of a "natural light," which says nothing to me but the emptiness of a world in which I no longer exist. It is quite close, on the other hand, to Kant's *coup de force*, the unprecedented step by which the world suddenly split in two, with "phenomena" on one side ruled by determinism, and "noumena" on the other no longer governed by the laws of the senses or of science. I am tempted to say of the individual I am advocating what Kant said of his Freedom: He has a hope of escaping from the philosopher's pessimism and the scientist's scepticism only if he exiles himself elsewhere, into a heaven of principles in which he will finally be assured that he will not be dissolved in the merely phenomenal.[6] He is no longer the necessary basis nor even the corollary of the three existential facts in which I located signs of his existence, according to a categorical logic whose authority he now denies; but he is the postulate, the unconditioned condition, the governing idea of a new practical reason, which simply orders that we not kill, that we resist misfortune, and that we recognize the radical nature of evil. Individualism, in a word, is an idealism without metaphysics, a transcendentalism without transcendence, the transcendental idealism of a soul that consists of nothing but the unsupported axiom of a refusal to submit.

Once again, what does it mean that the nature of my wager and what is at stake are such that, as soon as it is made, it escapes investigation? If I were to attempt to endow it with an arsenal of attributes of which I would then, like a psychologist, draw up an inventory, any such list of attributes would simply restore it to the cunning ontology from which I wish to release it. Shall I attempt to know more about it, beyond the assertion (which I repeat for the moment) that "there is something of Man in man"? As with Pascal's infinite, I know clearly *that* it is but, on the other hand, I do not know *what* it is. Besides, how could I go about expressing this fiction—half-obvious, half-concealed—which I can perceive only glancingly? Like the One of negative theologies, this governing idea is perceptible only by faith—others would say by the "heart," I would simply say by an ethics. Can I not at least articulate this ethics in masterful and masterfully organized language? What distinguishes it from ontology is precisely the fact that it does not relate the existent to Being but to the myriad of other existents, in the improbable disorder of their furtive and empirically determined encounters. Does this represent a defect, a failure of analysis? The substantial individual, hypostatized in a clear definition, is, in the contemporary era, the individual that tyrants prefer, programmed by the "human sciences," whom I want nothing to do with at any price. Then how is it possible to escape from this hypostasis? By thinking the paradox of a soul which has no essence but the impossibility of having an essence, which is not a substance but something wrenched away from substance, which is not a thing at all but a kind of self-transcendence that is irreducible to the status of a thing. Consequently, when I speak of transcendental idealism, this is a way of dismissing the dilemmas in which every philosophy encloses me. When I assert that "there is something of Man in man," the formulation is adequate, designating as it does the opposite of an object, a region of the world, or a category of Being. When I say "Man" in this formulation, this nonobject is nothing but a perspective on the world, a point of view on Being, the point of view, simply, of a desperate but unrelenting resistance.

Immediately, I can see the consequences of this lack of definition. First of all, the subject, in this account, is no longer the given he is believed to be, primeval and present at the origin, but a conquest over the given, a denial of the origin. He is no longer a reality, created from all eternity, whom evil societies have progressively rarefied, but a belated surreal being for whom society is not a graveyard but a ground on which he can flourish. He is not a source, a principle, and a creator of effects, but an effect first of all, the effect of his effects, the fruit of a long and painful process, an interminable movement. Rather than the conclusion and the fruit, he is the process as such, movement as movement, which does not so much remove him from his shell as tear him away from the illusion that he has a kernel and that he is natural. I am not, I become; I am the process of becoming a shell in an inexhaustible production of meaning that never unites me with some forgotten home. The private is less peace than war against peace, against the inhibition of the simple, against the nostalgia of primeval mornings, against the laziness of enduring which creates the "happiness of stones" of which Camus spoke.[7] The soul is not the beach beneath the paving stones but the paving stones above the beach, appearance against truth, the mirage of frivolity against the gravity of Being, the play of the symbolic against the paranoid fixation on the solid ground of supposed "roots." Carved from the organizations of the society in which he is located, the individual I have thus presented is less in the stone than in the chisel, less on the page than in the pen, less in the content than in the style. An activity in the body of the existent, he is not a being of the world, nor an existent in the world, but, literally, a *coup d'état* on and against the world.

This is still not a definition. But it is a formula for an individual whom I can call free. Perfectly, sovereignly free. With an *a priori* freedom, which has finally escaped from the traditional and insoluble aporias. For where did these aporias come from? What is this "problem of freedom" which philosophers have harped on since philosophy began? Everything depends first of all on the fact that they have always looked for freedom prior to the free act, in the instant before its advent, in a stock of virtualities which I am supposed to draw on before acting. Further, the subject is supposed thus to possess a capacity for indifference, a substantial autonomy—at ease in the possible, used up in the actual—an autonomy whose characteristic is to choose between dismal possibilities offered to its whims. The philosopher then has no difficulty in seeing these whims as a mirage, this equivalence as a naïveté, and this presumed choice as the retrospective illusion of a consciousness ignorant of the real chemistry through which, while it thought it was deliberating, objective necessity had already chosen for it. Nothing of all that stands up if I hold to my wager. The argument collapses at one stroke in the face of my transcendental, displaced, and insubstantial subject. Freedom is no longer to be looked for before the act, at its imagined source, in that essential place where it is supposed to be activated before it is set in motion, because that place, by definition, no longer exists. I am now obliged to search for it not at the threshold but in the midst of the free act, in its effective fertility, in the concrete involvement in which I am enclosed and in which I invest myself, in the fundamental action that is identical with the self which acts. And in this way I can reduce to nothing the claims of a causality that is admittedly unbeatable in the false debate about the autonomy of human nature, but that no longer has anything to say to me on the real question of what happens when I move and involve myself *in* an act of freedom. In the face of belated etiologies and archaisms about the truth of freedom, I am assured of a freedom precisely delineated by the intensity, the dynamism, the impetuosity of my resolution. Against determinist certainties—which always know that they will have known and eternally foresee what has already happened—I know and I sense that I am; for I am endowed with a power which, contemporaneous with its advent, is nothing but a certain form, a certain quality, a certain modality of the will. This is another version of the *cogito* of resistance: I exist when I will, for I must will in order to be.

Still, one must will. Yes, simply will. And this is not so easy or so immediate as it seems. In effect, when I look within and around myself, I observe that my ordinary state is not to will badly but not to will at all. I see everywhere nothing but forces—whether silent or loquacious regularities—about which I determine that, being "scientific," "necessary," and sometimes even "divine," they excuse me from acting and thinking with my own mind. I cannot become indignant at this without immediately hearing the rumble of the universal admonition once more calling me to order, ordering me to submit, either to the necessities of nature or to those of history, the state, or society. Even if I wished to master them, to act justly with them, to wish them rather than their wishing me, I would not be sure of succeeding. In fact, I would be certain of the very opposite, because I lacked a basis, a rock on which to stand, For this is indeed what I lack in order to will: in the desert of non-intention, in the hell of the insignificant, in this world in which evil is a mechanism rather than some wickedness, one object, a single object, about which I can assert without fear of error that it is the pure object of a will that is mine. This is what I need, and what is needed by all the sleepwalkers, drunk with irresponsibility, sick with surrender, impatient, oh so impatient to lose themselves in the dark undergrowth where, doing nothing but execute necessary and natural laws, they can never again be "willingly evil." They need a Law, the pure product of their brains while simultaneously located outside them, radically absent and simultaneously perceptible by the heart, which they can, by relying on it as one used to rely on God, make into the corollary of their consciousness.

To press the argument further, why, in order for me to exist, do I need the postulate of this absence, this externality, in fact, this submission? Because my fate is such that I really have a choice only between that submission—perfectly imaginary, I agree—and very real submission to the "force of circumstances" of Saint-Just and Hegel. Because the other term of the alternative is again a mute, blind consent to the laws of a material or social externality, which I think I have thoroughly mastered only after it has dispossessed me of all my freedom. Because I know very well, in other words, that without the hypothesis of a sublime heteronomy to which I can exile myself and on which I can make the self-transcendence of my will depend, I have no recourse but the immanent exile, the tacit consent to the laws of the perceptible, which made Eichmann and the *kapos* of the century say that they did not will what they did, did not know what they willed, were nothing but the executors, the agents, the acted-upon of an imbecile thing. If Kant therefore could say, without a shadow of paradox, that the categorical imperative is a principle of freedom, this is because, although this imperative may very well enslave me, it is the only means I have, against the robot sleeping within me, of stretching and restretching the bow of my will. And if Kierkegaard later insisted so firmly on the difference between this commandment and the one imposed on me by the tyrant, this is because, since it is simultaneously external and internal, it has the overwhelming particularity of being a source of dialogue, of "opposition," and finally of a soliloquy between my soul and its double, between myself and myself.[8]

For this is indeed the wonder which I recognize and which makes me, too, join the tradition of this obedience. Contrary, for example, to the scheme of Rousseau's sovereignty (according to which, believing that I was adhering only to a law I had prescribed for myself, I was in fact making a contract with the whole social bond), the face to face confrontation with the Law, with this pure "noumenon" that I arbitrarily posit, is a pretense by which I escape from myself the better to find myself and come close to myself. Contrary to what has always been thought, the initiative of the individual who wishes to be moral does not have as its primary theater the relationship to others, others as they confront him, but the relationship to himself, in which "reason" struggles to win out over "passion," the will to the universal over the desire of the particular, the rejection of barbarism over resignation to its base deeds. Since the I whose task is to inform the empirical self manifests itself only within that empirical self, and has to do only with that self, the struggle for freedom, the battle for the ethical, are the most intimate and most personal tasks imaginable, in which the subject looks only within himself at the conclusion of a labor that concerns only himself. It is not very much then to say that this contemplation of the Law is a principle of freedom and that it wrests me away from the hidden burdens of *amor fati* that drag me down. We must add—and this is essential—that it is a principle of individuation, since there, and there alone, resisting the *fatum* in myself, I discover myself quite simply as a self which can resist. The individual does not make the Law; the Law makes the individual. And if being the Law is being a self, we must agree reciprocally that being a self is always and first of all being the Law.

I said being a self is being the Law. I repeat: the Law makes the individual. And I insist again: if there is something of Man in man, it is that Law and it alone which humanizes the capital letter. In other words, I am so irreducible to all other existents not because I am a biped, a mammal, a being endowed with reason, but because I am the only one who sees myself as and wishes myself to be an animal of legality. If, as I discovered at the outset, it is forbidden to kill me, legitimate that I resist, intolerable that I suffer, this is not because I am alive and because life as such is "sacred," but because I am the Law and that Law, in me, is venerable. If it is true that I am a body, and that that body is inviolable, I am nevertheless not made of blood, earth, and dust, but carved out of finer material, invisible, impalpable, which does not altogether belong to me even if it manifests itself only in me. It is not true, if you prefer, that there is a "soul of the world"—a great and good nature, a powerful and wicked mother, which makes me an atom, a fragment of contingency, and from which I have laboriously been extracted. The fact that I am the child of a Law means, as for Freud, that that Law, being the shape of my desire, makes every definition a negation, every determination a castration,[9] every humanization the fruit of a repression, without origin and perpetually continued. Instead of being repressive, arbitrary, and censoring, the Law makes up the skeleton, the most intimate element, the gap which is the closest to man insofar as he is man and has the name of Man. Outside of it there is, as we know too well, only the release of instinct, the triumph of death given and received, and hence the arbitrary affirmation of the barbarian impulse, faceless and limitless.

From this there follows a decisive reversal whose consequences I can now only guess at. If it is true that confronting the executioners who treat their victims like animals, I must assume in the victim a kind of "human nature," then it is also true that this nature is precisely anything but "natural." If it were, instead of discouraging and shaming the murderer, it would on the contrary comfort him with the classic sophism that the animal is also nature, that nature is also bestiality, and that therefore nothing in nature is opposed to the will to murder. Did they say anything different in Auschwitz when they claimed they were only gassing lice, and in Kolyma when they said they were only imprisoning "hyenas"—in camps throughout the world, nature, always nature, nothing but men reduced to their pure natural essence? Is a racist doing anything different when he treats difference as a form of identity, reduces an individual to his chromosomal identity, considers him a creature explicable by zoology, and makes natural science the zero degree of humanism?[10] No, the truth is that, if the idea of human nature has any meaning, it is as a monster of humanity, a prodigy of denaturalization.[11] That, in order to provide even a minimal obstacle to totalitarian madness, such human nature must be reasoned, overreasoned, torn away from the evidence of its raw immediacy. That, in the face of a biologism which always leads sooner or later to fascism, such a nature must be resolutely legalistic, legislated, legislating, merely a homonym of the human nature of the scientists. If, as distant from me as he may be, another appears to me as a fellow creature, this is because he is neither a primary given nor an immediate given of my consciousness; neither an atom of society nor a cosmological molecule; but an intermediate being, half real, half unreal, about whom I know and respect only the Right that creates him and again the Law that shapes him.

In turn, what does this Law say? What must it prescribe for me? What must it will, so that, by willing, I may be? Spontaneously, I am tempted to conclude that it says nothing, prescribes nothing, literally wills nothing. Since it escapes in principle from an empirical reality that would otherwise deny and submerge me, how could it do anything better than reiterate its monotonous formality? If its whole role is to raise me up, to rescue me from the danger of essence, wouldn't the slightest determination make it fail in its mission and make me lose my non-definition? If the subject that it establishes is nothing but a point of view on things, how could it be anything better itself than an empty and useless perspective on that subject? Hegel was wrong, in this connection, when he saw the French Revolution as the triumph of formal legality, avoiding any "content" as a "restriction." He should rather have said the opposite and deplored the fact that it had been too intent on translating its Law into laws, its *virtù* into "virtues," and its duty into terror. This was the tragedy, not only of Robespierre but of all the subsequent revolutionaries, this degeneration of a formal Will into this will or that will and, always, at the end of the road, the will to wound. My Law is exactly the opposite: a totally abstract form, a judge and never a participant, masterful and never servile, which, rising to its full height between the earth of men and the heaven of principles, claims to dominate the order of the universe. It is not exactly empty, will-less, and powerless; one might rather say that it is full, abounding with a single will, which demands that we sanction, specifically, that we relativize, the contents of all laws and the claims of men to absolutize the particular will. It is formal in the very precise sense that it organizes without ordering, bears witness without being embodied, and formulates a code without detailed prescriptions. But it nevertheless has a function, which is to place me apart, in disagreement, in discontinuity, in perpetual *dissent* with respect to a world that pales in the face of its sanctity. Then what does it say? What does it prescribe? Simply the eternity of a formidable No to the reign of history in which we have seen, from Epictetus to the Marxists, the power of submission.

At this point, I am far from the classic moralities in which a Good, posited at the outset, prescribes the subject's duties in detail. The good that I intend is rather the corollary of a primitive and fundamental duty which has no foundation. It is no longer a sketch of one of those "moral conceptions of the world" for which philosophies are celebrated but which continue to be haunted by the shadow of politics; but a posture, a moral *attitude,* in which the attachment to an impossible principle takes precedence over every possible code or morality. It is no longer even a question of Kantian ethics, still too contaminated by Stoicism so that a subtle necessity sometimes wins out over the demand for freedom; but the vestige of an older tradition, whose impress I am not sure I can find in philosophical ground, and which rather leads me in the direction of the Prophets of the Bible. For is this position of dominance, this excess, this will to be in discord with the world, anything but the definition of the Law of which Malachi says that it must be "no respecter of persons,"[12] and of which the God of Moses says that it is like a great "book" from which the very names of "sinners" are gradually "blotted out"?[13] Is this formal imperative void of any content not the same one that Edom, Ishmael, and all the nations rejected by declining the gift of a Torah in which they saw only a collection of particular laws, in each case intolerable to the spirit of their habits, their customs, their ethos?[14] According to the Bible again, wasn't it the historical virtue of Israel to have understood the meaning of this unattributable non-prescription? And what does being the "chosen people" mean, according to Deuteronomy, but the unprecedented, senseless, extravagant choice of abstract obedience preceding any particular attribution?[15] "Chosen" means postulating a Value which gives value to all values but receives none from them; and this is why it is said that Israel, alone among all the nations, decided to "do" and then to "listen"; to do, consequently, *before* knowing what had to be done; to act absolutely before hearing relatively. "Chosen" also means wagering on an authority which is so high, so removed from the course of history, that it summons me as much as I bow to it. And this is why Isaiah says that Yahweh called him "from his mother's womb";[16] Jeremiah, in his first lines, that God "knew" him "before" he "was formed in the womb";[17] and, finally, this is the meaning of the paradox in Genesis, which has disturbed so many commentators, that makes Noah a "just man" *before* the promulgation of the Law.[18]

I shall return at length to the principle of this Law. To this mysterious precedence which makes me, when I choose it and it chooses me, older than my own name. To the radical externality of a scroll which I must "eat"[19] like the prophet, but which is nevertheless engraved in my "bowels" as on a "tablet."[20] To this ethics of the detour in which a just action is of value only with reference to a Referent which it exhausts no more than, according to Rabbi Akiba, a "lemon" is exhausted when I "inhale" its "odor."[21] But, for the moment, it is time to pause. I asked, What must I remember in order to continue, in spite of all the denials standing in the way, to think of myself as and to name myself Man? I have answered up to this point: I need nothing less than the evidence of a *cogito* that weaves its own truth from the postulate of a Law sufficiently empty and formal never to degenerate, never to crystallize into terroristic legality. I can now confirm: I needed the memory of the monotheist function (or should I say fiction?), whose first and last words are perhaps to wrest the subject away from the burdensome weights of the world, of nature, and of the history it calls "idolatry," and I, in more modern terms, call "barbarism." Why not say it, then? What I had in mind, throughout this journey, was a Number, simply a number, the number "One" of a monotheism whose testament knows neither the word nor the category "religion";[22] whose tradition has at least one singular characteristic, namely that, being refractory to any mysticism, it never ventured to establish either an ontology, a cosmology, or a triumphal world system; and whose effect in the world was thus perhaps nothing but a perpetual suspension of all adhesions to ontology or cosmology in which men get lost, dissolve, and busy themselves. In a word, the "One" of a resistance.

Destroy the Sacred Groves

But we must go still further, drawing all the concrete lessons from this basis in legality, and completing the outline of the individual subject. The fact that he is first of all something wrested away from nature and a will to discord with the world, that he is not a thing or an existent among other existents, implies a chain of consequences in which the function of the monotheist fiction will begin to appear clearly.

The first consequence is that, contrary to the commonplace, a consciousness will never derive what will enable it to affirm itself and to revolt from the obscure depths of a "libidinal economy." Contrary to what the spirit of the age tells us, it is not by listening to the body and some undefined whisper of the flesh that consciousness will discover the source and the nourishment for its resistance. The first nature, in fact, which it must resist is the nature in itself, itself insofar as it is nature, the very natural character of its instincts and desires. For what is this desire, whose imperative has so insistently been asserted recently in the obscene jubilation of its rediscovered excess? Rigorously thought out, it is a process of negativity about which we know, at least since the *Philebus,* that, obsessed by its object, relentlessly attempting to join with it, it is always in the end an aspiration to rest, peace, immanence.[1] Its infinite anxiety—the tireless urge that constantly projects it beyond itself and its works—is never anything but the reverse image of a tranquility and lassitude that are promised as the conclusion of a dialectic confusedly presumed to be bound to break off and consume itself. Lived through in the brutality of its release, in the prodigality of the self that seems so seductive to our vitalists and romantics, it always conceals a hidden appetite for nothingness, a nostalgia for an unmentioned order, a concealed postulation of an identity between soul and soul which, as Rousseau says in his meditation on the shore of the lac de Bièvre, makes him desire nothing so much as no longer to desire anything at all.[2] And finally, attached to the horizon of a future beatitude, it still dreams of a dismissed and literally mortified time, which has fled only in order to flee from itself and to contract into one single instant indefinitely dilated in which, enjoying an interminable platitude, the subject can only wish (like Mozart in a letter to his father)[3] for the pure and simple annihilation of his particular being. Here, in this dream of happiness which haunted the entire eighteenth century and is the real meeting point of Marie-Antoinette and Robespierre; in this preeminence of pleasure which has curiously returned to haunt us in our new age of innocence, sophism, and imposture; in all cases, finally, in which one wagers on nature rather than the Law and its censorship, there is the vestige of a recurring nihilism that undermines any personal will and condemns it in fact to death.

To die of desire? It will be argued that I am making things too easy for myself by reducing desire to its Hegelian and classically dialectical definition. That I am therefore ignoring all the modern attempts, after Nietzsche, to think of it outside shameful negativity, purged of its bad conscience and its anxiety, in the glorious positivity of an immense "yes" to the world. And that there is thereby, in this "liberated" thought, a new relationship to the body and its materiality, which has the specific characteristic of establishing the rights of life against those of the death instinct toward which the Platonic Eros was inclined to move. This is probably true; but it is also true that one does not escape at will from the Platonic enclosure, and that there is in this perspective another version of the illusion, of the same naturalist mirage. What inhabits it is, as always—as I have tried to show elsewhere[4]—the denial and therefore the fantasy of a necessary consumption that repeats in reverse the circuit of the old pattern. The trap into which it falls is the one set out by Stirner, Sade, and a few others, in which the proclaimed innocence of the process of becoming and its currents abolished any scale of good, evil, perversion, and even murder. What is the criterion for distinguishing the oppressor from the oppressed when you sing the praises of untrammelled pleasure and assert the equivalence of all pleasures? What reason is there to choose resistance rather than submission when you make a principle out of desire and the equivalence of all desires? Why should you condemn racism, anti-Semitism, and the concentration camps, when you think that the victims found advantages and pleasure there, and that only pleasure counts according to the standards of liberation? In the name of what, finally, can we continue to speak of the rights of man, if the characteristic of man is to become everything that he is, and if his first duty is to will everything that he can? The truth—the terrible truth of a certain contemporary leftism—is that if desire is indeed, as it assures us, the measure of all things, then there no longer exists anywhere a means for taking the measure of those objects. And if all human chemistry is exhausted by this circle of desire, why should it not be time to rehabilitate a Drieu, to hear a Darquier de Pellepoix,[5] and, in conclusion, to make the natural (so very natural) horror of the century banal?

The truth above all is that, in this naturalism of the left, there is a fearful temptation—again neo-pagan—which might very well end up by not being satisfied with making fascism "banal." As in all *real* fascisms, in effect, it is the individual as such who disappears down the trapdoor of this proud and joyful wisdom.

As in the thirties, we can see the old idolatrous refrain returning with all that that supposes of blind obedience and sacrificial fantasies. And, as in the Greek pattern, the very idea of a subject of resistance becomes again an absurd and improbable myth—a hypothesis as useless as it is illegitimate. The hypothesis is indeed *illegitimate* when, like Callicles, our mutants and decadents decree that all values are arbitrary, repressive, and superfluous, a thin crust on a volcano from which we must await—at once imperturbable and trembling—the eruption and the earthquake. It is *useless* when, like Socrates in this case, they nevertheless recognize a sovereign value in the Number that makes them live in harmony with the world, in the rhythm of its currents, at the whim of its syncopations and its mechanisms of ontological libido. It is *preposterous,* in a word, when, thus reconciling against himself (in surprising complicity) the two antagonistic figures of the famous dialogue, the subject finds himself caught on the horns of a dual necessity, which prescribes on the one hand that he obey the blessed disorder of his own intensities, and on the other that he surrender to the almost organic order of dominant matter. Callicles plus Socrates? Socrates in Callicles? Beyond the image, this is the key to an unprecedented compromise between the order of things which, we are told, is structured like a desire, and the order of human desire which, we are told, is homogeneous with things. Beyond the compromise, it is the cult of a physics which, because it is identically valid in the domain of the instinctual microcosm and in that of the general macrocosm, is the very opposite of ethics and the ground of its impossibility. Beyond this physics itself, it is the return, once again, of ancient Stoic harmony and the commandment it conveyed to men to embrace what they do not control, adore what does not depend on them, and bow to the rule of the inevitable—to renounce, abdicate, collaborate.

It is therefore not surprising that this materialism of the libido fits so well with materialism in the ordinary sense. In Italy, for example, in the late seventies, there was a movement of "autonomy" that was inspired simultaneously by slogans of "liberation" and the most antiquated commonplaces of Marxist dogmatism. In France, at the same time, the old anti-Semitic passion was as strong in libertarian circles as in the party of the working class.[6] Even more strangely, at a moment when repression was at its peak in Argentina, a weekly of the extreme left was capable of arguing—in opposition to an article I had written after a visit to the country—that it was the desire of the "masses" of Buenos Aires to devote their attention to a sporting event, thus aligning itself with the exact position of the Communist International.[7] This series of apparent paradoxes is explained as soon as one admits that materialism remains materialism and that, however it may dress up its denial of the Father and the Law, it can do nothing but provide infinite variations on an identical adoration of order. One who finds the criterion of every politics in the pleasure derived from it by ordinary people is saying rigorously the same thing as one who makes the direction of history the measure of every value. The same procedure leads the one to say that no human rights are worth the "kicks" men get from their concrete violation, and the other to say that freedom cannot be better defined than as "understanding of necessity." An identical necessity is determinant in every case and stands on the twin pillars, synchronous and interchangeable, of a vulgar and vulgarly historicist Marxism on one hand and a leftist and mechanically Freudian brew on the other. In this holy alliance lie the risks of a fascism that will surprise only the myopic, who are determined to look on the right for what always comes from the left.[8] And for me, in any case, there is a clear choice which—against the cult of desire, nature, and the particular—proposes an individualism of reason, principle, and abstraction, no longer engraved in the flesh of things but on tablets of stone situated on the level of the most exalted duty.

It is therefore obvious that the heart of the question is, far beyond the pathetic "ideology of desire,"[9] a notion that stems from much further back, armed with the reputation of all the just struggles the century has conducted in its name, glorified by the dignity it has sometimes granted to countless ridiculed communities—I mean the notion, the affirmation, the claims of what, since the awakening of the "minorities," has been called "difference." For I must stress that if it is true that a consistent antifascism compels me to this duty and abstraction, I have difficulty in seeing what I could make of this antifascism by "listening to my difference"[10] and its "ethos." If we agree that an authentic subject is a monster of humanity who, deaf to any nature, denies his own natural character, then we must doubt that his most precious possession lies in that irreducible particularism he is variously enjoined to cherish and to cultivate. If it is correct that individualism presupposes a wresting away from essence, thinghood, substance, and being rooted, on the contrary, in the Law and its transcendental displacement, how can we not see that claiming to root it in an essential "minority" means turning one's back on it? Further, if we remember that a self which resists is defined less as a region than as a point of view on the world, and that this point of view is first of all one that forbids us to kill, can we not imagine a "politics of difference" which would be paradoxically terroristic and murderous? In fact, this is what would happen if, with complete consistency, we granted the executioner, the pervert, or the Nazi his sacred right to difference, and thus his right to kill, to rape, or to imprison.[11] This is not an imagined notion but the concrete position of Callicles and his contemporary heirs, who are so ready to oppose to the dictatorship of the singular the dictatorship of force, to the empire of the general the rule of violence, to the arbitrariness of the Law the law of caprice and madness. It is not even an accident but the strict corollary of the anti-wager which, claiming to establish an ethics on the primacy of difference, thinking to make it the single article of a conception of the world, would people its universe with supermen, usurping as it establishes itself and excluding by affirming itself. Their first conscious discovery would be—it always is—the discovery of corpses lying next to them.

I want to be clearly understood. I am not saying that any particular sexual, national, or ethnic minority is wrong to assert itself: aside from the fact that nobody needs me to provide him with reasons to rebel, this would be both peculiarly rash and pedantic. I am certainly not condemning the feminist, Breton, or Provençal struggles, and might add, in further clarity, that my spontaneous instinct is to support them. Nor am I claiming that the "difference" on which these battles pride themselves is a delusion or a mistake; it obviously exists and draws all the proofs of its existence from its obviousness. What I am saying is simply that the struggle of the Breton people often comes close to the abyss of a dangerous "Celtitude," and the struggle of women for their autonomy to fearful fantasies of murder and castration.[12] That this kind of temptation begins precisely at the point when one chooses to make the fact-of-difference nothing but a fact, and to make its just proclamation the blind affirmation of a partial, local, and exclusive particularity. And that therefore the only means of averting the threat is to make this particularity simply one variety; to make this brutal exclusion a form of inclusion; to make this real difference a *supplement* of identity; and thus to make the positing of the fact into the demand for and the inscription of a right. In clear terms, this means that, in order not to sink into barbarism, the subject must presume that before he is "particular," and before he cautiously enters the community supposed to name his particularity, he is first of all a subject, a pillar of humanity, and that his reconquered singularity can and must be carved out of that humanity. It is not enough, in order to define himself, that he infinitely add up the series of his differences; for an individual will never come out of this addition, and out of this stock will never come the imperative not to kill and the right not to be killed. An anti-racist struggle, for example, runs the risk of one day turning into a reverse racism, perhaps of becoming confined to a tribal dogmatism, if it is not very careful to postulate, beyond the difference it is defending, a basis of non-difference against which that difference stands out. It is demagogic in this sense to proclaim, as some do, that "we are all minorities," if we do not immediately add that at the heart of every minority lies a dream, if not of majority, at least of tolerance. There is no particular right which must not first of all be brought into relation with the "man of diverse origins" of whom the ancient Hebrews spoke, the abstract and generic man who was the true subject of their Law,[13] and this is the meaning of the reproach we have already quoted of Yahweh to Malachi, who was guilty precisely of making distinctions between people within the Law.[14]

Let us dwell for a moment on the case of sexual difference, which is, if not the most important, at least the most exemplary. I am perfectly willing to accept that no anthropology is possible if the division it establishes is not only taken into account but made the governing principle of analysis. I know very well that it is *de facto,* that is, in the order of Being, absolute, primeval, and probably a founding division. But I still believe that *de jure*—that is, in the order of value and the rejection of violence—we must strive to presume that it is relative, induced, and secondary. This is virtually what the Bible does in Chapter 2 of Genesis, in the famous episode, which has made so much ink flow, of the birth of Eve from Adam's "rib."[15] This passage is in effect completely incomprehensible if it is not illuminated by the first version, in the preceding chapter, in which an enigmatic plural has the Elohist saying that God "created *man* in his image, male and female he created them."[16] The formulation returns again in Chapter 5 where, taking up the narrative for the third time, the chronicler explains that "male and female he created them . . . and gave them the name 'Man.' "[17] Nor must we forget that this "name 'Man' " itself, this *common name* of man and woman, this generic and abstract name against which their difference is established, is expressed in the Hebrew text as "Adam."[18] Even more disturbing, the parable comes—though everyone always neglects to mention it—after five days in which the creator has constantly separated, divided, distinguished: the "heavens" and the "earth," the "waters of heaven" and the "waters of earth," the "dry land" and the "sea," the "greater" and the "smaller" light, the "fish of the sea" and the "birds of the air."[19] And thus for the first time, at the dawn of the "sixth day," at the moment of the decisive action through which humanity is born, the divine artisan holds back the mechanism, the infinite process of duplication, of redoubling of otherness, which had been up to that point the very rhythm of creation.

Why? What is the source of this interruption? If God suddenly gives up distinguishing, this is perhaps because it is less a matter of discriminating—and devaluing—the Eve of flesh and blood than the "femininity," as we would say today, on which she might pride herself. What is at stake is less her femininity than the way in which it would confuse and complicate the relationship of beings among themselves and between themselves and the world. Less her, then, in this relationship, than the entire relationship, inasmuch as the monarchy of otherness would give primacy to nature—as we shall soon see with the story of original sin. The "woman" as such is not represented as "inferior," but the sexual relationship is first of all decreed to be secondary. She is not "humbled"—she has the "name 'man' "—but that man, herself included, would be, will be perhaps, if in the beginning were desire, temptation, and their infernal round. Instead of a supposed "inequality"—it is the *same man* who is "created male and female"—it was the form of an absolute equality which alone made possible the mediation of the difference that ordinarily enslaves and condemns those who bear its symbolic burden. How can we speak, as is sometimes done, of biblical "misogyny" or "sexism," when it is sex itself that is thus declared non-essential, a simple and insignificant episode of human structure and human destiny? This is rather a beautiful and bold image of total reciprocity between partners who, before being divided, are related by their humanity. It is a wager on a primarily interhuman relationship, in which one chooses not to exclude but to *desanctify* the immemorial wound which the war of the flesh inflicts on the body. And it is the basis (perhaps the only basis) for a morality of respect and recognition in which there is no "particularity" that is not placed—as soon as it is recognized, at the very moment and to the degree to which it is recognized—in relation to a horizon of right and universality. If the biblical woman is a "rib," this is because she is a face before she is a womb.[20]

But finally, the suspicious will say, isn't Judaism itself a cult of an otherness brandished all the more vigorously perhaps because it is denied to women and to non-Jews in general? Precisely not, for this otherness has the particularity that it rejects the idea of being rooted in a womb, of blending with matter, of being established on a real soil which, splitting humanity into natives and foreigners, can only bring war and discord between human brothers. God did not come for you alone, said Moses to the Hebrews, but for "whoever is not here today with us."[21] Nevertheless, isn't there a colossal spirit of particularism in Mosaic Law, so jealous of its prerogatives, so attentive to its purity, enclosed within the arrogant proclamation of its own election? We can understand nothing of the grandeur of the biblical message if we see privilege, chauvinism, nationalism, in an Election whose first concern is to tear the subject away from the age-old localities, the archaic geographies, the savage and spontaneous rootedness that are always and inevitably a source of cruelty. It is the "wicked," in the Prophets, who "take root," and Yahweh constantly "tears them up by the roots."[22] Isaiah says nothing different in the famous phrase when he speaks of "destroying the sacred groves" and, along with them, the old pagan spirit and its cortège of obscurantism and evil adhesion. "Sinners," he says again, "will be ashamed" because of "the *gardens* that charm" them.[23] The Talmud says the same thing when it gives Babel the "same status as Eretz Israel," and thus to Jerusalem the status of a land without territory, which derives its sanctity only from its message of vanity.[24] This is also the meaning of Jeremiah's words recommending that the Babylonians "strengthen their position in exile,"[25]

that they strengthen, in other words, a nation without nationalism, an identity without incarnation, a loyalty without a fatherland, breaking forever with the murderous mystery of the dark
spirit of the woods. And it was perhaps this infinite exile, this
fundamental rejection of stasis, this fantastic freedom in the face
of fixed and sedentary forms of existence, that gave to this people
of strays—wandering in a desert where they never settled, pray-
ing under pitiful tents they carried with them everywhere—[26]
the strength, as Levinas says, to recognize man in man rather
than in nature; the capacity to understand the universe on the
basis of others better and more completely than on the basis of
things.

From this there follow certain concrete and immediate lessons.
All those who lament the famous "roots" whose memory has
been lost by a perverse modernity should be reminded that all
speech, every institution, even every memory, presupposes a necessary and essential uprooting, and that, free through the law,
the spirit is enslaved at its roots. Against the monotonous com-
plaint of a nature worn out, tormented by the iron plow or the
cancer of industrialism, we must present the obvious fact (pointed out by Levinas again) that ethics begins at the point and only
at the point when one feels more at home among men than in the
privacy of one's home, in the undergrowth of the city than in the
ghetto of the woods. On the philosophical level, it is urgent to
have done with the nostalgia—inspired by Heidegger and German romanticism, but with much more inadmissible offspring as
well—for a "world" before "objects," for a "poem" before
"speech," for a "thought" before "knowledge," for an ecstatic
epiphany man could experience provided only that, in the shadow of the "tree" and its great wisdom, he be capable of following
the "paths" that wander across the fields, and of methodically
moving through the chiaroscuro of the "forest" of Being. In the
political realm, it is time to remind the supporters of the revolt
against technology that the struggle against technology is, as
such, obscurantist; to remind the apologists for an ecology that

has "moved to the left" (!) that nature also kills, and that everything that kills is "on the right";[27] and to tell the theorists of a
resistance gone to earth in its homeland that the longest resistance known to humanity took place in the Diaspora. For if, in a
general sense, to be a subject is to obey a law and obey only the
law one has established for oneself, then we must agree that the
first act of the free subject is to break with the place of his birth;
to free himself from the burdens that keep him in subjection; to
cut all the bonds he has not consciously willed; to tear apart the
organic tissue which situates him and which he has not chosen—
exile again, the exile of which the Prophets speak constantly,[28]
the radical cosmopolitanism that remains to be reinvented
against *all* communitarian illusions.

I do not deny, of course, that there are also always adherences
without allegiance, preceding any devotion, older than any
choice, and which make the being they inhabit as old as—even
older than, in a sense—the oldest of things. I would deny even
less that, as a Jew, I have often said that I felt in my belonging
an indecipherable and ineradicable mark, always already there,
rejected or accepted for my benefit or misfortune, like a fatality
of old in which I was "born" before I "became." But what must
be said, simply, is that however much this mark may exist, and
however indelible it may be for every man, it is of value only
through a second mark that gives it the seal of the universal, the
coat of arms of the imperative. And this is why the Bible constantly de-baptizes, nicknames its heroes, from Abraham to Jacob and Esau to Sarah.[29] If I insist so much on the category of
exile, this is because it expresses nothing but the primacy of tra-
versal over territory, of right over fact, but also of writing over
speech and the letter over the spirit. And it is in the austere letter
of an ethics that an identity can and must come to reestablish itself, though it may very well, afterward, declare itself and experience itself as prior to its legal age—the injunctions of the Torah are written in the "heart" and inscribed in the "bowels."
When I speak of "choice," I do so precisely to distinguish, on the

one hand, between this ethics according to the letter, this scrupulous concern for the letter which makes every origin a point of transit,[30] this attention to Scripture which, separating what should be from what is done, alone allows the subject to escape from the dictatorship of what is; and, on the other hand, an ethics according to ethos, customs, the appropriate, which, no doubt more faithful to the truth of its etymology, preserves it in the state of muddled confusion of an unmastered nature. This, too, is the meaning today of a return to Judaism. On this side of any mysticism, the attachment to a religion which—believing in nothing but the form of this ethics, in the hegemony of the letter over the spirit, in the necessity of the second mark—leads, as the poet says, to the definition of a "spiritual nation," whose "native land is the Torah."[31]

I said beyond mysticism; to be more precise, I should say beyond any sanctification. For, in the economy of being, the magisterial function of Judaism is that it wishes for nothing, in the end, but a desanctified universe from which all the most ancient forms of veneration have been eliminated. We can understand nothing of the nobility of its one God if we forget that He was never assigned any task but that of disenchanting, of illuminating the fog in which the crypts of the pagan cosmos were steeped. I have referred to it myself, as I have said, only because—against the pompous eloquence of "forests of symbols" and the providential marriage of man-as-the-world with the world-as-fable—it has never ceased to offer the purity of a text that speaks from man to man, on the ruins of all forms of allegory. There is a Talmudic text which, distinguishing between the two states of faithlessness and blasphemy, evokes of course the abandonment of truth, but also and above all the spontaneous attachment to mythological beliefs, to the old Baals of the past whose charms were so relentlessly vituperated by the Prophets. There is also a little fable which tells the story of Abraham, the son of a seller of idols. One day, while his father was out, he broke all the statues except for one, the largest, which he intended to blame for the massacre. When the merchant returned, he refused to believe or even imagine that an idol, even the most sublime idol, could destroy all of his fellow idols.[32] No sanctified being, in other words, has enough strength, dignity, or eminence to conquer paganism. Far from succeeding to the ancient "numen," representing its truth, or descending directly from it, the Hebrew God appears only with a resolute rejection of superstition. Monotheism is not a theism that takes its place in the long sequence of eternal forms of worship, but an historic revolution which, at one stroke, breaks with the whole stock of pieties, beliefs, and fetishes usually associated with the notion of religion. For a Jew or a Christian, religion is indeed, in the deepest sense, the name of a broken bond. To believe in the perpetuity of its message is not to adhere to the diffuse spiritualism that has recently returned to haunt modernity. To return to the Law is, on the contrary, to break with these fraudulent recurrences and the contraband of obscurantism, irrationalism, and the supernatural of which Judaism and Christianity are by definition inveterate opponents.

No, the world is not full of gods, of "Life," or of obscure forces that speak secretly to the hearts of their faithful. The God I believe in is nothing but the great wind constantly dissipating the swarm of souls and household gods surrounding me. Is it necessary to repeat that I reject nothing as much as the "loving understanding of the earth and man," which "delivered" my beloved Camus from his part in "humanity"?[33] The subject I am calling for is not an enemy of technology but is rather closely related to it, determined, like technology, to disenchant the world. The soul is a wager, not a fervor, for it refrains from all fervor and from specious transports—"Dionysian," as they say—that will always carry it into the seas of ferocity. We know it well, we whose ears have burned from childhood with the yelps of those who unearth the "Yid" in a man. Anti-Semitism, for example, is not a politics, an ethics, or even a perversion, but a mysticism, a theology, precisely an authentic fervor, and this is the only way in which it is possible to understand the strange and irreducible racism that leads to greater hatred of the other because of his very resemblance to the self.[34] This is also known by the survivors of the camps who refuse to relativize a suffering at the limit of all possible suffering: so perfect a holocaust, so perfectly programmed, was not a particular case of murder but an absolute defeat of the spirit, an extinction of all light, an immolation without precedent or precursor, and could not fail to be, as I have said, of a religious order and a religious nature. More recently, although not on a comparable scale, we have seen the evil effects of mysticism and its accompanying messianism when a sect of fanatics—hailed incidentally by the eastern European press[35]—turned an obscure mystagogy into the route for a terrifying sacrificial ceremony, which led it in one moment from the "sacred groves" of Guyana to the hell of false martyrs and real assassins. Against all this madness, against all these ecstasies, against this faith lost on the roads of the sacred, there stands the value of the pendulum of the Law, and the monotheist principle around which, until now, I have indicated that the Law gravitates. Against these monsters of theology and these mournful syncretisms, against this profusion of tribalisms and dark ecumenicisms, against those who wander everywhere proclaiming their hunger for myths, there stands the value of the biblical wager on the universal, "diverse origin," fundamental uprootedness. Contrary to what is always said, the infinite distress that marks our century does not originate in an obscure "logocentric" sin which, ruining the glorious morning of the world's foundation, is dragging it toward its destiny of complete nihilism. I would say, rather, that the misery of the Europe of concentration camps and the war between nations and races comes from the fact that Christianity, despite its millennial labor, had not indoctrinated it thoroughly or deeply enough. And there is now probably no real salvation, for a real individual, except in the very orthodox position of an instance by which what I must call, in a kind of shorthand, the "Mystery" would be finally abolished.

Why not say it, then? If, concerned with encounter and a

faithful dialogue between the two monotheisms; if, convinced as I am that from this alliance can spring a united front of resistance to neo-paganism; if, even though I began with an impassioned journey through the major stages of the Christian adventure and the crucible that it was for the individual, despite all that, I return slowly, with so much determination, to the realm of a Judaism that can for the moment almost define the limits of my perspective; this is perhaps quite simply because there is in its history a purity of action and a rigor of demystification that unfortunately have largely been lost by Christian evangelism. It would be necessary to tell the story of the fifteen-centuries-long war waged by the Church of Rome against the civil, imperial, or peasant religions it inherited for its misfortune from the end of Antiquity. To recall the whole crowd of cults, soteriologies, cosmic worships, which persisted in surviving, being reborn in its path, and which it integrated as well as it could into its festivals and place names. To mention all the hasty assimilations, the dubious syncretisms, the ruinous short circuits that in one place baptized a good storm spirit as "St. Eloi," and in another baptized as "St. George" an archaic hero whose reputation as a dragon killer was lost in the mists of time; or again, gave the name of "Holy Virgin" to some ancestral goddess of fertility and the harvest. And finally, to show how—at the conclusion of a hand-to-hand combat probably lost in advance—the heirs of Jesus always came to terms and, from pact to pact, from voluntary to imposed compromise, ended by recognizing and consecrating their historic defeat when they reordered their liturgies, sacraments, and calendars during the Renaissance. This is neither the time nor the place to retrace that odyssey.[36] Of course, it takes away nothing from what I have said about the contribution of Christendom to the emergence of human rights. It simply explains the reason for a privileged position which, here and now, and speaking only for myself, I grant to that other monotheism which—whether by will or necessity—has never ceased in the depths of its isolation to believe and to proclaim, against the local spirit, the testament of the Universal.

We Are All Children of Israel

Yet we must be more precise, for things are not so simple. This point by point opposition, as such, does not mean very much. And in order to understand it, we have to work out in more detail the pattern of the dialectic.

I am not, I repeat, a historian of religion. But it is obvious that Christianity would not have encountered the spirit of the particular if it had not looked for it and deliberately found it. It would not have had to compromise if it had not—on its own, and perhaps to its disgrace—resolved to debate, to conquer, and then to negotiate. Of course, it was not an attraction for limits but a passion for the limitless that made Christianity set its cross everywhere in the moving soil of the "sacred groves." Christianity was not haunted and undermined from within by the spirit of the woods itself but, on the contrary, by its hatred, a militant antipaganism, and a dream of worldwide baptism. It was because of the Gospel, if you prefer, because of preaching and absolute claims, that it progressively degraded, expended, relativized the letter of its message. And because Christianity wanted to extend itself too far, it ran the risk of extinction. In the exercise of intolerance, it created its strange laxity; from an excess rather than a lack of faith, it allowed itself to be corrupted, sometimes even ruined, by superstitions. It is hardly necessary to explain that this history of Christendom and its cosmopolitan dream is not at all identical to the history of Christianity and its spiritual message.[1] It begins *afterward,* during the decline of the Roman Empire, when Constantine and Theodosius made the ecclesiastic institution a support for their civil power.[2] It ends *beforehand,* at the dawn of modernity, when the French Revolution broke the long-standing bond between altar and sword, and made the guillotine the name of its new altar. But the fact remains that at least one lesson can be derived from this long adventure in which those who were catechized so often saw the priests as the advance guard for the gunboats, from this imperial dream in which the Church itself came close to losing its soul at the same time that it was mortifying the souls of the "infidels": The universal is not the antonym but the synonym of the particular when it takes the risk of thinking in the form of what I call, for want of a better word, a "universalism."

There is a rather good example of this unfortunate combination in the very wake of 1789, in a literary text which, although it has never been a monument of orthodoxy or of genuine piety, nevertheless has value as an indicator, a symbol, and a document—*Les Martyrs* of Chateaubriand. This is a book which, in effect, intended to prove to its time the supreme eminence of the "genius of Christianity," but about which Sainte-Beuve (and everyone else in the century agreed with him)[3] could nevertheless say that it "will be much admired by lovers of pagan mythology, to which the author has involuntarily granted such great superiority." There is a profound misunderstanding in this universe of canticles and mysticism where the pure sound of a bell is enough to interrupt Atala's "horrible outburst," but where the reader can nevertheless not bring himself to believe in Chactas's repentance, Eudore's divine wisdom, or the chaste feelings of the beautiful Cymodécée. How is it that the poet who wished so much to move, to delight the "heart" and the "imagination," to stir a sensibility left "cold" by the Greco-Roman supernatural, succeeded in showing us, as Flaubert said, only "typical martyrs," perfectly conventional, without human reality, frozen in the evocation of a Hell, a Purgatory, and a Paradise hardly more credible than "time's scythe," the "thread of fate," or the "scales of justice" they should have replaced? It is perhaps precisely because Chateaubriand was too intent on replacing, demonstrating, converting. He did in literature what others do in politics: catechism, preaching, defense, and illustration. A proselytizer more than a believer, he was not satisfied with asserting and deciding in the absolute; he also wanted to compete, to vulgarize, and to triumph. Inspired by the old dream of empire, transposed to the realm of language, it was not enough for him to believe in the infinite; he wanted to see all finitude pale before its grace. Too zealous a preacher, he would have liked all nature to imitate his God, and the earth, the heavens, the sea, all those sublime landscapes he takes such pleasure in describing, to raise their voices in harmony with the voice of the Lord. This is of course an exacerbated, but all the more eloquent, form of propagandistic universalism, which paradoxically concedes to the genius of the particular the essence of what it asks: the "images," "pictures," "mosaics"—the word recurs often in the *Examen des Martyrs*—in which the minor sacred elements, the demons of the soil and the woods, can only return in a climate of mystery, wonder, and diffuse pantheism that is the very definition of pagan religiosity.[4]

If, on the other hand, we consider biblical monotheism, we find a contrary dialectic and the opposite of this paradox. Does this monotheism sustain the values of the Universal in all their purity? So much so, in fact, that it refrains from preaching and diffusing them, and that, in the first Hebrew kingdom, outsiders were fellow citizens without being fellow Jews.[5] Were the Mosaic commandments not valid for all men for the "man of diverse origins"? In theory, yes; but it is nevertheless true that the Noachids were explicitly exempted from having to observe most of the prescriptions of Leviticus.[6] Weren't these prescriptions worthy of ruling the universe and of overthrowing the barbarism

that was everywhere enthroned in their place?[7] When the Hebrew army, at the hour of its greatest glory, triumphed over a
pagan army, it refrained from transmitting its Bible with the
point of its sword; and although it sometimes imposed "penitence" on the vanquished, it never spoke of "conversion" or
spiritual "baptism."[8] Was this because the idea of empire was
unknown to the Hebrews? What is certain, simply, is that the
Word and the Law are not elements of an empire, and when
Deuteronomy distinguishes between "optional" and "obligatory" wars, there is a careful explanation that, in the former
case, Israel is entitled to demand only civil submission, and in
the latter, obedience to the minimal morality of Noah's seven
commandments.[9] But was this a sign of contempt, the other side
of an unacknowledged intolerance? I know few hymns to tolerance as beautiful as the passage in Jeremiah in which Yahweh,
in his anger, proposes to his children the model of piety and lesson in devotion offered by "the sons of Jonadab son of Rechab"
although they are not Jews.[10] We could multiply examples from
diverse sources. In every case, the lesson would be clear: while
an excess of apologetics leads to the variousness of localisms, a
position of radical localism preserves the possibility of the One
and the Absolute. While an inconsistent imperialism is the har-
binger of pagan tribalism, a superior tribalism becomes the
means of maintaining a consistent monotheism. That the Universal alone has value is a conviction shared by every form of
monotheism; but on the condition, the biblical chroniclers add,
that this Universal is rooted in a particularity, a new minority,
an irreducible separation, the demand for which the people of
Israel must embody.

In this case as well, of course, we should not oversimplify.
Exodus shows us a crowd of "gentiles" and "servants of Pha-
raoh" leaving Egypt, listening to Moses's prophecy and setting
out after him.[11] It would not be at all difficult to detect the traces
of the innumerable encounters of the Jewish people with the
Greco-Roman mystery, as much in ritual practice as in details of

the Law[12] or some architectural feature of Solomon's temple.[13] The Talmudic rabbis later had no trouble acknowledging that in matters of religion and understanding texts, they were often indebted to pagan thinkers, philosophers, and theologians.[14] The Kabbalists went even further when they saw the long sojourn in Egypt as a ruse of providence to incorporate into the mind of Israel all the "sparks" lost in the temples of impurity.[15] And it is quite clear, finally, that at various stages of its history—in North Africa, for example—Israelite prosyletism was sometimes equal to that of Catholicism.[16] But what is nevertheless certain and of particular importance to me here is that there is in the Bible a model, perhaps the exact model, of a faithfulness without partisans, a preaching without zealotry, a Revelation without offspring, which is absolutely unique in the history of religion. It is impossible to understand anything about the structure of our Talmud, for example, if you look for a catechism, or even a "teaching" in the traditional sense of the term,[17] in the concise, tight, terribly esoteric dialogues written in a language sometimes approaching the limits of a quasi-mathematics. The idea of a Hebrew *Martyrs* or a *Génie du judaïsme* is unthinkable within the space of a Scripture always less concerned with testing its validity against the outside world or winning new lands of faith over to its cause than with tirelessly deepening the understanding of its Law, amending its text, adding glosses, in a process of meaning that left little place for the concerns of a politics. This is, in a word, an entirely different dialectic, an entirely different intellectual wager, in which the Universal and the Particular are still not antonyms, still strictly synonymous, but molded and as it were woven into the form of what may be called, again for want of a better word, a "singularity."

Universalism against Singularity? The two discourses are clearly not speaking of the same thing. They are two distinct models, even if the terms they use are sometimes identical. In order to identify the differences more precisely, let us consider a passage from Spinoza's *Tractatus Theologico-Politicus,* which probably provides the key for this dual reversal.[18] Everything depends, he says in substance, on the difference between two rival and largely antagonistic conceptions of the priest and his ministry. On the one hand is the missionary who "uses argument everywhere" and, through his sermon, counts on hastening the advent of the good news; an indefatigable traveler in pagan lands and among pagan souls, every man is a parish for him, and he measures the value and the extent of his truth by the number of his conquests—in short, he is an *apostle*. On the other is the biblical priest who, testifying rather than making speeches, speaks "in dogmas and decrees," in the image of "God Himself," whose will he interprets without claiming to incarnate it or to open the gates of the terrestrial city to it; an impenitent analyst of the profundities of the Law, a minister without a parish, and a shepherd without a flock, he speaks a Word that does not need to affirm itself by counting the number of its subjects—in short, he is a *prophet*. Between the two, if we do a little violence to the text, there is this decisive difference: the prophet, whose Hebrew name[19] means "called," and who is thus called by the Almighty rather than calling himself, is not an omniscient augur prophesying the future world, but an impotent oracle, a speaker of the pure present, simply called upon, here and now, to manifest an order. The apostle, on the other hand, whose Greek name says that he "sends" his truth "abroad,"[20] makes himself an oracle of the future already shaped by his activity. Further, if we pursue the parallel and carry it to its conclusion, the apostle, because he is a missionary and a pilgrim, now becomes a voyager, a nomad, a vagabond; and the prophet, on the other hand, because he is satisfied with speaking, with revealing the divine message of which he is the improbable and irresponsible bearer, enjoys an immediate, unshakeable, almost inert, and, as it were, already eternal proximity to the Law. With complete rigor, and contrary to the commonplace, we should be able to say "settled Jew" and "wandering Christian."[21]

Starting here, we could point to the contrasts in every area.

The apostle vulgarizes the Law; the prophet divulges it. The former is its preacher; the latter its preserver. The first casts it in every direction; the second exhibits it as a monument. One wishes to be its agent; the other a pledge or a sign for it. In one case, there is the ambassador, the demiurge in this world; in the other, the echo, barely the vestige. On one side, a caste of men who bring their word to men; on the other, figures of humanity who add a category to being. Or again, representatives of a social priesthood that soon turns into a band of rulers as opposed to participants in a pure ontological function. It was Ezekiel and Jeremiah who invented the idea of martyrdom, while John, Luke, and Matthew are the real pioneers of messianism. The apostle was already what we would call today a militant; and the West thus perhaps owes to the institutionalized Church the strange ideal which claims that every value in this world derives its worth from a basis in politics. The prophet is probably the first name for the "unnecessary man" of whom Solzhenitsyn speaks, or the "marginal being" Mallarmé evoked in speaking of artists and poets—those men whom he did not know how "to name in order to praise them, gratuitous, outsiders, perhaps futile," but of whom he was certain that, instituting a minority in the face of the dubious "unanimity" of the nations, they embody the "need for exception" which is, "like salt," the *a priori* condition, the abandoned and sovereign element that alone permits the utterance of a truly universal language.[22]

There is also, between the two poles, a whole series of possible combinations, some of which have a real existence. For example, there have been Jewish apostles: all the apostates, from Spinoza himself to Marx, and from the medieval converts to the Bolsheviks of the October Revolution, who thought that the road to the Universal passed through the denial of their Jewish identity, their particularity, and who thus sometimes turned themselves over to the mercies of their executioners.[23] There have also been Christian prophets: all the mystics, the men of the cloister and of silence, the martyrs of past and present who, believing in the impossible God of the deserted tomb on Easter morning, in a heart-felt faith not dependent on the order of the world for any proof of validation, carried its banner high through the depths of persecution.[24] There have been secular apostolates: every time an imperial Universal was combined with a local particularism—illustrated today by the monstrous mixture of the "International" according to Stalin and the "Nation" according to Déat, which has delicately named itself "Eurocommunism." And finally, there have been atheist prophets: every time an "unnecessary man" has taken the risk of formulating, in action and speech, his untimely maxims—this is always the case with those intellectuals who, from Moses to the Russian dissidents, have not waited for history to reach the True and the Good before daring to declare the obvious on their own. My Christian friends should understand me clearly. They no doubt realize that it is finally not so much religious realities or sectarian categories that I am thus characterizing but rather principles, perspectives, points of view on the order of the world and of time. I give the name "apostolic" to that specific form of relationship to the truth which, because it understands truth in terms of an abstract Universal, always carries within itself the seeds of the "totalitarian temptation." And, on the other hand, I call "prophetic" the entirely different stance which, because it understands itself in terms of covenant, that is, as a particular Universal, is always inspired by a dream of solitude and absolute individualism.

We must indeed consider whom the Bible is talking about when it presents its prophets, and therefore who is concerned by this model of particularized speech. Is it always the Hebrews, descendants of Abraham, Isaac, and Jacob? If prophecy exists as soon as a covenant is established between man and the Law, it suffices, says Isaiah, for a foreigner to agree to "observe the sabbath, not profaning it," for Yahweh to "bring" him to his "holy mountain," which will thereby be "called a house of prayer for all the peoples."[25] Is this covenant not a privilege reserved for a few chosen ones, the memorable heralds who gave their names to a few famous books? Those books are filled with more obscure murmurings, arising from a crowd of characters, sometimes faceless and nameless, who, like Eldad and Medad in the camp of Tabeerah, suddenly began to "prophesy"—oracles for a day, ephemeral glossolalians, but men whose advent was consecrated by Moses in the Book of Numbers.[26] Are these only exceptions, paltry anomalies, signs of a teratology of the divine that needs more regularity in order to manifest itself? Moses again, in the same passage, says explicitly the opposite when he answers an indignant Joshua, who advises him to "stop" the prodigy, that he feels no jealousy and would even accept that "the whole people of Yahweh were prophets" provided only that the Almighty "gave his spirit" to them all.[27] Every individual, really, women as much as men, the humblest of the humble as much as the man of distinction? This is exactly what God says to Joel when He evokes the day of glory on which "whoever calls on His name will be saved," and on which, pouring out His "spirit on all mankind," He will anoint "the daughters" as well as "the sons" of Israel, and also their "slaves, men and women" who will prophesy with them.[28] Prophecy, in other words, is a state of grace but not a reserved state. A prophet is any man who simply commits himself to the rigor of the Law. Every man is a prophet from the moment he is fully, unconditionally, and absolutely a man. And even the supreme word of truth, even the most universal of all universal speech, even *messianic* speech and activity, according to the Talmud, is within the reach of the "rabbi himself, or perhaps me, if the Messiah is among the living, or Daniel if he is among the dead."[29]

It then becomes clear how fragile, or rather, inadequate, was my definition of the individual reduced to the "man of diverse origins" who tore himself away from enslavement to his roots and from his immanence in the world. In fact, just as the claim of difference without the postulate of identity is a synonym of savagery, so a dream of identity with no difference at all would soon become the source of the madness of barbarism. Just as pa-

gan localities were caricatures of freedom, dissolving every form
of resistance in the great cosmological sleep, so apostolic imperialism is a parody of ecumenicism, forming men without age condemned to slavery. If Hitlerian romanticism could ape even the
notion of the chosen people while obliterating its governing reference to the order of the Law, how could Stalinist collectivism,
in the opposite direction, refrain from making that Law a norm,
simply forgetting that, in order to be expressed, it had to be
based on dispersion? The great lesson, in fact, of this "prophetic
model" whose outline I have sketched is that we must now begin
to retrace our steps: instead of moving upward from the naturalness of the body to the induction of its consciousness, we must
move downward from this too general consciousness to a new
particularity. If it is a *model* precisely, a model for modernity,
this is because it confronts us with an individual who is a twofold and fundamentally equivocal creature; divided, says the
Talmud,[30] commenting on the "double Yod" of the verb "to create" in Genesis, between high and low as much as between right
and left. He is drawn as if by magnets by two opposing forces,
two rival allegiances, which place him at the midpoint between
the heaven of the Law that is read and the root of the self that
reads. This schema, in the tension at its midpoint, expresses the
arc of a subjectivity that joins the edifice of humanity all the better by first seceding to the intimacy of its catacombs. To be fully
a subject is to live at the height of the paradox that orders me to
aim for the Universal—my passion, my first circle—only by first
separating myself from it and returning to the privacy of my
subjectivity—my obligation, my second circle.

   This results, consequently, in once again choosing the path of
exile, but an exile that has also changed meaning and sign. It is
no longer only a question of escaping from the massive and mute
presence of things, but in this case of really fleeing from the
great cities and the empty babbling of the noisy crowds. The
problem is no longer to wager on the letter against the spirit and
its hidden enchantments, for the letter also destroys when it is

made by man; and we must always, like Samuel, go further away from contingent gatherings, always set up our solitary tent elsewhere.[31] The risk is removed of being a thing among things and a pitiful piece of humanity shaped out of matter. But the urgency remains, as Numbers says, of "camping in solitude," of no longer being "numbered among the peoples," and of making oneself a Pharisee, consistently and in a way that will create such an abyss between the city and me that finally, perhaps, I may speak to the entire City.[32] Thereafter it would be impertinent to formulate a maxim that would be immediately, directly valid for all men and would touch the heart of their fraternity. The object of my quest is now an ethics of the detour, a choice through evasion, a practice of mediation in which I will focus all my care on discovering the point of extreme withdrawal, the place removed from sight, the ground of judgement without sanctions or tribunals—these are the only true sources of universal speech. For I really believe that in these times when human speech seems to have lost for good the right to speak; in this season of suspicion when every utterance is immediately reduced to an image of the world, a reflection of its structures, at most a tremor in the geology of its epistemes; in this totalitarian age whose totalitarianism perhaps begins in the order of ontology, with the decree that makes being full, without flaw or defect from which might arise my murmur against the thunder of history; confronting this disaster in which some hail the advent of a triumphant absolute spirit, I believe that the time has returned to rely on a language which is no longer borrowed but *begins absolutely* with the prophet who utters it, the author who authorizes himself by it, exiled but returned to himself.

This choice of exile can be understood literally, first of all, as the test of a self which authoritatively removes itself from intercourse with men and from their complacent grimaces. This is the attitude of Rousseau, for example, the Rousseau of the *Confessions*, in the admirable Chapter 8 in which he tells how, "applying all the strength of his soul to break the chains of opinion," he had to resolve "to do courageously everything which seemed good to me without worrying at all about the judgment of men."[33] Should we see this as another symptom of the unhealthy misanthropy that made Voltaire chatter so much? It was the opposite, in fact, and the bold expression of a paradox inaudible in the sociable city: The only way of cherishing and joining with one's fellows is, unfortunately, to isolate oneself from them and appear to ignore them. Can we read it as a pre-romantic profession of faith, in the image of those liquid hearts who cultivated the self only to be better able to bury it in damp cosmic soil? Rousseau speaks of "courage," "strength of soul," "breaking the chains," and therefore of a struggle of the spirit, a bitter and stiff resolve, a heroic return to the values of authentic reason, ridiculed, according to him, by all his contemporaries. How, it will be said, can one live a truth of reason against everyone? Is one still justified by the Universal when one has chosen no longer to count at all on "the judgment of men"?[34] Yes, of course, he replied, applying in the strictest sense the formula of the prophetic ideal. For, in a world of lies in which only the particular is of value, there is no other way to coincide with the Universal but to return to the self and to adhere, simply, to what "seems good." Yes, a hundred times yes, he would repeat again today, today more than ever, in the shadow of that modern reason which has so often assumed the hideous face of madness while what he called "opinion" drifts everywhere over the charnel houses. For there is no other basis for lucidity, no other method for a thought of resistance, no other recourse, sometimes, for a consistent antifascism, than to settle in a hermitage and to put oneself in a position to be right against the whole city.

One can also understand the notion in a more figurative sense, and this is what another solitary man did who, landing in New York one July morning in 1940, having lost his wealth, banished from his country, wrote proudly on the ritual form of the American Immigration Service: "I will live in my name." And when this man is named Alexis Saint-Léger Léger, alias Saint-John

Perse, the quintessential singer of anabases and exiles, poet of leavetaking and proud privation, child of the islands as much as of the land of France, who drifted throughout his life between wandering and fidelity, then the quip is more than a quip, it is the mark of a necessity. When we know in addition that this man of glory and misery, jealous of his indigence and his rich poverty, was associated by force of circumstances with the human adventure of the few irreducible men who were capable of opposing to Nazism the strength of their rejection, then the necessity is better than a necessity, it takes on the value of resistance.[35] Finally when, in 1960, covered with honor and praise, the aging artist declared in Stockholm, on the occasion of receiving the Nobel Prize, that if "poetry is first of all a way of life and of complete life," nevertheless nothing maintains form or measure "under the incessant flow of being,"[36] how can we not recognize in such a long solitude the stubborn and perhaps desperate temptation to break the circle of lead that is finally closing being off from every particular speech? Of this great man of letters of the twentieth century, this creature as demanding as his work, we could then say what he himself said of Dante, the "born rebel":[37] that, certainly, "born for everyone," his first concern was "never to be alien to himself"; that, being a man of "presence" and "affluence," he took care to withdraw into "absence" and "refusal"; and that, bound to his century, he found the strength to be involved with it only in the extremity of his disengagement, the most inaccessible of confinements, the most elevated solitude—that of any individual worthy of the name, worthy of bearing his own name, and especially of speaking the "words of a living man."

Could it be that there are also words of the dead against which we must resist? It is certain that there are words of death, words which sow death, and that the twentieth century is the century of those words. Hobbes foresaw them, predicting "discords" and "battles," which would be conducted with "all the more ferocity because they would have to do with doctrines"[38] and would involve battalions of supporters of doctrines. The nineteenth century named these death-dealing words when, in the ebb of the "frozen revolution," a member of the French Institute[39] invented—to designate the "new science of ideas," which would give its followers a "mathematical" power over souls—the novel term "ideology."[40] The young Henri Beyle understood; at twenty, he wrote a brief *Caractère des femmes françaises* in which he applied, literally, the laws of human machines according to Destutt de Tracy; and the work established him, curiously, as the first ideocrat, the first to have dreamed of "making others will," or of "precipitating" in them a feeling with as much certainty as a chemist precipitates his compounds.[41] And the later dictators also understood, who, with more success of course and infinitely more seriousness, rejoiced, like Hitler,[42] in the miracles of a "theory of ideas" that gave "mathematical certainty" to their victory, or, like Stalin,[43] in "that force of the highest importance" represented by ideologies in "the solution of the new tasks imposed by the development" of socialism. In 1952, Sartre criticized Camus for "neglecting Marxist philosophy."[44] Camus could have answered him that Marxist philosophy, as such, does not exist. That what exists, everywhere, are ideologies, that is, concrete philosophies, that is, machines for multiplying crime. That he was not so much "neglecting" them as freeing himself from them and turning his back on the madness with a human face which, in the present age, speaks the language of philosophy. And in fact, the author of *L'Homme révolté* occupied in his turn a strictly prophetic position, which he understood in a third sense: a solitude, not with respect to his fellow men—to whom he intended to return at the end of his detour—but to the ideocratic metropolises, the great necropolises of knowledge and science one must force oneself to avoid if one wishes, modestly, to attempt to restore meaning to human universality.

For this is indeed what is at stake. And Camus was aware of it, answering sarcasm with haughtiness, and replying to the pack of his critics the famous "Solitaries? You would really be alone without those solitaries."[45] What he meant is that the characteristic of the language of exile is to move away from the specious combinations made by ideologies only in order the better to reestablish a truer solidarity, which is built, face to face, between solitary individuals. What he said is that there is no exceptional speech which, however singular and fragmentary it may be, even *because* it is singular and fragmentary, does not wish to be accountable, does not experience itself as potentially responsible for the entire world. And what he rediscovered, in fact, was perhaps the ultimate meaning of Kantian morality carried to its conclusion: A subject becomes moral, and thus really a subject, only from the moment he is bold enough to believe that, in the last instance, the fate of humanity depends on the utterance of his maxim. Folly? If so, it was also the folly of Gabriel Péri, shouting at the firing squad whose guns were already aimed at him: "Imbeciles, I'm dying for you!" It was the folly of Kafka, saying that "whoever strikes a Jew strikes down humanity." It is always this folly which, as Barthes has written,[46] inspires every artist when, refusing to fall into line or to be inscribed in a "category," he takes the risk of speaking out and universalizing the singularity of his name.

At this point, we are far from the mythology of the man-god, what Freud called "his majesty the ego." This ethics of solitude is the opposite of the egotism of power which, following the naturalist tradition, grants the individual a sacred right to the holocaust. The prophetic model, carried to its logical conclusion, reverses itself once again, pointing to another subject which is never so much itself as when it *answers for* others. The "Other" is an idea in the subject like the idea of the infinite in Descartes, like an excess of thought, a supplement to the will, an obligation to tolerance and to the rejection of barbarism. Universal? Particular? It no longer makes much sense to oppose one term to another, for the two threads of the dialectic, ascending and descending, end by weaving themselves into an inextricable bond, which gives such great scope to this strange "individualism." When Cain asks, "Is my sin too great to be borne?" the Talmudic commentator answers, "The sin against man is the only one for which man cannot be forgiven."[47] Similarly, against today's neo-pagans, who call for unlimited expansion for each individual, we can now argue that the soul, overcome by the soul of the other, burdened with all the weight of the world, again a total part, but a part of the totality of human suffering, is not primarily a demand for survival but the impossibility of inflicting harm. And it is finally clear why I have spoken so much of "Law" and not yet really of "Right." Because, outside this precedence and the order of reasons it expresses, outside this monotheist basis and the mechanism it implies—incidentally less because of the transcendent grace from which it derives than because of the ethics it presupposes—there are no human rights that are not always, now or soon, the rights of the human corpse.

12

The Kulak and the Commissar

Given these conclusions, we can now return to the more familiar domains of phenomenology. We can, without great danger, go back to the locations of egotism, which are in the end the bases for that strange being in the world, the dispersed subject. We can also reevaluate some of the lessons of an *Aufklärung*—of Locke's philosophy, for example—which recovers some pertinence by being thus bounded and limited. In other words, sheltered from the twin dangers of abstract universalism and untamed particularism, we can recall the system of real rights attached to a real individual from the moment he commits himself to a real resistance.

There is first of all the obvious fact that an individual is finally primarily a body. But a body that is more than a body; a body that is more than the sum of its parts, but whose parts can be thought of only as vestibules to heaven. The needs of my neighbor—the Talmud says in substance—are for me spiritual needs, spiritual demands. This truth is worth repeating in an age of revolutions that make the body nothing but a body, see its matter as nothing but matter, its needs as a capital, and its flesh as the clay out of which the new man is forged. "Health," said John Locke, is the first human right; and the absence of suffering the condition for any kind of freedom. This commonplace is also worth recalling in the time of those philosophers who—armed with Sade, Nietzsche, and their epigones—liberate sex or desire by submitting them methodically to the operations of industry, by establishing every human relationship on the model of piecework, by sometimes tolerating rape, kidnap, or even murder in the name of the collective appropriation of the body of each and every one. Have you ever heard the poor speak of their own body?[1] They speak of it as of a thing, a thing among things, and, with a fearful and almost superstitious curiosity, they watch from the outside its collection of miseries, pains, illnesses, as though it were the body of another, a stranger, a neighbor. Their body is a simulacrum, which no longer belongs to them; their body is a great wound, something like a neurosis of the flesh; like the Job of the Bible, they always speak of it in the third person.

Thus today we are all poor and must proclaim loudly the fundamental right to private ownership of the body. This right is not self-evident when we consider all the time that it took for women, Western women, to achieve the elementary right of control over their own wombs. It is all the more valid for that half of humanity whose bodies are broken, exhausted, tortured, in infernal laboratories, in the shadow of scaffolds more fearsome than those created by the Middle Ages. It is disregarded even here, in a certain sense, in the welfare societies which every day dispossess us of the right to suffer in peace, in silence at last, without the murmuring of words, of busy speeches whispering to us the meaning and the reasons for this pitiful hovel which is, if they are to be believed, the other face of paradise. It is literally displaced in those societies of generalized surveillance which deprive men of the penultimate privilege of choosing the time, the place, and the manner of their last breath: so few Tolstoys taking to the road to die proudly in a railroad station, and so many miserable people stretched out till the end of time in absurd hospices, full of pomp and uproar. A hospice, it will be said, is not a torture chamber, and it is true that it would take a great deal of thoughtlessness and foolishness to dare to compare them. But I am simply saying that a world in which, today, I can no longer suffer or die in peace is a world which, tomorrow, can martyr me. And that the new declaration of human rights which it has become urgent, if not to imagine, then at least to look for, must begin with that, with an extended habeas corpus.

And yet we have to know what a habeas corpus is, how it is derived, and what are its implicit consequences. Intellectual historians know that it was born in a precise territory, that it presupposes a philosophy and a general anthropology, those of Locke who, in a few well-turned arguments, and in spite of the considerable limitations I noted earlier, established its tradition. First, man is effectively free if he has pleasure in himself and if he is the only one who disposes of his body and his actions.[2] Second, as a corollary, he has this *right* only because he has first of all the *duty* to assure its preservation, because he cannot give to others more power over himself than he has, and because he is not free, in other words, to choose, against the "law of nature," to reject freedom.[3] Third, more concretely, this duty itself presupposes another right—the right to "make use" of everything in this world which may help to preserve it, and to draw at will upon all the "nourishments" and "commodities" that the "Creator" offers in abundance to the appetites of "natural intelligence."[4] Fourth, decisively, this use is itself possible only if the individual possesses a specific means, "work," but work which belongs to him like his flesh and his "hands" and which, already delivered from the Christian curse, is an integral part of his body and a support for his power.[5] Fifth, finally, and this is scandalous, everything this work can do, everything a "hand" or a "tool" does, everything a "horse," a "wage earner," or a "capital" works on, is removed by definition from "common property" and abruptly enriched with a personal sign, is broken up into unprecedented and legitimate "appropriations."[6] I am oversimplifying, of course, but this is nevertheless the essence of the argument. The impeccable movement which, from the ownership of the self by the self, leads to the ownership of property. The frozen mechanism which makes a free subject *de jure* into a possessive individual *de facto*. The origin of a theory which, from the date and the place of its baptism, has finally bequeathed to us the historically unquestionable fact that without the right to property, there is no habeas corpus.

Is this really a scandal? That is not the question. The question is rather the genetic one of the trace in the present of that old tradition, of the weightiness, here and now, in the course of modern history, still possessed by those five arguments of the primal scene. Roughly again, we can understand the first as a wager on an individual who must, in order to resist, act and think as though he had no obligation to any man or any social bond for the person he is and the singularity he affirms; and it is true that the wager still holds, holds more than ever, of a resistance conceived as the absolute monarchy of a pure *de jure* subject. The second, which converts this right into a "divine" duty, is perhaps nothing but the expression of what we would call in modern terms an "inalienable right"; conferring on the "Creator" eminent domain over bodies is a way of adding to them an ontological inviolability without which the very idea of a human right or a prohibition of crime would be literally unthinkable. The third, because it posits the reign of the creature over the goods of this world, remains a weapon against the romantics of every age, those clowns of the mists who make the self a substance blending with the great "Substance"; hence the argument which is indispensable for any form of freedom is Lockean—the self is not of the world, it is of value against the world, it is always worth more than the world and its homicidal naturalness. In the fourth, which makes work a property, nothing but a property of the body, there is already a counterargument to the Marxist madness that saw it as *the* property, in the sense of the essence of a man who, now "alienated," is promised a reconquest by which he will one day attain to his truth as "human capital." Scandalous or not, Locke's property owner remains an alternative to the "Worker" who, for Stalin as well as for the Nazis, is one of the principal figures of fascist modernity. Finally, as for the fifth argument—the one that strictly speaking is the basis for the principle of appropriation—how can we not see in it something like a premonition of the great madness which, expropriating the homes and goods of ordinary people, depriving them of the very place that gave them an identity and a name, creates peoples without faces, humiliated, their heads bowed in shame? On this point, as on the others, the lesson of the *Second Treatise* is still attested to by the century; and it is not certain that we have any means, without it, of thinking of integrity, the inalienable right of a subject to escape from violence.

It can certainly be objected that the subject in question is a "bourgeois" subject, as though there were another one that should be preferred. The whole history of socialism unfortunately expresses the opposite, that the form of the individual is, as such, a bourgeois form, born on the ground of bourgeois thought, and that the only possible choice is between that form, with its original flaw, and no individual at all, as the Cambodians, the Chinese, and a few others would like. Since I have sometimes conducted it myself,[7] I am aware of the case against its will to preservation, its obsession with survival, which makes it a conspirator of fear, persevering egotistically in the imperious tradition of a sterile mode of existence. But the entire history of revolutions illustrates that there is no alternative to this debased and timid peace except in war against bodies, the atrocious dismemberment of the flesh, and the great pools of blood left in their wake by souls who storm heaven. I know, as everyone does, that "property is theft," and that in a condition of scarcity—a scarcity which Locke excludes, not by accident, from his model—it is a source of poverty and indubitable oppression. But then what can be said of those states that, confiscating theft, monopolizing scarcity, finally reign supreme over the dispossessed masses and have found no antidote to capital but the merciless abolition of every personal will? I agree, finally, that capitalism is horror, and that, at least since Thiers and the Communards shot in Père-La-chaise, the figure of the property owner has been its emblem. But when will we finally understand that a society without any property owners at all is still a capitalism, the worst of capitalisms, the only capitalism in the world in which, not satisfied with exploiting men, the state takes away even the ground in which their will to live is rooted, and that these "petty bourgeois" are given, in exchange for the little wealth which is all they have, the great works of history that are the fate of the leaders? If the dilemma, in other words, is between a philosophy of history and a "petty bourgeois" thought, I willingly assume the role of petty bourgeois. If the debate, the division, is between the kulak and the commissar, I choose without hesitation the kulak over the commissar.

To those who would still hesitate, I would recommend that they read the strange *Utopia,* for example, imagined by Thomas More four centuries ago. The constitution of the state is familiar; because it abolishes every form of "property," it also does without laws, "reduced to a very small number" for which "the crudest interpretation is accepted as the most correct."[8] Every citizen is a "doctor of law," and law is only a vestige of the splendors of the old world. Everyone remembers the form of this state which, because it crowns a society without classes, "castes," or "corporations," is relieved of all the weight of political arbitration but is entirely in control of the organization of production and the distribution of wealth.[9] The state is apolitical; but it is weighty, stifling, omnipresent at every moment in the life of ordinary people. The organization of daily life is also famous: regulated joys, programmed pleasures, standardized punishments, distributed by the administration to its citizen-functionaries. Dispossessed of the fruit of their labor, they have no more control over their time or the space of their emotions.[10] This is a model, which has since been realized, of a justly egalitarian will; but one which, realized in this way, is paid for with the loss of freedom. It provides evidence that equality can be expressed in two senses, the political and the social, and that the two senses intersect but are not contemporaneous. It provides proof, widely recognized today, that the former presupposes, demands property; while the latter, denying it, presupposes and implies the suppression of Right. Had Locke read More when he asserted that private property is the first human right?[11] What is certain in any case is that, in the light of this model, this evidence, and this proof, the argument is not as strange or as scandalous as it seemed. At bottom, it means that a social bond which is organized first of all around social equality is certain never to recover the guarantees of political equality; and this was discovered much later by the totalitarian systems. A society which begins, on the contrary, with scrupulous political equality is the only one that can, later and by a detour, achieve more social equality; and this is what is concretely called "democratic procedure." The rule is simple, but so constantly ignored that it is perhaps of some use to recall its obviousness.

Then what happens if, conscious of the limits of the model—limits which, as you remember, are not those comonly thought—we attempt to generalize it, displace it, radicalize it? If, armed with its lessons (which, whether we like it or not, cannot be circumvented), we now return to the mysterious habeas corpus I evoked at the outset and about whose "broadening" I proposed to think? If, holding firmly to the thread and substance of Locke's argument, we attempt to broaden it as well, to extend its definition, and especially to extend the range of its object? The first thing that happens is that—based on the work of a body which is more than a body, more than form or matter, something better than the brute presence of an element in the world—"property" in turn is more than property, more than "goods" and "wealth," something better than simple "control" over the "nourishment" and the "commodities" with which the author of the *Second Treatise* stopped. We reduce it, paradoxically minimize its meaning, by seeing in it an assault, an evasive expansion, the conjunction with the world of a soul tracing around itself its circles of products, works, and labors. We completely misunderstand it if we reify it, substantialize it, while it is fundamentally the closing in of those circles, space and time cut off, the body and the soul within their own circle, in the area of a suffering, a personal death, or a consciousness. And if I praise it so highly and attempt to exalt it, this is because it no longer derives in any way from philistine egotism, but from a refined individualism that possesses nothing better than the desert solitude of an inner landscape. The "I" is not another but a pure sovereign, of which the self is the kingdom and the inner heart the citadel.

I say this without any play on words, with all due respect to the apostles of the division of the self and the disordering of all the senses. I say it with others, with all the men and women who struggle everywhere against totalitarianism and who often have nothing to propose but this property of consciousness. We are indeed talking about a citadel when hounded men who have lost their own path have nothing left, in order to rediscover themselves and cry out their distress, but the recourse and the refuge of a pure insurgent will. Are we aware of all the power of a will when, withdrawn into itself, it opposes to the killers the tranquil disruption of the first person? A few consciousnesses in the East have greatly disturbed the order of things. Do we realize all the capacities of inertia, the massive inertia of a soul throwing its whole weight behind the simple refusal to bend, to serve, to fall into line? Along with laughter, the grating laughter that makes the world weep, this is probably the supreme form of refusal, defiance through contempt. In fact, I know no definition of dissidence but as a redoubt, a refuge for subjectivity—a "rock," says the Bible—which, carved out of the very body of the state and the institution, opposes its entrenched camp to the "camps" of the "right" and the "left" that Bukovsky has spoken of. Finally, I know no better definition of freedom than the refusal to adhere, the "stiff neck" as the Prophets say,[12] which leads us to withdraw, to remove ourselves from the world, to seek elsewhere, in the depths of the intimate self, the strength to resist.

I am not thinking, of course, of La Boétie's dead end, the hypothetical withdrawal of "desire," taking back one fine day the sap it had given to the tree of lordship. But, more concretely, of the millions of rebels who, in the United States, for example, in the late sixties attempted to block with their bare hands the most formidable colonial war in history. And they effectively achieved their goal because they did nothing, these "radicals," but think for themselves and speak in their own names, disregarding all established logic and all established interests. I am thinking still less of the Stoic apathy which, from Epictetus to Malraux, has left at the very heart of hope a kernel of resignation; but rather, concretely again, of those other rebels, the students and workers who in the France of 1968, against the parties, the unions, and the established doctrines, unleashed the greatest general strike in history. They were "bourgeois individuals," millions of bourgeois individuals, crowds of "possessive" subjects, in solidarity because they were solitary, who joined their voices together because each one was starting from the most distant point of his inner fortress. There is, in fact, no example of resistance which was the act of programmed individuals, soldiers of a dogma, even a reversed or defiant dogma; the Trotskyites know this well, since they paid for the illusion with their lives. There has never been a great antitotalitarian rebellion that was not the act of "property owners," fighters for inwardness, highwaymen of solitude, heroic partisans of the fortresses of the personal will. And the French communists, like Nizan, learned this when they were able to reject Nazi barbarism only at the price of the torments we all know about: absolute secession, and finally martyrdom. It is in this sense that I say—far from Locke at this point—that "property" is, of all rights, the first and most eminent, as much in the order of being as in the order of reasons.

Would you like another example? There is once more the case of the Jewish people, this dispossessed people, torn away from itself, whose murderous uprooting has covered all the time and space of the West. Isn't this the most magnificent example of the ardent consciousness that burns but is not consumed, and that has nevertheless formed a shield against millennial genocide? Isn't this the clearest illustration of the property of the poor, the poor metaphysical wealth which can be weakened by no poverty and undermined by no dereliction as long as a will survives that can continue to say no and to believe in higher values than those of the world? Like the just man of whom Isaiah says that, if "misfortune" strikes and the "epidemic" rages, he must return to his dwelling, take refuge inside his walls, and "close the doors behind him," the Jew is the victim of persecution who for a long time had no refuge but within himself, in that house of dreams whose stones and roof he carried within his heart.[18] This metaphoric dwelling—Jerusalem the "open city," said Zechariah—is the mirage of a promised land, which is in no way a real place but a land in the mind, irrigated by waters from above, the illusion of a messianism of which the Prophets tirelessly repeat that it must not so much be embodied as form a barrier, precisely, against the madness of utopia. The "People of the Book," the Jewish people, is the one that believes, that has never ceased to believe, even perhaps with the return to Palestine, in a fictitious fatherland, made of laws and magic spells, in the shadow of the cathedrals of dust that are its monuments. The "chosen people"—it is the one that knows, that has never ceased knowing, that Israel is also the blessed name of a useless property, an internal exile, a hunger for the universal which it carries in its flesh like a wound and which has simply never allowed it to surrender.

I have long wondered about the reasons for the hatred felt against us by all totalitarian régimes without exception, but notably by the socialists. I have always found the latent anti-Semitism which persists in Western communist parties, in the guise of "anti-Zionism," for example, somewhat mysterious. But I have never found most of the common explanations for the phenomenon very convincing—notably the obsession with the mythical "wandering Jew," merchant and moneychanger, circulating like currency through society. For, in reality, if it is true that there is no fascism not intent on rooting out the refuges of will and subjectivity in every individual, this is the reason for the hatred of Judaism, perceived as a theory of this refuge, a cult of this subjectivity, a basis for resistance to the total illumination of totalitarianism. If we agree that every citizen in a fascist régime may at any moment suddenly have to explain, like the deputy in the Convention who felt himself observed by Robespierre: "He is going to suppose that I'm thinking something," we can understand that the Jew, seen within the confines of this fantasy as a pocket of opacity and incongruous darkness in the world, is the principal enemy of the Robespierres of every age. Our terrorists have no quarrel with the wandering Jew, but with the opposite image of the rooted Jew, rooted in his solitude. They do not persecute in him the one who circulates but exactly the opposite, that is, at bottom, the owner of property. They do not fear "imperialism" in Zionism, but a metaphoric and worldwide alternative to the socialism of souls. For the strange status of Israel is that it is less a region of the world than a category of thought. The meaning of this category is that we are all, you are all, Jews of that Palestine. There is no freedom which is not situated in Israel, if it is true that to resist is always to choose the side of the underground of inwardness.

Is it necessary to specify that one will find few examples of this definition taken literally in the textbooks of philosophy? Is it necessary to recall how those texts cooperated, in their way, in reducing and rooting out that inwardness, creating men without shadows, purged of all darkness. We can find means of thinking about and illustrating this resistance among artists and writers in fact, just as much as in the Bible. In Stendhal, for example, whom I have called an ideocrat but who was also the inventor of egotism—he devoted one of his *Chroniques italiennes* to a description of the *maquis*, precisely, from which arise the rebels, the lawless, the men from below. No one was more concerned than he with secrecy, obsessed with mystery, and we know from his life of his taste for anagrams, rebuses, puzzles, pseudonyms. After Mme de Lafayette, and with a talent even Sartre could not equal, no one described so well the dangers of the gaze, that indiscreet scalpel, that pitiless weapon plunged into the depths of the soul by the "spy," the "confessor," or the possessive lover: it is with curtains and shutters closed, safe from the gaze of others, that Julien finally takes the portrait of Napoleon from under his bed and reads his beloved *Mémorial*. All of *Le Rouge et le Noir* is an apology for shadow, darkness, intimacy—the intimacy of Vergy, for example, where Julien agrees not to play Sorel any longer and can surrender himself, for the first time, to the incomparable pleasure of being himself. And the pleasure of dissimulation too, of the virtuous duplicity demanded from chivalric souls by a society of philistines that "kills, excludes, imprisons, or humiliates" the man of heart and talent. An ethics of impossible happiness, a relentless quest for a pleasure which slips away as one approaches it, all Stendhal's work is perhaps nothing but the demand for the inalienable and sacred right to silence and secrecy.

It is also nothing, above all and very directly this time, but a kind of field manual for a guerrilla warfare of inwardness. *La Chartreuse*, as everyone knows, is the narrative of a plot, an astonishing collection of intrigues halfway between a vendetta and a court crime in Suetonius. There is a minister of police who, while he "dressed like a character in a play," weaves his plans for regicide, covered by his position on the councils of the kingdom. A great-hearted duchess who, like a Balzacian courtesan, rides in the enemy's carriages and pays her respects to him, but only grants him the appearance of her assent while preserving within the most implacable hatred against him. And finally, a young curate of twenty-three, inspired by a frozen ardor, a passion indifferent to good and evil fortune, which has no more effect on him than a good hand of cards. These three characters, out of the ordinary the author tells us, make the first discovery which Julien glimpsed, but in a still confused manner. The struggle in which they are engaged, with their entire soul and strength, is a hopeless and perfectly futile struggle—but with a splendid futility that removes nothing essential from its style or its reasons. There is also a further discovery, which was beyond the grasp of the *carbonari* of the *Chroniques italiennes*. It is granting too much to the prince to declare war on him, for you sanctify and recognize him by entering the realm of illegality. Authentic dissidence, the only kind which goes to the heart, is a dissidence that makes cynicism into a battle weapon and sovereign contempt into the most absolute weapon of all. And last, there is the crowning touch of the novel: At the end of the journey, in the depths of one's dungeon, confronting death on the edge of eternity, the tunic becomes detached; one removes it at will and is again intact, miraculously identical with the self one became, long ago, one evening on Lake Como. Fabrice is a Lorenzaccio who succeeds because, to the very end, he has held to the wager on inwardness, the double game, reserve.[14] Desperate, cynical, and nevertheless faithful to himself, the Stendhalian hero invents, in other words, a manner of resistance which others have rediscovered since, in the real world. Confronting the gaze of the prince and monolithic thought, the mechanisms of surveillance that detect rebellion in our very faces, we have the right and the duty of a fundamental hypocrisy.

Perhaps this defense will surprise those who have heard me argue elsewhere for the hatred of lying and the duty of lucidity. But this would be to confuse domains, to play dangerously with words, to forget that "truth" is spoken in at least two senses which must be scrupulously distinguished. On the one hand, *the will to truth*, the determination to say it and to have it said completely; and we know the use that can be made of this in a world which does not so much censor as force its subjects to speak and reveal themselves. And on the other hand, *the imperative of not lying*, of which Stendalian hypocrisy is not the opposite but an image, a form among others, its mode of resistance and clandestinity—still a truth, but silent and internalized, buried beneath a mound of silence, when revealing it in its nakedness would expose one to the danger of death. There is a crime of truth mentioned by the Talmud, for example: the crime of the witch who, because she looked too far and pushed her curiosity too high, deserves to be punished for her excess. Above all, there is *a drama of the will to truth*, the drama whose hero is Hamlet—the man whom fate has placed in the impossible situation of being the only one who knows what is hidden from everyone else, of being obliged to shed light on what lies in darkness. On the ramparts after the ghost has left the stage, when he tells Horatio and Marcellus that he might soon "put an antic disposition on,"[15] Hamlet knows that folly is the only way out, the only means of speaking the truth in a world of falsehood. He knows, and these are his last words—after he has given his "dying voice"[16] to Fortinbras, the man of action—that "the rest is silence,"[17] that one cannot live with truth, that there is a madness in telling all, and that one can die from that madness too. Like Hölderlin criticizing Empedocles for having wanted to bring full and complete transparency to men, Shakespeare teaches a superior hypocrisy whose motto might be: Nothing but the truth, not the whole truth.

This apparently anodyne motto is perhaps decisive in these refined times when bodies are also exterminated with the weapons of this madness. It is far, very far from self-evident in an age of police clad in the colors of Hegelianism who crowd the benches of history in posthumous trials wherein they condemn the living in the name of the truth of their actions, not visible to the actors but dialectically demonstrated. I maintain that fascism begins—multicolored fascism—with the concern to place a man in the prison of that truth, to lock him up in the Bastille and the enclosure of *his* truth, to reduce him, simply, to the label of his concept. Anti-Semitism, for example, is also a reduction of the Jew to his Jewish narrowness, a manner of defining him by the exclusivity of his difference, and hence the denial of the character, essential to any kind of freedom, which consists of being always elsewhere, something other than oneself, better and more than the self of one's truth. And this is the final meaning of this principle of hypocrisy: the fundamental right of everyone to deny, to betray, to deceive, not always to act according to what he is and what others want him to be. Baudelaire—an artist again—called in 1861 for a declaration of human rights that would include the right to contradict oneself and the right to go away.

Is this power of non-definition finally compatible with the right of property with which I began? It is its corollary, its most intimate companion, the keystone that supports it and gives it full scope. It is the ultimate condition for the enlargement of the personal and the broadened habeas corpus, which now appears rigorously deduced. It is the very work of dissidence which, rooted in the inwardness of the soul, keeping itself strictly in its place, within its boundaries, nevertheless constantly undermines those boundaries, breaks them down, displaces them. It is the last human right, if you like, without which the subject risks becoming a mime without a face, hung on the cross of his self, bogged down in routine and the inhibition of the linear. And so we come to the end of this brief itinerary, which, drawing out the metaphor of "possessive individualism," has extended its scope to the dimensions of a resistance. Having presented the phenomenology of that resistance, it remains to establish for it a theory.

PART FOUR:
THE BIBLE OF RESISTANCE

I am no longer so desolate about humanity. I see clearly what makes man, even when he is paralyzed with horror, a figure whom nothing has ever been able to crush. I can also imagine what will ensure that even in the greatest dangers he will never cease from winnowing his just rebellions. Yes, I can imagine it; but we must still move forward. And this is why, more certain of man's horizon and the solidity of his name, I can attempt in conclusion to replace him in the context of the world. So that we can complete, after having deduced his essence, the formulation of the principle of his resistance.

You will not therefore be too surprised to find me entering more vigorously into the thickets of the biblical text. I shall rearrange the fragments of that opera of dreams whose ultimate message, I repeat, is a message of rebellion. I shall gather its Word, like a precious stone which, while others linger in suffering, offers a hope. To summarize without anticipating too much, monotheism is the thought of resistance of our age, because it proposes a definition of evil, a doctrine of justice, an ethics and a metaphysics of time. And also because in the first place it supplies us with the fragments of an answer to the eternal question: What can I do, what must I do, in the face of the despotism, the lies, and the oppression of history?

13

The Seven Commandments

What then is to be done? I know what has been made of this
old question in the past, and what is still made of it by countless
time-serving thinkers, courtiers of Syracuse and experts in the
ideal, who have surrendered their minds and the rigor of their
science to the executioners. I am all too well aware of what the
question is worth when our valiant concepts, suddenly displaced,
take to the streets and march in step with the pack, and when, as
Hegel predicted, arguments become events, documents become
movements, and logical necessities become murderous. Indeed, as
I have often said, it is the nature of the true, the only, revolution
of the century that, since thought has taken power, there are no
camps which are not concentrated philosophy, realized philosophy, the "pudding"[1] finally eaten, the word finally made flesh,
the world "transformed," as they say—those people, that is, who
are weary with having so long "interpreted" it. For all those
who cannot bring themselves to believe that so much savagery is
the banal product of an appalling misunderstanding; for all
those who hear, in the howling of the *kapos* of Buchenwald and
Kolyma, the savage interpretation of century-old dreams scrib-
bled by their masters in their innocent treatises; for all those, finally, who hold to the simple precept that an intellectual must

never serve as an auxiliary to assassins, there is a great temptation to take refuge in silence and in the harsh irony of a fashionable rejection of "every ideology."

The fact nevertheless remains that one cannot long dwell in
this skepticism, which would quickly become an alibi for surrender. The question of what is to be done is also a challenge, and,
however scalded we may be by a sinister memory, or even petrified by the horror of ideas that kill even more efficiently than
bombs, we cannot perennially drone on about futility. As an intellectual, then—but perfectly inorganic, without supervision or
control, yet not a deserter for all that—I believe it is my duty to
answer, against the cohort of intellectuals who openly pursue
their work of submission in the realms of the right and left alike.
A professional of history, a preserver of memory, and especially
privileged in my voice—nothing but my voice yet my whole
voice—I believe it is urgent to recall, to formulate categorically,
the few simple maxims which, on the level of daily human existence, are the breviary for those who struggle. And this is why I
take the risk of asserting these maxims, of giving body to these
rules which, although they are imperative and reasonably based
on the derivation of the individual, are nevertheless indicative,
relative, as we shall see, to the most concrete cases of the refusal
to submit. I have reduced them to the symbolic number of seven,
thinking of the seven commandments of Noah in which the ancient Hebrews saw the minimal morality applicable to any society, once it claimed to escape from the traps of barbarism. Perhaps Noachism today is simply called antifascism.

First commandment: *The Law, your Law, is holier than the
event.* Universal history is not, as you have been taught, the infallible guide, gathering the last words of the dying and deciding
among the words of the living, which decrees that this one is following the line, condemns that one as a deviant, and leads the
survivors, heads bent and spirits broken, to its prescribed end of
wonder and mystery. You must no longer lend credence to the
philosophers' fable—that Bible of despots—that there is a

"providence," says one, an "absolute spirit," says another, a "dialectic," says a third, whose key is concealed from you by "narrow perceptions," some obscure "ruse of reason," or perhaps your "class origin,"[2] but this key will not forget you and will not fail to punish you. Keep yourself from the enchanters who, confusing truth with the laurels of its victory, wait for it where armies pass by, hear it where the guillotine falls, and leave you the choice only between joining the caravan with your lot of deserved suffering or meeting in hell with the population of madmen who were unable to attend the meeting with the inevitable. For to be free is precisely to refuse the meeting, that ambush, and the blessing it gives to the untold crimes and suffering which are, it appears, the price for its inexorable process. It is to adhere to values which, even if they are ridiculed and denied by innumerable facts, nevertheless continue to be valid, to believe in their sovereign right. It is to posit that good and evil exist, not necessarily in every place and every time, but no matter what time may do with them and whether or not it ratifies their persistence in existing. This is how the people of the Bible lived for two millennia, and their history was never anything but an obstinacy in saying no, in denying the manifest verdict of centuries. This is how its rabbis thought and wrote, throughout their strange books, teeming with confusions, blinding anachronisms whose calm assurance testifies to an extraordinary freedom with respect to the very notion of annals. And thus we can explain the inconceivable perseverance of a tradition for which countless thinkers, down to Spengler and Toynbee, prophesied imminent and necessary disappearance. So true is it that to resist means perhaps first of all to resist history itself, denounced as absurdity, aberration, and immemorial misunderstanding.

The few men and women, the tiny minority[3] of heroes who dramatically entered the legend of the twentieth century on June 18, 1940, were saying nothing different; and this was the basis of their resistance. When a *pays réel,* drunk with its defeat, assembles fervently around a providential marshal, and when the good people of Vierzon massacre a tank officer trying to defend the bridges of the Cher,[4] it is hard to defend the expression "popular legitimacy" for those who nevertheless decide to continue the battle. When a sovereign assembly, sovereignly elected by the most regular procedures, and having come moreover from the glorious Popular Front, overcome with gratitude and repentance (already),[5] invests the saviour, by 569 votes to only 80,[6] with full powers to "restore" the "unhappy country," it is difficult to find the slightest hint of "democratic and republican" legality[7] in favor of London. Finally, in the succeeding years, when the French anti-Jewish police deported one hundred thousand "kikes" and carried out a census of two hundred thousand more[8] while from its depths the Nation made not the slightest public[9] gesture of solidarity with the victims, we must agree that Vallat and Darnand were indeed, for the moment, and for a moment whose duration no one knew at the time, consistent nationalists,[10] and Charles de Gaulle in his proud exile a "treacherous" officer in the pay of a "foreign power." It is of course easy today, for prophets after the fact, to see in the Resistance the signs of a precocious and brilliant lucidity; the truth is that at the moment when the communists themselves wanted "neither Pétain nor de Gaulle," "neither cholera nor the plague," and preached reconciliation between "German and French workers,"[11] the seven thousand exiles of Free France could justify themselves only by a pure moral wager, posited in the absolute, "against all opposition," as one of them said,[12] hovering over a world from which the obvious itself had disappeared. The worst insult one could offer to this handful of irreducible men and women—disdainful of any success and of the verdict of events, who nevertheless stubbornly persisted in crushing the horror—would be to say that, everything considered, dead to shame, the "real meaning of history" was there, feeling its way as usual, but clearly manifested to those who were clever enough to read it. For the meaning, the *only meaning* then available, was on the side of collaboration, since everything conspired to attest to its insurmountable fatality, its regular normality—exactly what the least Hegelian of modern generals revolted against. "The following days were cruel," he noted, after the failure in September of the uprising in the colonies.[13] Yes, not only cruel but literally senseless, such was the challenge hurled, beyond men, armies, and diplomatic authorities, against the very course of events. By this improbable act for whose arrogance, parenthetically, he would have paid dearly in case of defeat, he did nothing less than drag history in person into the dock, decreeing suddenly that it was guilty, absurd, impertinent.

Hence the second commandment, which flows naturally from the first: If there is no event worthy of calling forth the sacrifice of the Law, then the world is ripe at every moment for judgment—and *it will always be the time, for you, to manifest the good.* In the most harmless circumstances as much as in moments of tragedy, the only true courage consists in saying and doing what, in conscience, seems to you necessary to give value and honor to existence. You will distrust the meteorologists who whisper to you that it is not time yet, that you must let time take its time, that the mole of future time has not finished digging; in fact, future time never comes until the day of reckoning has passed and the thunder which ordered you to act has fallen silent. To the professors of patience who never weary of waiting for the twists and turns of meaning to accumulate until its totality arrives, you will oppose meaning to meaning, answer blow for blow, and retort that there are values that do not have the time to wait. The Psalmist says: "Let nothing prevent you discharging a vow in good time";[14] no, nothing should force you to involve it in history, mediate it in tactics, defer it because of a scruple that is always the other side of a ruse, an intrigue, or a plot. One day, Genesis recounts,[15] when Hagar and Ishmael were wandering in the desert of Beersheba after Abraham had driven them away on Sarah's orders, there was no more water in the skin, and the mother, at the end of her strength, "abandoned the child under a bush."[16] Elohim was moved and, "from heaven," opened the unfortunate woman's eyes. She saw before her "a well," and went to give water to the boy, who afterward "grew up" in the desert.[17] The angels were astonished, adds the Talmudic commentator, indignant at seeing the Almighty so lightly save the one who, one day—they knew, those clever readers of the providential design—would rise up against its people and make Israel suffer. And what did the Lord reply? Again according to the Talmud, he answered with this magnificent and extremely significant statement, which makes calculation, delay, and finally lying the first crime according to ethics: "The end of history is of little importance, for we must judge each man according to what he is rather than for what he will become."[18]

This is more than an aphorism; it is the sign of a necessity. The supposed dénouement does not matter when, at the crossroads of the moment, necessity shifts and the rigor of a choice imposes itself. Necessity is a snare and the angels' premonition an illusion, and in the face of it the only thing that counts is the imperious ultimatum of saving a dying body. Since the idea of an ethical process is nothing but a mirage, the only idea that is not a mirage is the idea of an action that is not lived in the humility of mediation but is on the contrary always experienced in the sufficiency of a sublime non-mediation. In modern terms, we would say that the battle for human rights is chronologically, logically, and ontologically the primary human duty; and this not in virtue of some vague provisional morality, humanitarian stopgap, or undefined political minimalism, but as a rigorous and perfectly well founded conclusion, which refuses to see history as the sovereign lord. Thus, for example, a few years ago I became involved in the fight of the Bengalis against Pakistani oppression. While some bright lights saw the corpses of the Ganges Delta as "bad" corpses, who were shaking the bases of unity of a reputedly progressive state, I thought it was urgent to revolt against this dictatorship of progress.[19] This is also the reason why, in an entirely different domain a little later, it was impertinent to consider it suspect to listen to Solzhenitsyn while a Marchais was speaking or to relay the message of the Russian dissidents on the eve of a French election.[20] The argument could, in fact, be valid only for those who—assuming what had to be demonstrated—postulated the idea of a total, totalizing, totalitarian meaning, which would provide a label and a definition for any particular real misery. In the name of the same principle again, my friend Marek Halter, at about the same time, testified, for long alone, against torture in Argentina. Confronting him were parties that all preferred to keep silence about a suffering which had the dubious impropriety for some of not being the Gulag and for others of not being Chile—and for both of not fitting exactly into the regulated pattern of the landscapes of history.[21] In a word, if the battle for human rights is indeed the primary struggle of the late twentieth century, this is because what is at stake is neither a new strategy nor a charitable action, but a different philosophical perspective on the world which says, like the Prophet again, all deadlines have passed for resisting barbarism, whatever its face and whoever its victims may be.

Further, more profoundly, in virtue of a different relationship to time, we can formulate this third commandment: Whatever the presumed consequences or the objective scope of your action, *you must in every instance assume that the future is not your concern.* Besides, how could it be, that evanescent and rigorously risky future, which will never cease unfolding and improvising its own past? How could it enter into the problem and the choice of action when it is itself problematical, undecidable, constantly playing with you—betraying you and endowing your present with unexpected consequences? Don't you see that an action dependent on the future and wishing to be relative to what will one day come from it, would be relative to the infinitely relative and would thereby simply lose any hope of being undertaken? Even if you were to attempt it, in the name of what would you justify it since, caught in a chain of indefinitely postponed proofs, it will by definition be indefinitely unjustifiable?[22] No, the truth and the most elementary logic demand that—in the face of the irony

of history, which disfigures as it inspires the result of your enter-
prises—you declare yourself incompetent about the result and
preoccupied by the intention that moves you at the moment.
Strictness and true moral intransigence presume that, rejecting
the historical responsibility which the prudent take on the better
to temporize, you free yourself of positivism and so-called objec-
tivity in order to assume, without fear or regret, the inconse-
quence of the beautiful soul. To the eternal Hegelian[23] who
summons you to choose between the "man of the present" who
does not accept his action "to its full extent" and the "heroic
character" who ignores the conflict between "subjective" and
"objective" views, you will answer that you have nothing to do
with a "heroism" that conceals the most deceitful desire: acceptance of the world as it is, following every twist of its wanderings. If he insists again and objects that the future whose sanction you disdain constrains you whether you like it or not and
will make your resolutions "turn out differently from what you
would wish," his insistence will strengthen you rather than
weakening your choice. For the wheel of sanctified history may
turn and turn again; it will intimidate only its worshippers, and
will merely invite you to harass it all the more in an interminable guerrilla war. It may very well be your master, but it will no
longer be your god; and one obeys a god, but one resists a master. It is certain that it will humiliate you and mock your pure
"intentions"; but no one forbids you to answer its sarcasm with a
renewal of pure intention and its decadence with new insurrections. The fact that the future is not your concern means that
your lot is impatience, anxiety, the turbulence of a will that never ceases to deny its incarnations. To resist means to *begin again*
to resist, and to reply at every turn to the false "tragedy" of historical action, which disarms only the apathetic, the will-less fu-
turologists. "Do not meddle with matters that are beyond you,"
says Ecclesiasticus;[24] but work all the same, never stop working.

Can we give a specific contemporary example? This commandment applies almost exactly to those intellectuals who agi-

tated in succession, but without the slightest recantation, for the liberation of Saigon from the aggression of U.S. imperialism, and then, once Saigon was liberated, for the dignity of the refugees who left, again *en masse,* the new communist régime. It is the key of the paradox, but not a disavowal, which led them, in other terms, from the "rank-and-file Vietnam committees" that supported the just struggle of the Vietnamese bombarded by American napalm in the sixties to the committee for "a boat for Vietnam" created toward the end of 1979[25] to help those same Vietnamese, crushed from the inside this time, under the boot of red despotism. On this occasion, the editor-in-chief of a major French newspaper repeated point for point the argument of the "heroic character," explaining in substance in a message to one of the founders of the committee[26] that he could not join the initiative of individuals whose earlier struggle was responsible, in his view, for the present disaster and who nevertheless refused to assume that responsibility "to its full extent." His interlocutor answered,[27] as a perfect "man of the present," that the current struggle was the logical consequence of the earlier battle; that antifascism seems contradictory only because fascism is constant in its essence; and that it was not a matter of prediction, strategy, and finally abdication, but one of urgency, imminence, and indefatigable indignation. The one began with the obvious fact that the future came from the past in order to draw from that the sophism that the past came from the future, from which it has received its coloration and its retrospective truth. The other admitted the terrible misunderstanding which, in fact, inscribed the death camps in the "objective" line of the war of liberation; but since he had no other line but that of resistance to oppression, he entered this misunderstanding not so much in the debt ledger of men's conscience as under the liabilities of a logic of history which is precisely the ground for that resistance itself. So we have on the one side a commissar who, observing that in the course of ten years the same men and women fell under the blows of colonial war and then of internal dictatorship, deduced that all those who hastened the dénouement of the former were objectively guilty of unleasing the latter, and saw this responsibility as a motive for keeping silent and letting the horror have its way. And on the other, a committed man who, from the indubitable fact that the same men and women suffered in both cases, concluded that, since the same causes produce the same effects, a maxim that was just in one case was just in the other, and saw this distance not as a motive for repentance but as a reason for persevering, indeed for committing the same "crime" again. In a word, going now beyond the anecdote, the objective consequences of an act can be considerable politically, but they are nevertheless morally negligible. Historic error is not only a right that morticians in their magnanimity might grant us; it is an unavoidable duty.[28] Political wandering is not an argument against an ethical maxim; but an ethical maxim, in its innocence of the kingdom of ends, is always a sharper weapon against the wanderings of politics.

Then what is the basis for this maxim and what determines its formulation? Where can you get such assurance and the calm acceptance that you may be mistaken? Is your resistance nothing but a blind, confused, and powerless reaction? Are you a plaything, a wisp of straw buffeted by the winds of history? What is certain, in any case, is that contempt for the future as such is not enough as a basis for rebellion. If it is true that the justification for your maxim can lie neither in its end nor in the consequences you intend, it remains—but it is also necessary—that it lie in the cause and the form of its motive. If history is a miscalculation not of your making, you are on the other hand responsible—and absolutely—for the rigor of a principle in which all the coherence others search for in the wandering course of time must be restored. If your initiative is rigorously without a future, it nonetheless has a source and that superior lucidity which will allow you, if the case arises, to reject the false alternatives wherein, in the name of the "direction of history," the wise men would trap you.[29] The fact that the future is not your concern, in other words, does not mean that you must replace the Hegelian dialectic with Stoic submission to the moment; but that you must weight that moment itself with a density of intention, of planning, perhaps of eternity, which will make its imminence more than a caprice or a particular folly. This is why the good maxim will be one that, without damage or contradiction, you can make into an object of "prophecy," in the sense in which I have defined the word. The single criterion should be that in case, hypothetically speaking, someone else, elsewhere, were to apply the same law, that law should bring about less murder, less horror, less barbarism. And from this my fourth commandment follows: Whatever you may wish and whatever unremitting time may do with your will, *you will undertake nothing that is not immediately worthy of being instantly and perpetually repeated.* This is substantially what Isaiah says when, lamenting that he has "toiled in vain" and "exhausted himself for nothing," he nevertheless consoles himself with the knowledge that his "cause is with Yahweh."[30] What he means is that even if it is untimely, without successors, disavowed as soon as it is spoken, his speech has, in and for itself, by virtue of its transcendental character, the absolute criterion of its eternity. What he says to us, profoundly, is that if all the nations of the world finally opened their eyes and, like him, held themselves close to the Torah and its prescription, for example, against killing others, the world would go on a little better than it does right now. In a polysemous universe in which history, like a cancer, causes meaning constantly to proliferate, this is the question which, following him, you must never forget to ask: Does the meaning which I now, sovereignly, manifest deserve or not to be universalized?

It is a clear criterion, and I think that if it were applied methodically, it would allow us to avoid a number of academic arguments. It is obvious, for example, that the maxim which drove the intellectuals of the thirties to protest, in the salle Wagram, against the arrest of Thälmann, and to applaud, in the salle Pleyel, the conviction of Bukharin, could not be universalized without sophistry; but it is also clear that, fifteen years later, Camus's rule condemning alike the executioners of the right and the executioners of the left could be, and was in fact, universalized. I am perfectly willing to be told that the entry of Russian tanks is progressive in Prague and the intervention of the CIA reactionary in Chile, but on the condition that you add that the distinction is political, that is, of the moment, that is, contingent and finally deceptive; while, on the contrary, the rejection of imperialism in all its forms is a moral attitude which, in any hypothesis, economizes human lives and could be shared without danger by everyone. The idea dear to the left, still, that there are good and bad, "just" and "suspect," dissidents, is probably an efficient idea if it is a matter of cutting off a head, but effectively impracticable when you attempt to formalize it. For if Solzhenitsyn's fate can be rather quickly decided, what can be said of Bukovsky, Pliuchtch, or Maximov? Where does good resistance end and bad resistance begin? Where is the "deteriorated" socialist and where the inveterate "counterrevolutionary"? At what point does religion become the "opium of the people" and up to what point is it the "sigh of the oppressed creature"?[31] In the China Sea, should we save economic refugees and sacrifice political refugees? The enumeration of these dead ends would be amusing if it were not so horrifying, and if each one did not contain the rejection of the rather simple truth that the order of ethics begins when—and only when—one agrees to the principle of universality: a life is a life, a body is a body, from the moment they are in danger of death or a loss of dignity. Finally, on a more general level, it is clear that in the famous dilemma, the primacy of the "end" over the "means" is a *morally unfounded* position since, as soon as one attempts agreement on the determination of ends, the attempt engenders discord and a multiplicity of opinions; while the opposite position can easily be formulated as a universal rule because, since means are nothing but the concrete point of convergence between concrete men and concrete history, it would, at least theoretically, be possible to draw up an exhaus-

tive inventory of them with a minimum of cacophony and legitimized murder.

The situation is clear now. What is at stake in each case is the
autonomy of ethics with respect to neighboring and opposing
disciplines that aspire to reduce it. And this is therefore the fifth
commandment: Despite tradition and against those who would
promote surrender, you must assume and convince yourself that
truth, your truth, *is foreign to the order of politics.* For what is
this politics which I have already tried so often to demystify?
What would it mean to say: "Truth is political"? What do intellectuals mean when they proclaim with so much assurance that
"Everything is political"? It is in fact a very ancient argument,
as old as philosophy, and hammered out by two thousand years
of theories. It was probably born with Plato, and we can find
traces of it, for example, in the early dialogue entitled *Euthydemus.* "Politics" is the name Socrates gives to the "supreme" and
"royal art" that the Athenian Clinias is looking for and that
must "govern everything."[32] If it has this privilege over the
crowd of competing forms of knowledge, this is because, he adds,
it has the merit of "making everything profitable."[33] This "prof-
it" itself means that, properly "brought together," the myriad of
passions or pitiful things men call "opinions" can attain to their
order and their secret harmony.[34] Apprehended in their "synthesis" as well as in their "divisions," these opinions would appear
as "mistakes," fragmentary and partial perspectives on the
whole, about which men can complain only if they are ignorant
or in bad faith. And Socrates then asserts that, in the face of this
supreme and "governing truth" which is the privilege of the
leaders, the humble can only keep silent and stagnate in their en-
durance. This powerful demonstration recurs in Aristotle, Leibniz, and Hegel. It can even be read in Spinoza, known as an
apostle of "freedom of conscience," since he devoted an entire
Tractatus to establishing and clearing the way for the *political*
conditions for the advent of truth.[35] There was perhaps no philosopher in the great tradition who did not consider it axiomat-

ic—and who did not go to great lengths to prove it—that truth is a matter of state in the strictest and most banal sense of the term.[36] And you know, of course, the fate of this proof among the latest heirs of the tradition, those prodigal sons who tried to "transform the world" according to grids of "interpretation" bequeathed to them by so many centuries of the thought of order. I am speaking of Marx, Lenin, and their epigones who, converting the old theoretical assurance that had graced the West in its cradle into a practical rule, have never since ceased legitimizing a devaluation of ethics whose concrete results are obvious.

This was the case, for example, for the attitude of the communist left in Germany in the thirties, with its incredible failure to block the rise of Nazism. Why, until the Reichstag fire, did the Party keep to its suicidal line that the principal struggle was against "social democracy," which was the concrete equivalent of collaboration with Hitler?[37] What was the mysterious reason for the countless specific actions carried out with SS thugs, the 150 votes supporting the Nazis in parliament, and the incredible summer of 1931 when the Party campaigned with the Steel Helmets against Otto Braun's left-wing government in Prussia?[38] Was it simply out of loyalty to Stalin that Neumann, number-two man in the organization, inspired in August 1930 a "declaration program for national and social liberation," hailed by Röhm, Niekisch, and Strasser as the entry of the Communist Party into the "German resistance front"?[39] And in what name could the same Neumann, two months later, negotiate with Goebbels on the shore of Lake Constance a possible reversal of alliances in return for an intervention of the Red Army to aid Hitler's national ambitions?[40] Must we conclude that it was a terrible, but banal, error of judgment when the Political Bureau, at the same time, ordered its militants to infiltrate the SA and to establish the notorious "beefsteak groups," red inside, brown outside, in which Nazis and Communists would fraternize while the first concentration camps were being set up around the country?[41] No, the descendants of Bebel, Liebknecht, and Karl Marx knew the truth about the camps, the SA, and Hitler; but the truth for these political minds was first of all the *truth of* the general crisis of society, which was shattering Germany and whose dénouement had to be *politically* hastened. They certainly heard the lament that was beginning to arise from the ghettos and even from the communist cells; yet, in the Marxist game, a lament is not a lament but more than a lament, something better than a lament, the perceptible and insignificant echo of the earthquake affecting the social body which will make possible, in the end, the seizure of state power that remains its objective. It was not for want of information that they were blinded for so long, but rather from an excess of science, of theory, of dialectics—that "royal art," as Socrates said, which teaches that the true is not what is true but what resides in a "supreme Truth," reducing what is true to the level of a symptom and assigning it to its place, its servile and humble rank, in the historical order of things. If this omnipotent Party, deeply bound to the working class of the time, with a rich tradition unequaled anywhere in Europe, still growing rapidly in the early thirties,[42] could "saddle," as the anarchist Friedrich said,[43] "the horse that Hitler would ride through the Brandenburg Gate," this was because it functioned according to a conception of the world that saw subjects as simple bit-players on the stage of history and victims as the inevitable price of a sure revolutionary process. It therefore could not conceive of any raw and direct evidence that would not necessarily be objectified in the deadly realm of politics and its "organizations."

From this there comes a sixth commandment, which is the corollary of this tragic experience and could say, parodying the famous expression: *Without a theory or a revolutionary party, you will practice resistance.* For, beyond the KPD, what failed then was the old Enlightenment idea that the more one knows, the more chances one has to resist. Men evidently never succumbed more easily than at the moment when they were more thoroughly ideologized than ever before, and knowledge is therefore not enough when it is not made fruitful by ethical determination. What also failed was the prejudice rooted in Marxist brains that strategies of rupture can accomplish lesser actions (resistance) because they can accomplish greater ones (revolution). In fact, their radicalism, which is often nothing but the mirror image of the leaders' will to power, during the course of this century and in the name of a hypothetical end of time, has never stopped turning ordinary people away from the imperative tasks of the present ends of history. And finally, what failed was the old conviction, rooted everywhere in the Western left, that large-scale organizations—purveyors of radicalism, ideology, and hope—are alone capable of putting together and organizing collective rebellion; the opposite has always been observed, the massive and methodical organization of surrender. Do you know of a single one of those organizations that can pride itself on being at the source of a single significant antitotalitarian revolt? Can you think of a single one of those revolts they did not first try to stifle, delay, and sometimes even prohibit? Are there many well-behaved, faithful, militant intellectuals who, still today, do not condemn Pinochet with the arguments of Brezhnev and Brezhnev with the arguments of Pinochet, and in both cases with fascist arguments? Ultimate incarnations of the "objective mind," these parties are not the sum of the subjective minds of which they are made up. They have an independent existence, and they leave its imprint on the bodies and souls of their followers. Deriving less from the categories of consciousness than from those of history, they immolate every consciousness on their new altars of discipline and rigor. Servants of the spirit of the world, self-proclaimed underpinning of the present and future odyssey of humanity, these great machines for mobilization are the monstrous mechanisms of the pagan theater and its tragedy of abdication.

How can we forget, for instance—to go directly to the most painful example—the case of the Jewish organizations in Warsaw, Berlin, and Budapest which drew up lists of deportees, took from the unfortunate the money to cover the expenses for their own deportation, and went so far as to establish Jewish police forces that would round up Jewish men, women, and children for the death convoys?[44] And how can we forget that, a little later, the insurgents of the Warsaw ghetto had to pay a heavy price to get weapons and dynamite from smugglers or German deserters, because the Polish Communist Party and the Armia Krajowa, the principal resistance organization in the country, showed themselves reticent, if not hostile, toward these vagabonds, these insurgents of hope who intended to die with guns in their hands, assuming in solitude their dignity as free men?[45] The fact is that, concretely, the only organizations ever to provide individual subjects with anything but misery and accepted despotism are those which, devoted to a particular, momentary purpose rather than a perpetual mission, die out and disappear once their task has been accomplished, and so alleviate concrete suffering rather than flourishing on it, "capturing" it, as Ezekiel said superbly. The difference between the "coordinating committee" of the ghetto and the Armia Krajowa, for example, is that the first was an underground whose network matched in nearly perfect detail the topography of the sewers and cellars of Warsaw, and the second a mechanism whose pyramidal structure already prefigured the new social order and perhaps the new hierarchies of liberated Poland. Again, the difference between the Algerian FLN and the French CNR was that the latter disappeared at the end of the Resistance, even if it entrusted others with the task of realizing its ideals; while the former, institutionalizing its just war, could only become the framework of a society and soon be tempted by totalitarianism and the war of all against all. What distinguishes, in the late seventies, an organization like Amnesty International from a classical political party is that, precisely because it is apolitical and completely indifferent to changing man, life, or the world, it is satisfied, by saving bodies, all bodies, and nothing but bodies, with establishing solidarity between solitudes that it strengthens and comforts, instead of abolishing.

We are thus far from the traditional notion of "commitment," which can now be seen in a new light. For from this follows the last of the seven commandments, which alone can make the preceding six coherent: If it is true that to join a cause is to give up committing yourself, *you must, in order to commit yourself, begin by detaching yourself.* Is it necessary to recall that André Gide, for example, really contributed to the honor of mankind and the humble only before he was enrolled, at a time when, detached from any allegiance, he was nothing but an unhappy consciousness carrying his indignation with him to Chad or the Congo?[46] Is it necessary to repeat, once again, the lesson of the Prophets and their distrust of those slogans which, creating order in the world and disorder in souls, bring all speech into line with pagan attachments and forever block its path toward the apprehension of justice? If politics and truth are indeed what I have said they are, then there is no ethical action, in effect, which does not presuppose a withdrawal of the self, an area of dissidence, a promontory apart, from which one may judge, decide between things. If history is your master and the master of all masters, then the *a priori* condition for any possible resistance can only be the decree—and the continued effort—that will make you alien to the course of that history and thereby rescue you from the snare in which it tends to imprison you. This does not mean, of course, that in the name of some undefined aestheticism you will take refuge—like Jünger—justifying his surrender by a bad *Treatise of the Rebel*,[47] in the world of the prompters who make fun of the human pantomime from above, sometimes condescending, between two meditations, to relieve it out of charity. Rather, it means, quite to the contrary, that dismissing once and for all the twin delights of the aesthete's renunciation and the politician's optimism, you will have all the better grasp of history because it no longer has any hold on you. You will harass the potentates all the better after you have left their temples and broken their laughing idols. And I believe that thus, and only thus, will you be able, as they say, to "restore hope to Billancourt."

Where was hope alive in Nazi Germany, once again? At a time when the agents of the Comintern turned over to the Gestapo the poor hotheads in their ranks who wanted to leave the game, there were Catholics, for example, or Protestant ministers who, in the name of Christian faith and hatred for paganism, said no to Rosenberg.[48] At the point when the official left was endlessly mouthing its criminal fables about the historic course of things and the fate of capitalism, there were soldiers who became dissidents, like the old general of the Reichswehr who, discovering the inscription "Jews and dogs prohibited" on a public bench, sequestered himself at home and quietly let himself die. While in 1934 Manuilsky was still declaiming that "there is not the slightest doubt that the line followed by the German Communist Party, which consisted in avoiding open combat against the fascist gangs, was absolutely correct,"[49] there were men of the law who, in the name of Weimar legality, refused, like Carl Goerdeler, the burgomeister of Leipzig, to allow the swastika to be hung at city hall.[50] When someone finally comes to write the true history of that internal resistance, we will discover irregulars, pacifists or anarchists, "a-social" or "petty bourgeois" figures who, persecuted from both sides, cried out "Never again war" with Carl von Ossietzky, Erich Mühsam, Ludwig Quidde, and a few others, almost all of them mutilated or dead in the deportation camps.[51] We will see arising from the shadows the anonymous crowd of Jehovah's Witnesses who, also alone, preferring torture to blasphemy, refused to join to the name "Hitler" the fervent "*Heil*" that could only apply to God.[52] We will rediscover heroes, forgotten as soon as they were martyred, because they dared to think differently, like the Berlin printer Ernest Friedrich, the madman who devoted his life to establishing a "Museum of Peace," which the SS transformed into a barracks in 1933.[53] Or Martin Gruerwiehl, an uncommitted worker, who broke the law of silence by publishing, in 1934, under the title *The Story of a Prisoner of Dachau*, a minutely detailed narrative of his season in hell.[54] We will perhaps also find traces of the improvised *samizdat* which was circulating (already!) in defiance of Party orders, in defiance of the orders of *all* parties, among ordinary individuals who, one by one, entered heroically with a firm, determined step into a present doomed to catastrophe. This "true history," of course, has not been written, nor is it about to be. It would be the most stinging rebuke to the memory of organizations that for twenty long years drowned out the tumult of empires and nations with their futile gibberish. It would be the finest homage to the discreet commotion ordinary people always make in moments of greatest surrender, once they have ignored the crude beacons of history and challenged the forces of deception and the arrogant cynicism of the leaders. I hope that with these few lines I have simply, and humbly, contributed to ensuring that one day, finally, they will no longer be so alone.

14

The Order of Evil

This catalogue of commandments is not, of course, a catechism, and I have no intention of asserting that it is either exhaustive or definitive. It is rather a series of points of view, furtive and fragmentary perspectives on those undergrounds of the will, those cellars of *chouannerie,* whose whispers I began by suggesting we should hear again. Through these examples of struggle or surrender there appears something like a procession of horror, but also of hope, which from beginning to end gives evidence of the necessary decline, the metaphysical descent that removes ethics from the heights and installs it in the lower depths. And we can perhaps begin to glimpse, from these few cases, the basis for this resistance from below; the choice it implies beyond politics; and what it means, both metaphysically and in fact, for the reasons men give themselves for living, dying, or simply suffering.

For if I had to sum up, gather these methods and lessons into a single perspective, reduce these commandments of insurrection to a single article, I would finally say that they are all opposed to a *diktat* which is really no longer political in the ordinary sense; which, if necessary, can do without state, police, or ideology in order to bend the bodies of the humble under the burden of suffering; which is, in fact, supported by a collection of simple, discreet, unexpressed principles that are nevertheless prodigiously effective in making a mutilated soul keep silence. And first of all we must attempt to recapitulate the sequence of these principles.

To begin with, then, there is a principle one might call *economic* because, following Leibniz,[1] it weighs, measures, and calculates the suffering of concrete men according to the standards of a view of the whole, the great cosmic picture whose forms and contours it emphasizes in contrast. Thus we are told, for example, that the "balance sheet" of sixty years of socialism is "globally positive,"[2] or that unemployment in the West is the "price of growth"—and too bad for the one who pays, for the price is in order, it is an orderly part of the world, it is never anything but the shadow and the negative side of the good. Secondly, there is a principle which derives from *statistics* because, in the manner of modern "human sciences," it allows us to recognize in particular suffering the simple specimen of a universal law, a typological disease that abolishes the self, the "I" reduced to the "one" of a common name: one is "neurotic," another a "deviant," a third a "misfit," and to hell with his obscene and sovereign discomfort for, thus labeled, he becomes regular, summed up in a rule, the shadow of an evil now banal and generic. There is further a principle of *chemistry,* with a Hegelian flavor, which assures its victims that there are no open wounds, no hideous rivers of blood, that do not derive from their opposite, and do not end by coming together in a promised harmony for which they were the unsuspected but abominably fruitful prefigurations. This is the procedure of all the "progressive" apostles of "just" or "revolutionary" violence; for violence, to them, has its reasons, it has tomorrow's reason on its side, it is the royal road to the arrival of high noon. And lastly there is a principle from *optics*, because it crowns the preceding ones with the ultimate argument that misery, all things carefully considered, is nothing positive, but a visual illusion—a mirage of the diseased eye, dissipated as soon as one puts on different glasses and agrees like Descartes to "change one's desires rather than the order of the world."[3] And in the name of that "wisdom," the starving man is ordered to stop dreaming of bread and the slave to free himself while remaining in chains—for his servitude is nothing, the lack of bread nothing either, nothing in each case but an erroneous point of view on the sweet spectacle of the world. Economist, statistician, chemist, and optician: the executioner is all of them at once, and to oppress is always to implant in our brains the four corners of what must be called a "mechanism of meaning."

This is the reason why expressing a servitude or a misfortune, "giving it meaning" in the purely semantic sense of the term, "giving an account" of it as the expression goes, is often enough to collaborate with it and help conceal it. This was already the method of the good Stoic masters who, to the question of how to make bearable the scandalous distribution of wealth between the good and the evil, invariably replied: All one needs to do is to put it into sentences, elucidate its mystery and its logical basis, contain it within a tight network of arguments. And those arguments, moving gradually from the anodyne order of "causes" to the surreptitious sequence of "ends," will make it at one stroke as "necessary" and "natural" as the production of "figs" by a "fig tree" or "olives" by an "olive tree."[4] This is still the sure method of contemporary Marxists who, to the imperious obligation to exculpate red fascism and the concentration camps in the East, answer in exactly the same way: All one needs to do is to "analyze," "explain" the phenomenon, bring its "origins" or "historic conditions" to light, and thus to make it so clear, so evidently "limpid," so regularly deduced from the "backwardness" of the Russian masses, from "imperialist encirclement," or the consequences of the "civil war," that it becomes ordinary, mechanical, and almost inevitable. Nor am I very sure that the complacency of some who rationalize the Nazi horror—insert it into a history or sociology of the ignoble, refer it to some "crisis of capitalism," some "international situation" in which it was entirely steeped like a pale consequence in the stream of its antecedents—is not one of the best means of diluting its specificity. By thus reducing its brutality, smothering its harsh colors in a reassuring penumbra of occult motivations and sound determinations, such theorists sometimes succeed, better than forgetfulness, in legitimizing it. It is not true, in other words, that resistance to fascism always comes through "theory," as the left believes. Theorizing for the sake of theorizing takes the risk of using a rhetoric that, throwing a smokescreen around evil, blunts what there is of Evil in evil. Nor is it true that the Stalinists lie about the Gulag, as the right imagines. They lie less and less, they speak more and more truly; there is no end, in fact, to their accumulation of truths, and one need only glance at the Stalinist library on Stalinism to see how countless strong and subtle arguments do nothing but move back the threshold of the intolerable while bringing the threshold of the acceptable that much closer.[5] It is finally false, as everyone says, that in order to understand anything about totalitarianism we must make it familiar to the eye and the ear. If this familiarity is sometimes a victory of reason, it is always an absolute defeat of the spirit, which makes us deaf and blind to the exceptional excess of barbarism. This is perhaps where the "banality" of which a famous deportee once spoke begins,[6] in this imperceptible but inexorable drift which, giving meaning to something that has no meaning, always places us in danger of justifying the unjustifiable.

Then isn't it bizarre that periodically there returns to Europe the specter of an imaginary—and entirely too comfortable—"rehabilitation" of fascism? If the Stoic-Marxist lesson is correct, the real danger is perhaps closer to hand, in the subtle, discreet, and innocent process of language which, acclimatizing the infamous to the order of discourse, simply integrates it into a terrible discourse of order. I have no objection, for example, if people passionately pile up all the elements in the file of a Drieu La Rochelle.[7] As far as the investigation may go, the deeper it penetrates, the more thoroughly it accumulates character traits and details about events, the more it will come up against the irreducible *hapax* of unspeakable ignominy, and the more it will confront the unfathomable leap which, in the same conditions and with equivalent "complexes," made one man a swine and another a Resistance fighter.[8] I am well aware of the aleatory and contingent components of this leap. But to dwell on that contingency, undo the knot, make an inventory of its strands, and become intoxicated with its rather banal mystery, is to behave like the philosophers who asserted that "one can love evil only because one takes it for good," and because "occasional causes" have disturbed the divine certainty of judgment.[9] And this is always, in the end, to excuse crime, to absolve the evil will, and even sometimes to pity the elegant uncertainties of a madman who criticized Doriot for not being enough of a Nazi.[10] I am not saying that it is not interesting to analyze a perversion, to investigate the incoherence of a pathology and interpret its symptoms. But not everyone who claims to be an analyst is one, and the Socratic principle is, on the other hand, something like a poor man's Freudianism which, reducing every monstrosity to thoughtlessness, all malignity to lack of will, every disorder to an improbable family, childhood, or sexual question, does more than excuse, since in this case it *erases* evil, relates it to what it is not, explains it by a defect in being, and so literally nullifies it. This is the mistake of those who believe that, seen from a distance, in the diaphanous perspective of time, the fascist is more clearly revealed, purged of his areas of darkness, irrationalism, and passion. There are no fascists for the historian, no evil for the psycho-sociologist; for them, all circumstances are extenuating, so that they can extenuate, for example, the anti-Semitic vileness (Drieu again) of a writer who was finally rather mediocre. There is a symmetrical mistake made by those who assert that, seen close up, in the opaque intimacy of its real activity, with a sympathetic understanding of its concrete motives, this vileness can be better understood. Everyone knows that, seen up close, the executioner is a fine man, and that in the dock at Nuremberg you would have looked in vain for the stigma of yesterday's devil in the emaciated

features of Goering, the frightened face of Rudolf Hess, the pitiful figure of Julius Streicher lost in his insignificant civilian
clothing.[11] Up close, from a distance: this is a dual and reciprocal
hallucination which operates in such a way that to give meaning
implies, paradoxically, to see nothing at all and, if not to take
sides with, at least to take the *point of view of* legitimized murder.

In a more general sense—and in this case, in the order of the
most trivial phenomenology—it is to take the point of view of
death, the point of view of the dead on the living. Do we really
know the meaning of that quite simple and innocent statement
which urges us to give, as they say, "a meaning to our existence"? The argument, from Socrates again through Plutarch, is
implacable, asserting that it is only at the "last moment," in the
reflected light of the abyss, that the whole myriad of actions, passions, and trials which clamored throughout the course of an existence can finally be organized into a retroactive constellation
and composed, on the edge of the grave, into a coherent and
clearly meaningful shape. Can one imagine a meaning *in* life, in
the heart of the course of life? The expression is contradictory,
as Benjamin Constant understood very clearly when he waited to
hear from the lips of his dying mistress the "last words" that
would be enough to magnify the absurd cacophony of her futile
words while she was alive, or Chateaubriand when he attributed
to Rancé the deathbed reflection that "What one is at the moment of death, one is forever,"[12] and that what one was, reciprocally, in the chaos of preceding moments, is of value only in relation to the moment of the horrible last judgment. Can one build
an ethics, an attitude of resistance, on this superstition of meaning? The very idea is absurd, impertinent, in an age that has
made man a perpetual phantom, dispossessed of his present,
haunted by a disaster that has become the single event of an insignificant odyssey, in a hurry to undo himself, already enchant-
ed by the reverse echo of the final débacle. And thus Malraux,
asserting like Rancé that death "transforms life into fate," was
never able to create anything but funereal silhouettes, seized by

the novel on the eve of their annihilation, hurrying with numb steps toward the waiting grave, and therefore removed from the human tasks of man's condition, alienated from the humble concerns that make up everyday moralities. I am not denying, of course, that Malraux's work has its grandeur. But in the confused "ardor" of his purgatorial characters, destined for posthumous and almost superhuman glory, "frenetically lying in wait," as Scali says to Alvear, I also see the temptation of an anti-ethics which, inherited from Nietzsche or D'Annunzio, is sometimes not very far removed from some of the darkest mythologies of the century.

In the end, it hardly matters whether this conception is true or false, for I am sure that it is true only from the viewpoint of the gravedigger who, reading every biography as an obituary, sings of the human adventure to the accompaniment of a death knell. I do not know whether death "makes everything that preceded it irremediable,"[13] but I do know that in this romanticism of the end there is a twist of atheist humanism which, starved for transcendence, transfers to the idol of death all the ruined attributes of the dead god. Here again, in other words, and even if Meaning no longer has exactly the same meaning, the same mechanism is operating. Only, after preaching silence, teaching resignation, and legitimizing murder, it now encloses ordinary people within a "tragic" conception of the world, which gives them no greater protection against the reality of misery.

What then? Well, I would say the opposite. I believe that we must reverse all these spontaneous networks; break, dismantle, the mechanism of meaning. I claim that there is no solution, no method of resistance, except in muting the senseless, deploying an ontological Luddism that will be able to dissipate these mirages of coherence one by one. And so it is with death. First of all, it is not true, it *must* not be true, that death has the slightest value or the slightest dignity; far from being the fate, the inestimable lot that I must cherish, accommodate, premeditate, it is nothing but a hateful, awkward defeat, a pitiful carnival of the damned far more than of martyrs, an implosion of misery, and a failure without nobility. And if it is correct, in a certain sense, that more often than not one dies at the level at which one has lived, then I know that I shall die low down, without a hint of light, without an ounce of redemption, as has been so clearly understood (from Swann to Meursault, from Jacques Thibault to Gide's Boris) by all those chance victims who populate modern literature. Nor is it true that death has the power it has been granted of triumphing over an existence and transfiguring it. The apogee of absurdity and the abyss of madness, pinnacle of open horror and absence of any truth, death ruins more than it monumentalizes a life, blurs its outline rather than sanctifying its features. And if it is also true that in the strict sense, death completes life and is life's goal, then it is a goal whose very futility can only—as Jankélévitch so admirably says—[14] end in removing from it, by retroactive contamination, the few fragments of meaning whose illusion it happened to retain in its course. It is a strange finality, this end in nothingness; the infinite boundary of "wind," as Ecclesiastes says,[15] which will never come to the end of its process of making the whole course of my life, for eternity, a voyage without an end and the wandering of a vagabond. Far more likely to be true, in fact, is the lesson of Job, who saw—rather than a divine signifier whose verdict was calmly awaited by "beings for death"—an invisible and cryptic profundity, an obsessive projection of horror which, while "beings against death" are still alive, relentlessly acts to overthrow, to "demolish utterly," to fill with "darkness" and "corruption" the futile shelters on the "paths" of time these "beings" struggle to construct.[16] A positivity without god, a negativity without theology, my death is not tragic but horrifying; and when it is brought to bear on what has preceded it, it makes it all senseless and not irremediable.

The same combination of mute positivity and blind negativity is found in the "other" death, that inflicted by violence. The story of Cain and Abel, of the original murder as told by the Bible,[17] is in this respect exemplary. Does this crime have a "meaning" for which an inventory of conditions, a complete catalogue of circumstances, would be enough to give an account in order to attenuate its horror? What is striking in the biblical text is that everything seems to occur in the interval of a moment, a brief and instantaneous thunderclap, in a contracted and somehow incandescent time. No one will ever know what Cain thought of the word of Yahweh;[18] nor will anyone ever know what "motivated" him to rise up against Abel.[19] All that we do know, all that we hear, is the abrupt "he killed him"[20]—the inexplicable passage into action without a real passage, the incalculable step without a past or a process, the catastrophic almost-nothing in which the very idea of "circumstance" is explicitly swept away. Was he motivated then, "responsible," as we would say, and did Cain "voluntarily" sink into evil? Yes, of course, says the chronicler, who explains that God had warned the man;[21] that he had shown him the monster lurking by his side; that Cain therefore could have "acted well," "dominated" the "urge" to evil, and then recovered from it;[22] and that, if he did not do so, this was not thoughtlessly, but in virtue of a vicious choice, a choice of perversion, an excess of evil will, that alone makes possible personal punishment, identifiable by the "mark" on his forehead which will pursue him throughout the time of his wandering.[23] On one hand, then, the sin is not really *in* being, it is not in order with the order of being, it could not possibly be reduced to any "explanation"; and this is confirmed by the Prophets when, in order to name the sin, they rehearse the lexicon of negation— "lack," "deviation," "distraction."[24] On the other hand, it is indeed *of* being, it makes disorder out of the order of being, to the point that the earth itself had to "open its mouth" and rebel against the rebel.[25] And this is what explains that, in order to designate sin, the Bible, usually so suspicious of the vocabulary of idolatry, constantly resorts, beyond the single episode of Cain, to the positive images of demonology—"prostitution," "fat" around the heart, animal "rut."[26] *Of* being but not *in* it, *part* of it but *out of place, placed* in being without creating a *harmony:* such is the status of crime according to the Jews that, equidistant from Socratic misunderstanding and the tragic flaw, it can best be thought of as a fissure in things, a rent in their fabric, a gap in their fullness, an immense and incommensurable *evil.* And then that is "sin"; a dense but senseless hole in being. And the sinner is a man who has a "heart," but who, according to the texts, turns it in the "wrong direction."[27] And this is what we have to assert with complete rigor against the subtle minds who "give an account" of the madness of a God and his fellow divinities—burdening the world with all its weight of nothingness, *that type of murder exists irreducibly only insofar as it is devoid of the slightest meaning.*

This is the explanation for the fact that, if the Old Testament is certainly the most magnificent book of morality ever shaped by the mind of man, the modern idea of a "psycho-sociology" of the ignoble is completely foreign to it. If it is filled throughout with the great clamor of the just reviling the infamous; one looks in vain in it for the fine singing of the intellectual and the abyssal representations of the sinning soul with which Paul and Augustine enriched Christendom. Never has anyone looked horror so completely in the face and feverishly prophesied against it, and yet never has anyone been so distant from it, so hostile to totalizing it, so determined not to reflect upon it. Ezekiel and Jeremiah had no doubt that a prophet was always, as legend would have it, a prophet of sorrow, confronting sorrow directly, reading its disorder as such, and never trying to reduce it or to whitewash it with pretenses. All Mosaic Law is perhaps nothing but this paradoxical demand for lucidity which, rejecting the effects of meaning whose ravages we have seen, teaches, if not the discord, at least the discontinuity of the ethical imperative of truth and of what, following the Greeks, we call the "will to know." A paradox? Perhaps, but it is precisely the paradox that haunts Freudian psychoanalysis, its interminable process, its critique of appearances, and the implacable scrutiny to which it subjects fantasy and fantasy's mad dream of harmony. Obscurantism? If you like, but I would remind you all the same that that obscurantism provided *The Gulag Archipelago* with its resources, its explosive force, its stength of conviction and almost of revelation. We can never repeat often enough that Solzhenitsyn is an artist, not a theoretician, and that this artist is a prophet who, finally giving up the idea of establishing yet another, decisive "interpretation" of the camps, chooses simply to show them, to rehearse their horror, to harp on their absurdity, just to express, to articulate, their senseless litany.[28] An illusion, then? Yes, certainly, but on condition that we add that this illusion is the best protection against the dual rhetorical hallucination I have mentioned, which, setting horror in order, inscribes it in the order of the good; and that it is probably in the fictions, the "illusions" of contemporary art, that we find the "truest," most clairvoyant and most prophetic, in all senses of the word, discourse on what I have called elsewhere "barbarism with a human face." What expert can express better than Kafka the arid, livid, gray anguish of contemporary man? What learned seismologist will go further than Joyce in Molly Bloom's monologue toward the pure and lucid recognition of the a-cosmic nature of the world? Isn't there more in the staccato style of Dos Passos, in the interminable interruptions of *Manhattan Transfer,* than in most treatises on industrial misery? And yet another writer, Philippe Sollers, is now showing us voices without faces and things in their confusion in the inferno of language he has the audacity— the irony—to call *Paradis.*

At this point, there is not much left of the mechanism of meaning and the eminent domain it conferred on the masters over the suffering of the humble. It only remains, in fact, to dislocate its four corners and make them pivot on their axis of desolation. Against the Leibnizian economist, we would argue that the "picture" and the order he attributes to particular stains of misery are of no importance. And we would add that because this misery is precisely nothing but absolute and frenzied non-meaning, a single man who suffers is enough, in the end, to prove that all harmony capsizes and sinks into confusion. Against the modern statisticians, we would argue that there is no name or title, no species or location, to express and classify sorrow; but this sorrow, on the contrary, by the simple fact of its existence, denies the pertinence of the sciences, indicating the point at which they fail and stammer the "one" of an inexpressive grammar. Against the Hegelian chemist, the necrophile of new pain, we would argue that this pain is not the location of any kind of holiness, miracle, or dialectic; but in a death camp or a starving slum, the only adequate discourse ought to be the discourse of damnation, of planetary infirmity, of a formless unreason gradually overwhelming the ebbs and flows of a creation suddenly stricken by an inexplicable falseness. Against the Cartesian optician and his indulgent lessons of wisdom, we would argue that what "disturbed" men was not vision but things, not the reading but the text; for the text of things themselves is fundamentally obscure, forever indecipherable, stuffed with barbarisms, drunk with barbarity, more cross-eyed in its opacity than the bad vision of ordinary people in its immediacy. To all of them, then, we will answer that suffering is not a servile raw material laboring clandestinely for the benefit of sumptuous regulations whispered in the corridors of power; but the very hypothesis of regulations, whispering, and corridors appears in its futility as soon as it is considered from the angle of dereliction. A proof of non-ontology: I suffer, therefore the world is not, it is not really the world but a foul pigsty. The evil spirit says that harmony is not of this world, that harmony is not even in disorder, but that the very idea of order, as such, is an unworthy and murderous fantasy. The argument can be reversed: If we agree to call "tragic" the conception of things which expresses the painful dramaturgy of evil transformed into good, and "pessimistic" the conception which recounts the simple and harsh painfulness of being a man, a man condemned to evil, to an untotalizable evil, then we must conclude (once more against the spirit of the age) that the tragic is the very element of oppression and pessimism, perhaps, the viewpoint of the oppressed.

For it is now not only a question of the dialectic of meaning and non-meaning. We have gradually approached the confines of another theme, a more ancient one, which comes to us from the theologians under the name of "radical evil." What exactly does Genesis say in the famous narrative devoted to Adam and original sin? What strikes me in this text is that it seems entirely organized to discredit the notions of innocence, the fall, and history, which most classic commentators have constantly stuck onto it. Innocence? They have seldom noticed[29] the rather disturbing fact that it is at dawn on the sixth day, in the serenity of the Garden of Eden, when Eve has not yet come into the world, before deadly concupiscence has arrived to disturb man, and therefore before he is filled with the feeling of sin, that Adam receives from heaven the fateful warning and that an "admonition" is given to man to make him bow before the prohibited.[30] A prohibition in the state of nature, an inexplicable taboo at the time of the earthly Paradise, a divine commandment before guilt: that clearly means that there is no innocence not marked from the outset, spoiled by a fundamental Law, which is established *at the origin* and before any sin. History? If the author of the narrative saw fit to introduce into his plot the mysterious "serpent,"[31] which the dramatic pattern as a whole could very well have done without; if, instead of making it a mechanism introduced unexpectedly for banal reasons of plot, he was intent on presenting it as a divine creature, made by Yahweh himself, in a fabulous action on which the preceding chapter dwells at length;[32] and if, finally, he took the risk, with this hideous reptile formed "from the dust and returning to dust,"[33] of resurrecting one of the old chthonic demons which Judaism, as we have seen, constantly drove out of its imagination; if the serpent is present, then, with so much evidence and insistence, it is perhaps in order to indicate that the evil he embodies is also there, always there, already there, always already present even before appearing. It is to say that, literally, this evil "created" before man has no history, that it is not history or coming into being, but tradition and eternity. And the fall, finally? In order to fall, Adam would have had to be elevated, and sin to have come to him by accident and from outside. But it is difficult not to see in the strange round of "exculpation"[34] which makes him attribute to Eve, and Eve attribute to the animal, responsibility for the crime, an extraordinary admission of guilt, we would say bad conscience, in which it appears that the demon was nothing but a version, a dimension, a temptation of the inner being, inevitable and as it were on the downward slope of the tradition of evil. In order for there to have *been* a fall, there would have to have been a real event, a passage from before to after, a procession of no and yes. But once again, as in the story of Cain and Abel, the event is so brief, the interval so instantaneous, the passage so anodyne and almost imperceptible, that it gives the impression of being a momentary suspension of time, a fold rather than a step, a blinding "superimposition" in which sin does not succeed purity but, in the moment, loses it.[35] Original sin literally has no origin. Evil does not *arrive,* it is this side of, preceding, any coming into being. "Radical evil" designates this enigma, this incredible paradox, this satanic circle, at the limit of all thought, which the Bible nevertheless leads us to think about, because of the parable: a horror that is contemporaneous with the very genesis of the world.

Hence another paradox, which runs through all the prophetic texts and concerns the strange, ambivalent representation by the Hebrews of this God of prohibition. On one hand, in effect, there is the Almighty Lord who orders Jeremiah, for example, to "take in his hands" the "wine cup of wrath" with which he will quench the thirst of "all the nations";[36] who announces to Amos "the end of the people of Israel" and the mourning of the earth itself, doomed to "devastation";[37] whom we see in Isaiah brandishing "his hard sword, massive and strong," to smite the just as well as the guilty.[38] This is the arrogant, the cruel, the wicked, the death-dealing "Yahweh of Armies," master of the holocaust and prophet of disasters, who reveals himself to his people in the terrifying traumatism of a promised cataclysm.[39] Then, on the other hand, there is a subject who is all weakness, a prince with sorrowful eyes, whom one sees in Isaiah cultivating a difficult vine which, despite all his efforts, will not grow;[40] a stranger on the earth, at the end of his rope, says Micah, incapable of "doing good," and "dishonored" by false prophets who mock his disability;[41] an invalid, in effect, deaf to men's laments, powerless, says Habakkuk, to hear the call for help they address to him from the depths of their cave.[42] This is the humble, the pitiful, the Adonai of exile moved to pity, whom we see in modern Yiddish folklore filling an eternally leaky cup with the tears he sheds for the sorrow of Israel. Is he good or evil? Benevolent or malevolent? The question does not lie there, but beyond, in the twofold imperative of fighting sometimes on the front of the pagan temptation—that of Plato, for example, imagining a God "withdrawn into his watchtower" and allowing evil to supplant him, to implant itself in his place, to occupy the absence of being which he leaves by his withdrawal.[43] The master stroke of Judaism is to present in opposition the idea of an omnipresent God, creating and establishing evil, covering with his divine body the place of malediction, even generating that place in a positive plenitude which becomes, paradoxically, not the denial but the best proof of His existence.[44] And sometimes, on the contrary, on the front of what would soon become the Christian temptation— the one which, from Augustine to Malebranche, allows us to hope for a world delivered from the fall by the threefold operation of penitence, retribution, and providence.[45] And the second master stroke of the Bible is to oppose to this, as though in anticipation, the mark of a vassal God, acted on more than acting, overcome, overwhelmed, transgressed by the free course of an evil of which he is the obligatory and the first victim.[46] In both cases, in other words, what appears—marked with the double coat of arms of Elohim's helmet, in the meeting of his two faces, which confront and answer one another—is the single and identical intuition that the world bends beneath the law of evil, and that evil, in return, is another name for the world. And "radical," in this case, means not simply the origin and the genesis but the horizon and the future of things; this mark of the impossible—a Freudian would say, of "mastery"—which forms an eternal obstacle to the totalizing paranoia of men, and for which the strange fiction of impotent divine omnipotence thus presents a guarantee and to which it bears witness.

Now we can understand more clearly the real scope of the crime of Adam and Eve, and the nature of the prohibition they violated on the seventh day. It had nothing to do with a crime of sacrilege—an offense against the divinity of God—since it was only later, after the birth of Seth, that the idea was conceivable and that men began, says the Bible, to "invoke the name of Yahweh."[47] Nor did it have any relationship to criminal violence—an insult to the humanity of man—since it was still later, with Cain, or even later, after the birth of Enoch, that the idea of humanity, and with it crime, took shape.[48] Nor is there a trace of an eruption of evil as such, since, as I have just said, the tradition of evil appeared infinitely earlier, before any historicity. No, what happened in reality, the only thing that really came into being, the only thing that could have historic force in the rarefied moment of the world's first sin, was perhaps the exact opposite of what is always said: not the discovery but rather the denial, the covering over, the Luciferian erasure, the literal *disavowal* of evil and of the impossible which monotheism means. For in the end is not "ignorance" the proper name for the "knowledge" of good and evil that the serpent hissed to Eve? And the Prophets knew the formidable mechanism of meaning underlying it, which misused it and always led to treating dialectically what should be distinguished. Isn't verse 6, which presents the temptation itself, the chronicle of a blunder and an illusion, of the stubborn naïveté that consists in finding "good to eat," "agreeable to the eyes," "pleasant to contemplate" a fruit about which it is nevertheless written that it is accursed? In the face of this passion, this will—for it is indeed a matter of will—to fail to recognize the malignity of a tree that was nevertheless there, "in the middle of the garden," must we not conclude that it was indeed *from innocence* that Adam sank into wickedness, and not, as is usually believed, *from wickedness* that he fell from his innocence? Then this would be the clearest lesson of the passage: If it is indeed true that there is evil and that this evil submits things to its law, the greatest human crime, the first crime of men in any case, consists in denying it—and Isaiah said that there is no greater evil than to "call evil good, and good evil."[49] Further, the text operates in such a way that it obliges us to understand the word in a dual sense, so that "evil"—understood in the sense of "sin"—derives from the exclusion of "Evil"—understood in the sense of "radical Evil." The reader soon learns the price in calamities—to be precise, the Flood—exacted by a confusion of this scope. Nor has modernity failed to remind us of that, in an age of totalitarianism whose most barbaric fantasies sometimes seem to find their origins in the ancient story of Adam. Wasn't it from the mouth of Adolf Hitler, in the twentieth century, that we heard once again the sinister reptilian temptation to "be like gods"? Wasn't it the Cambodians who repeated the mad denial of the threefold fatality of sex, death, and labor, which were imposed on the individual subject after the fall to remind him of his finiteness? And haven't Lenin and his epigones followed the dream of a "classless society," perfectly transparent to itself, in which every tree, even those of the concentration camps, would be "agreeable to the eyes"? In a word, in the general history of fascism we can see the eschatological will to erase, to forget the obsessive trace of the evil against which the first man stumbled.

But we can also imagine, to conclude, how the refusal to forget, the rage to recognize, the passion for lucidity, were and remain, symmetrically, the *a priori* conditions for resistance. It is indeed true that, because there is evil and because this evil is insoluble, it remains necessary to oppose it, to thwart it, to dispute it in an insurrection of the soul that knows no reasons but those of the intolerable. It is indeed, as Deuteronomy says, because "there will never cease to be poor in the land,"[50] and because no final solution in history will ever come to the end of that infinite poverty, that we must here and now, without further ado, urgently and in the present, oppose it step by step. The perennial existence of evil and of the myriad sufferings that are its living image does not foreclose the spirit of revolt; on the contrary, it liberates it, justifies its action, perpetuates its voice, and no secular messiah can any longer direct or control its irreducible protest. One never has a "reason," in other words, to resist—for that "reason" or those "reasons" will never do anything but disguise the unreason of the world. And it is first of all against those "reasons" that men rebel when, weary of being dispossessed of their misery as much as of their meager wealth,[51] they decide to rise up so that there may be in this world merely a little less metaphysical and material poverty.

This is a paradox which greatly disturbed the Christian theologians, leading them to say in substance that, since absolute morality requires absolute freedom and since that absolute freedom requires the possibility of immorality, there is no morality which does not presuppose and imply, more than the risk, the necessity of an absolutely immoral world. This is a circle whose viciousness the Prophets and the Talmudic rabbis experienced when they made man the literal associate of the Lord, collaborating with him, in an elliptical confrontation, in the great work of creation that is perpetually being recast but never really completed. And this is why, finally, to the two representations of the divinity which we encountered a moment ago, the Bible adds, grafts on, a third at least as insistent, in which the Yahweh of armies or of mercy now appears as a "refuge," a "citadel," a "shield," a "fortress," and above all a "rock."[52] So many terms to say that that which is, does, wills, and sometimes suffers evil is nonetheless, simultaneously, a rampart that provides the possibility of rejecting evil.

15

Thus Spake the Stones

But reject evil in what way? In the name of what and of whom? By what miracle and mystery? How can we resist an evil that has been described as so "radical"? We shall learn very quickly by methodically extending the metaphor of the "rock," following the sequence of its textual occurrences, and subjecting it to the test of the major concepts of monotheist ethics. For this enigmatic image—which is strangely absent from most traditional commentaries, almost always treated as an insignificant rhetorical device, but nevertheless remains astonishingly persistent in biblical literature itself—perhaps has more meaning and importance than we have been willing to admit.

What then is this "rock"? How and why is this mineral shelter made of rock? The first answer is suggested once again by Isaiah, in the opening of Chapter 51 (at the intersection of the two post-exilic cycles that make up the end of the collection), right after the advent of Cyrus, the good news that was hailed by Ezra and Daniel.[1] And what does the Prophet say, in this moment of glory and elation? First, he says this: that to "look for Yahweh" is effectively, very concretely, to look for a stone, a true and living millstone, a rich and authentic quarry from which, like a face in plaster, I have literally been "cut."[2] This God, strangely, is not yet the "potter" of Jeremiah and the Lamentations, who "shapes" "fine gold" from "human clay."[3] He himself is the "fine gold," the concrete and sticky "clay," the shrunken artisan, identical with his object and with the mass, from which, says the text, "we have been hewn."[4] The mere utterance of his name is enough to pulverize the classical schema of a bipolar creation with a dual causality, in which the Principle impregnates a Substance that awaits it, outside, "as the female desires the male."[5] There is, in fact, no longer any outside, any substantial externality at all, which this mysterious God does not make into a non-place, a hollow and vain gap, from which it was necessary, he explains, that we be "drawn out" in order then to be "hewn."[6] This does away with the womb, the fruitful and generous mother whose patient and trembling "power" is told of by every polytheism, every philosophy, and every science too. Confronting this "rock," the only "mother" is sterile, forbidden to bear fruit, literally unproductive; and this is the meaning of the evocation, a little further on, of the name of "Sarah."[7] It also does away with the idea of a material, a distinct and fertile matter, which would receive the imprint of a form bearing order and meaning. Matter, says Isaiah exactly, does not so much draw form to itself as it "draws it out" of itself, expels it, throws it out of its "cavity," its barren "ditch" of nothingness;[8] and the etymology of this "ditch" attests to its connivance with the essential aridity of the "female" womb.[9] All ground, all earth, snatched up into celestial androgynous generation, becomes dead, mortal, death-dealing nature. Nature, says verse 3, is always "ruins," "desolation," "wasteland,"[10] shameful and belated remnants of the dust from which once, in the world's first days, in an insupportable chaos, were drawn humans and animals, "serpents" and "innocents."[11] Earth, matter, and the mother: the fact that God is a "rock" means that, to the disturbing seductions of a threefold materialism, monotheism opposes a "gaze," a "hope" toward "heaven," a conception of man, of his progenitor and of his lineage, which might be called a consistent "paterialism."[12]

To be quite specific, this is today the best antidote against the central fantasy of all real fascisms: the fantasy of a "race" born, said Hitler, from "nature and the "mother," without the intervention of the works of the "father," at the conclusion of a monstrous and "bloody" parthenogenesis.[13]

We can find illustrations of this division, this fundamental line of separation, in the very first books of the Pentateuch. Thus, in the last instance, we can explain Adam's sin, for example: drowned in the material "flood" which "then rose from the earth" and "watered its whole surface,"[14] he was still nothing but a weak and pitiful "natural" son, a child of the lower depths swarming with the horror of things, incapable of "looking at," of "recognizing" the principle from above;[15] in a word, the perfect incarnation of the "unfortunate man" described in Isaiah,[16] who has "made his back like a pavement" and like "a street for passers-by." We can also better understand why the first dialogue between men whose trace is preserved in the Bible is also the first case of violence whose memory it records: because the birth of the two brothers "borne" by the "woman," with the simple "help" of Yahweh,[17] was inscribed on the ground of a fecundity with two entrances; because the very functions of the protagonists—"shepherd" on one hand, "farmer" on the other—[18] symbolically represented the fatal misery of origins; and because even the literal meaning of their names—"Cain" means what is "gained" from the earth and "Abel," on the contrary, immaterial "breath"[19]—carfully considered, already designated, perhaps *dug out,* the whole ruinous fissure of the materialist split. It is clear, on the other hand, that if the second biblical dialogue—another encounter between brothers, which later opposes Esau and his younger brother Jacob—does not despite its extreme violence degenerate into a physical confrontation, this is because times have changed and the horizon has shifted. It is the time of venerable mothers who, unlike Eve, "conceive" without "bearing,"[20] give birth in sterility, sometimes grow indignant, like Rebecca,[21] at their incomprehensible fate and, attributing to the Lord all the glory of their wombs, have already consummated the divine rupture. And what is certain, then, is that if the question of fratricide is the first—and perhaps the most decisive—of the metaphysical questions immediately posed to the prophetic consciousness; if this question arises moreover in the traumatism of failed, abortive, premature fraternity, hanging on such a slender thread, as we have seen, that it took a single instant for a shattering action to snap it; then the only concrete way to provide an answer for it, to remedy the catastrophe, to avert its possible and threatening repetition, is to establish the axiom that one never respects the "brother" except by recognizing in him the "father." And this is the lesson of the aged Isaac, admittedly blind but not as deceived as one may think by the "mother's" trick when, in the famous episode,[22] he blesses both in turn, and reconciles around his name as *father* the "man of the open country" and the "man of the tents."[23] It is not an accident, by the same token, that the image of the rock is explicitly associated in the text of Isaiah with the "imminent" perspective of the end of "oppression."[24] That, in the Psalms, it assures the man who leans upon it that he will be "delivered" from his "enemies."[25] That the Second Book of Samuel observes, still more directly, that it "saves him from violence."[26] God is a "rock," and this rock "engenders" man; that means, secondly, that he is the mountain in which is rooted—in a land of Law, of Right, we would say simply of rationality—the commandment not to kill others.

We can then understand, on this basis, why it is always a mistake to look in the Bible for any regrets over or postulations of lost paradises. The attention that Isaiah demands "from peoples and nations"[27] is exactly the opposite of those obscure nostalgias that enchant our contemporary apostles of archaism. Archaism, from Adam to Isaiah, is in every case, without ambiguity, a pure image of horror; and it was precisely from that horror that man had to disengage himself in order to become really human. It is a complete misinterpretation to see in his "gaze upward" a glance backward or a return to the sources, since what lies behind is, by definition, the location of wombs and of matter; since the sources themselves are naturally poisoned; and since he speaks, in verse 10, of damming them up, of "drying up the waters of the great abyss"[28]—and Nahum later spoke of "drying up all the rivers."[29] It is absurd to say that misfortune stems from a loss or a forgetting of the "origin," since on the contrary it always derives (in the wake of the notion's periodic revival) from falling again into the origin. And the entire effort of the Prophets is precisely to set up an obstacle to the origin, to block, dam up its flood tide, and to push always lower, more deeply into men's memories, its compulsive and bloody traces. Moreover, they go so far in this direction that their oracles are filled with stupefying episodes in which we see the Almighty abjuring his creation and his creatures,[30] dreaming of replanted trees and rerouted rivers,[31] in one place representing again, in the rigorous order of its first unfolding, the scenario of creation, [32] in another, exclaiming that he "is" not but has "become" a "father for Israel," and that Ephraim, who came so late, is his "first-born son."[33] And when we read, finally, in the latest of the books of the Bible, the Book of Wisdom, that "the whole creation . . . was once more, and newly, fashioned in its nature,"[34] how can we not conclude that, with this final retraction, as it were corresponding *en abyme* to the opening of the Pentateuch, the whole biblical corpus comes full circle on a genesis for which failure seems definitively to be the destiny and the law? For this is indeed the problem: the Jewish God is a failed God, who failed in his work, who failed in it forever, and who, if he exists up there, must be laughing uproariously to see so many madmen dream of an immortal Eden, a miraculous Golden Age, or a forgotten Nature, while he knows, from his "rock," of its unforgettable perversion.

Thus, by translating *Bereshit* as "Genesis," the Greek scholiasts probably, without knowing it, slightly confused the issue. They missed the capital distinction, the intimate homonymy, which gave the Hebrew word all its richness, affecting it by introducing a deep ambiguity between an "origin" that had to be erased and a "beginning" that must endlessly weight it with meaning. They forgot that, for biblical man, the idea of "genesis" perhaps simply has no meaning, and that it must be replaced by another theme, much more complex, of an uncountable genesis—a plural and serial generative process, which unremittingly repeats the work of its erasure. They make us forget that the golden number of this monotheism at its dawn was, paradoxically, less the "one" of the primordial than the "two" of repetition, and that the Prophets were so determined to reject the dualization of the principle of fecundity only so that they might be able to double, infinitely multiply, the principle of historicity. Moses speaks in Exodus of "two tablets of the Testimony."[35] They were written "on the front and on the back" and "on both sides," by the very finger of God.[36] Deuteronomy means "second Law," and it is always a "second" Law that is announced by the "oracle of Yahweh."[37] On Mount Ebal, Joshua speaks again of "a copy of the Law of Moses."[38] The "camp of Elohim" which Jacob sees after his meeting with Laban is called the "double camp."[39] And finally, the Talmudic tradition explains that there were two series of tablets, the true and the "broken" ones, kept in the Ark. This motif of duality is omnipresent in the texts. There is no register in which it does not intervene. Monotheism is not a monism; its fundamental category is not creation but beginning again. The fact that God is a "rock" means, fourthly, that ethics is a process that never stops contradicting, correcting, *resisting* the historic course of things and their cortège of silent and terrible natural phenomena.

This is also the deep meaning of the notion of "covenant," so often misunderstood and hastily assimilated to the other notions. It is not, as with Plato, for example, a terrestrial erotics, man's path toward God, a hemorrhage of the soul culminating, through asceticism, in contemplative communion with an originating will. It is rather a sublime artifice, God's path toward man, a harsh rent in heaven, from which "proceeds" and "descends" the constraint of a commandment.[40] It is from above, in the midst of lightning, through a gap in the clouds, that Yahweh in Exodus descends toward an immobile people, "fixed" and "confined" at the edge of the mountain.[41] Nor is it a pact, a contract between equals in which, in the manner of the pagans, two fundamentally complementary interests converge. Deuteronomy is much more pessimistic, describing unequal exchange, divergent interests, the unilateral promise, and the herd which is naturally, spontaneously resistant to its order. It is God who is "faithful," who "keeps" the terms of the oath, who even commits himself to it, says the text, "unto the thousandth generation," while the "human herd" is structurally "unfaithful" to a "will" that very clearly goes against its inclination and its "stiff" neck.[42] This divine faithfulness itself is nevertheless not eternal, in the Christian sense of the term, given once and for all, whatever sinners in their place may say or do. For one passage in Jeremiah in which God affirms that "just as the sand of the sea is measureless," so "my covenant with David cannot be broken,"[43] there are countless others in which we witness retreats, suspensions, long periods of darkness interrupting a covenant that is sempiternal, to be sure, but strangely subject to eclipse.[44] Nor is it the case, finally, that, as is sometimes said, the Jewish God is angry, capricious, and inconstant; he is rather worn out, exhausted with himself and with others, overwhelmed by outrages and wanderings, the great excessive one, the universal denier, the God against nature who so often experiences the repercussions of his inconceivable demand—personally "affected,"[45] physically "paralyzed,"[46] sometimes literally dispossessed by the wickedness of men and even that of his best "shepherds."[47]

A perfect covenant, in other terms, is a contradiction in terms; and Deuteronomy says this clearly when it concludes with the remark that Moses will remain the only prophet who has looked on the face of God.[48] The historic defeat of the covenant is analytically contained in the understanding of its concept. This is the meaning of the statement in Jeremiah, precisely the definitively defeatist oracle, wondering why Jerusalem is an eternal "apostate."[49] Nevertheless, from this eternity the covenant derives the reasons for its necessity and its constant renewal; which is why this act of force is called with complete rigor, at least at the moments of greatest lucidity, a "new" or reestablished covenant.[50] Because murder is the usual case and democracy the exception, we would say today that to make a covenant is to look toward a God who is also, and fifthly, a rolling stone, rolling downhill, but who then rolls upward again against the inclination of human desire.

The fact remains that things, too, never cease rolling; that desire never waits to give free rein to its movement; that human beings do not wait for God to form contracts and alliances. And a covenant can therefore only be an alliance raised to a higher power, an alliance on other alliances, a secondary Ark grafted onto the bonds with which men spontaneously enclose their homes of clay. What could be more spontaneous, for example, than the immediate relationship everyone establishes with himself which he calls "consciousness?" To take the monotheist point of view on this immediacy is simply to add that it is not innate but received, inscribed on the divine "scroll" with which Ezekiel fills his prophetic bowels;[51] and that the denial of this heritage, of this Man outside of man, of this man who is always already the "son of Man,"[52] is another name for egotism, the egotism of murder, as we see a little further on in the parable of the shepherds who, "pasturing themselves," sow everywhere around themselves "dispersion," "force," and "violence."[53] And what is more frequent than the strange will to servitude which drives free men to ally themselves with a king, "like the other nations?"[54] Samuel does not really deny this; he devotes a few verses to attempting to sway "the people," but seven chapters to opposing Right to Fact and the rock of the covenant to Saul's pretensions. Anointed by Yahweh, simply "master of his inheritance," strictly subordinate to "the authority of the judges," this improvised prince who had to be sought out "hidden among the baggage"[55] is neither the author of the laws nor the source of his own authority; and when he forgets this, on two occasions, that is enough for the "spirit of God" to withdraw from him and for him to lose the "royalty" for which he was only a mediator.[56] Is it not legitimate and natural, lastly, to ally with other men and to preach peace everywhere? Legitimate, yes, says Moses, when he announces to the men of Israel, in Deuteronomy, that he is not forming a covenant with them alone but "with whoever is not here, today, with us."[57] Natural, no, he adds, when, in Exodus, he adjures them not to "make a pact with the inhabitants of the land you are about to enter, or this will prove a pitfall at your very feet."[58] For here too the same distinction imposes itself between a direct and explicitly political alliance on the one hand, which, dreaming of a spontaneous harmony of passions and interests, begins with war and ends with war; and an indirect, strictly vertical covenant on the other, which, mediating differences in the mirror of the One, is alone capable of assuring an authentic and durable human universality. In this case, monotheism is no longer simply what interrupts the course of historicity in order to avert the return of the origin in history. It is also what interposes itself in the synchronicity of morality, politics, or psychology in order to prevent the confrontation of man with himself, his kings, or his neighbor from turning into a combat. Religion is a split rather than a communion. The rock is what breaks as much as what rolls. To make a covenant, in Hebrew, is always to "break" an alliance. "Covenant," in the Septuagint, is translated as to cut. The rock is that cutting, that breaking, that splitting; and what it "cuts" is precisely the snare—the "pitfall," says Moses—of a "conviviality" that is, inevitably, a principle of barbarism.

Yet we must make distinctions. For it is probably here, on this very question of conviviality and its splitting, that the two great monotheist religions are most deeply separated. Not, of course, that the Christians have a concern for their "neighbor" that is cruelly lacking to the Jews—pity, charity, solicitude for others are themes constantly present in Hosea, Isaiah, and even Jeremiah. Nor is it, as has been widely asserted, that the Gospels invented a law of love which is their specific contribution to the monotheist heritage: that law, it is too often forgotten, is explicitly inscribed, in both its parts, in the body of Leviticus, a passage taken by the Church Fathers as a source of quotation.[59] Still less is it the case that the originality of the apostles was to join together love of the Lord and love of the neighbor, which had remained distinct in the prophetic tradition. In Luke, it is a doctor of the Law who makes the connection, and when Jesus ventures the same thing, in Mark, he explicitly uses the authority of a reference to the Bible.[60] No, the real difference, full of moral as well as political consequences, is exactly the opposite: If it is true that the dual prescription is common to the two Testaments, it was perhaps the New Testament which, against all expectations, made them autonomous. Thus, in Matthew, it is Jesus who distinguishes, dissociates, hierarchizes "the first and greatest commandment" on the one hand, and then the second commandment, on the other hand, which simply "resembles it";[61] and it is Moses, in Exodus, who considers them indissociable, impossible to hierarchize or to be thought of one without the other.[62] The great novelty of the God of goodness and mercy is to wager on a grace, an atonement, on a redemption that will allow—once divine love has been given—the love of man for man to live with its own life. And it is the old God, on the contrary, who, connected to a radical evil and a pessimistic conception of the world, knows no love of man for man which must not constantly seek its grounds of legitimacy in heaven. It is John who speaks of looking at one's brother face to face, with no other reason or detour than his fraternal "unity," eternally established, forever and without interruption, on the principle of providence.[63] And it is Judaism—wagering on the fundamentally a-cosmic nature of the world that dooms every face to face confrontation to a shattering power relation—which prefers in the neighbor his proximity to God, looks in his face for the "gaze" and the vision upward, and engages in the work of communion only on the basis of a shared detour through the commitment to the covenant. For Christianity, in other words, the other man is lovable insofar as he is simply a man; for Judaism, insofar as he is *truly* a man, and proves it unfailingly by repeating his allegiance to the Law. The monotheism of the apostles is a religion of love defined as *agape;* the monotheism of the Prophets is also a religion of love, but defined by, based on, "equity." And this equity, which is another definition of the rock, means first of all *equal distance from the paternal principle.*

No one could deny, of course, the extraordinary cultural revolution implied by the Christian emancipation from the old commandment. When Jesus proclaims the unprecedented news: "I have not come to call the just but sinners," this is more than the paradoxical reversal usually understood. It is not that he suddenly discovers unsuspected virtues in the sinner, or that God has capriciously taken pleasure in granting the sinner greater dignity. It is not that the gracious acuteness of his vision can see beyond the sin and draw out of its shell the eternal divine spark slumbering in every man. We can understand nothing about Christ's "news" if we fail to see precisely that, by definition, it removes any notion of value, virtue, or merit. Breaking with the Jewish *nomos,* perhaps even more than with the Greek *eros,* it does not propose new reasons for loving but the unprecedented concept of a love *absolutely without reason.*[64] It is thus difficult to imagine the wound to ancient piety, for the believers in the God of equity who "renders to man according to his work and retributes each one according to his ways,"[65] represented by the message of this "King of the Jews" who now came to preach the equivalence of ways, the indifference of works. In the parable of the vineyard[66]—in which the master, in his unmotivated love, gives the same "wages" to each one, to the "last" as to the "first"—doesn't the whole Jewish order of the world totter and the trembling flame of Right abruptly pale in the face of a radiant sun that "rises on the wicked" as much as "on the good"? In the peculiar recommendation to "turn the other cheek" if "you are struck on the right cheek," were pious Jews not entitled to find an echo of the morals of Nineveh, where men "could no longer distinguish between right and left"?[67] The fact is that with this Christian transmutation of all accepted values—I have said it often enough—the figure of the modern individual finally arose from the limbo of the West. But also perhaps—and this is what is important to me for the moment—the fragile and subtle mechanism of resistance, so patiently constructed by centuries of Judaism against the eternity of evil, simultaneously lost its reason for being and its bases. "You shall not resist the wicked," explicitly says the God of Jesus.[68] "Keep me far from the wicked," implored the Psalmist of his rock.[69] What has been lost in the interval between these two propositions, in the interstices of this argument, is the muted conviction, as the Bible says again, that "all the ways of God are justice,"[70] and that in the *detour* of these "ways" is built the "fortress" of the "oppressed."[71]

For what precisely is this "justice"? In what way was it indispensable for the mechanism of resistance? It is clear that if I am dwelling on this millennial dispute, it is because this is not simply a matter for the theologians. And if, despite the sublime beauty of the Christian commandment of love, I nevertheless take the side of the ancient Mosaic position, it is because I sense in it the discreet trace, the only trace perhaps, of some of the concepts which, here and now, allow us to establish an ethical attitude in the face of concrete barbarism. The Prophets knew that there are offenses so monstrous that to perpetrate them is enough, at one stroke, to break the covenant and to separate oneself, irremediably, from the company of the living and the dead. This was the case for Cain who, because he had shed a brother's blood, was burdened with a "sin too heavy to be borne" and immediately condemned himself—it is he who speaks and not only Elohim—to the fate of a "fugitive and a wanderer over the earth," forever homeless.[72] It was the case for the Ninevites who, because they mingled their own blood with that of the "animals" of the city and associated all of them in a ceremony of fasting,

had violated the rules of purity that make a man a Man and became, says Jonah, "like beasts in great number."[73] It is the case
today for all the executioners who, fallen to the level of animals
and treating their victims as animals, killing the individual in
themselves and above all denying the individual in others, rediscover the twofold biblical image of crime and blood. That kind of
criminal is "perverted and an abomination to Yahweh," say the
Proverbs;[74] one who, in other words, not content with killing by
accident or from passion, erects his death instinct into a universal maxim—the racial "laws" of the Nazis, for example, or the
Stalinist "science" of terror. "Do not emulate the man of violence," says the preceding verse; "never model your conduct on
his."[75] Clearly, conviviality no longer has a meaning; there is no
basis for dialogue, and to attempt to engage in it with whoever,
by definition, thwarts it, is necessarily to fail, at the worst to be
deceived, betrayed, "assaulted."[76] "I will cut him off from my
people," Ezekiel later threatened.[77] I will take note of this ontological disaster: when the idolater, consciously, of his own free
will, chose that distance, that infinite separation, it was human
universality as such that was, by his act, ruined and so to speak
placed in suspension. "You must not displace," concludes Deuteronomy, "your neighbor's boundary mark."[78] No, do not listen
to the ambidextrous—the Ninevites again—who, today as in the
past, preach the virtues of union, social unanimity, the abolition
of divisions, and a political peace which, in each case, moves further away the frontier of resistance and indignation in the face of
horror. For the world, whether we like it or not, is indeed cut in
two, and no longer to distinguish between right and left, the
right of the assassins and the left of the victims, is, in this sense,
the greatest of crimes against ethics. Justice is nothing but that;
its function is not so much to mete out penalties as to delimit and
mark off places. And this is also the rock: the white stone which
marks off the distance and the interval between the good and the
evil. And this is monotheism: the impeccable definition of a
"crime against humanity," which makes the antifascist a consis-

tent geometrician. We can finally understand that when the Psalmist implored God to "keep him from the wicked," he had to be understood in the strictest, most topographical sense of the term: the assassin is not among us but outside us, neither my brother nor my neighbor, but one who is distant from me in space.

But also, as a corollary, he is not a dark stranger but a being familiar to me in time. There is in fact in the Bible a rather mysterious expression, which recurs like a leitmotif in the days of God's anger and which it would be wrong to treat as a rhetorical device. This is the famous curse which, against expectations and in defiance of the evidence, so often exacts punishment for "the sins of the fathers from the sons unto the third, the fourth, even the thousandth generation."[79] It is all the more disturbing because we read in other passages—sometimes even in the same ones—that the sons "will not be put to death for their father," but each one according to his own sin, the one he has in fact personally committed.[80] One might say that this represents the confrontation of two definitions of sin, two conceptions of guilt, not yet clearly distinguished, individual and collective, between which the Prophets are divided and finally incapable of deciding. On the one hand, the banal idea of a particular punishment imputed to the literal author of the sin, who alone must answer for it before the tribunal of men. On the other, the more subtle theme of a global responsibility, a metaphysical justice, an ontological tribunal, which maintains a record of that sin beyond any expiation. And what the Bible invents in this instance is the new and probably decisive concept that there is a time of crime, a temporality of the offense, a continuity which is proper to ethics, which intersects with but is not identical to the real duration of things. "From generation to generation" means profoundly that the crime against humanity—the crime of Cain, the crime of the Nazis—introduces into the order of the world so intense a disorder, so radical a split, that no sanction of history could ever erase its ravages. Understood in the strongest sense, the formula means: There are holocausts which are so perfect, so frightfully memorable, that no "distance in time," no casuistry, will ever prevent them from bleeding to the end of time. A statute of limitations, an amnesty? After what lapse of time? the Prophet would ask. Will it take ten, thirty, fifty years for horror to be no longer horror? The very arbitrariness of the period points to the fact that amnesty is a jurist's idea which, in justice, has strictly no meaning. The very contingency of the limit argues against a principle that, since it cannot be formalized, is the opposite of the universal maxims which alone form the basis of a moral attitude. Further, this amnesty-amnesia is, according to the Psalms,[81] the last weapon of the evil man, the supreme image of evil, which doubles and multiplies misfortune. And we know, we Jews, that it is always the eclipse of the old crime which makes the new crime possible; the erasure of the pogroms of the day before yesterday which cleared the way for the Buchenwalds of yesterday; and the veil thrown over Buchenwald which could tomorrow renew the shape of the old madness. Because it never ceases awakening the dead the better to kill them again, an ethics of forgetfulness is more than a contradiction in terms; it provides the very terms by which the will to murder perpetuates itself.

However, this does not mean that the only tenable attitude is one of morose and eternal vengeance. It even means the opposite for whoever is capable of listening to the rhythm of that temporality. The episode of Cain and Abel did after all come to an end with an action clearly representing clemency and indulgence. At the moment when he exiles him to the east of Eden, Elohim marks "the guilty man with a sign," which certainly has the capacity to recall his sin but also prevents "whoever might come across him from striking him down."[82] While he is marked for life, the life of the "fugitive" is safe, and he is symbolically protected from the one whom Numbers calls, in an almost identical context, the "avenger of blood."[83] It is even for fear that this avenger might pursue the criminal "in the heat of his anger," [84] and in his excess of zeal "fatally wound him,"[85] that Deuteronomy systematizes the strange institution of "cities of refuge"[86] where, separated from the community, "any homicide" can find shelter.[87] Exodus is even more explicit, in a passage close to one already commented on,[88] when it speaks of a God who "forgives faults, transgression, sin; yet he lets nothing go unchecked," who absolves them, if you like, without declaring an amnesty. Thus the entire Mosaic mechanism of justice could be contained in the spectacular but rigorous reversal that makes memory the *a priori* condition, not for rancor but for a free, radiant, and generous forgiveness. In forgiveness, in effect, there is gift; and to give, says the Psalmist, is not simply to give back.[89] What is given is not owed but literally abandoned, as a pure effect of goodness, to the monster who remains a monster. It is not that a belated repentance has exonerated him from his crime; but because nothing and no one could possibly lighten his burden, the just man can grant to the eternally perverted one the charity of his infinite power of grace. It is no longer because time erases or distance excuses that we must resign ourselves to laying old disputes to rest; but because time resolves nothing and because it is foreign to the time of evil, I can decide to acquit what is ineffaceable, to place in suspension what is inexcusable. Memory is not rancor but mourning, and to the extent that forgetting is not a moral category, the only true morality is one which, paradoxically, limits the imprescriptible, remits the irremissible, passes over the unforgettable which, far from being eroded, is confirmed in its very excess by this excessive forgiveness. And it is therefore not an accident that the irascible and vengeful Elohim is so often called "long-suffering"—literally, "long in the nostrils"—that is, "slow to anger."[90] That in the same chapter of Exodus, the One who "punishes the sons for the sins of the fathers" also "abounds in true benevolence," maintaining this benevolence "unto the thousandth generation."[91] That, finally, in the Psalms of David, we find almost Christian tones in praise of the indulgence of a God of mercy who renounces the "punishment of sin."[92]

I said almost Christian. For we are far from the simple alternative between hatred and forgiveness, and very far from a dreary dialectic of justice and love. We are on the edge of a conception of the world where dichotomies themselves lose their meaning and their cutting edge; and wherein, from the strict point of view of Right, it becomes as absurd to punish as it was a moment ago to grant an amnesty. For, in the end, how can we judge a man who no longer has a face, no longer has a "Thou" to which we can speak, but only a mask over the features of a beast? He is not a fallen neighbor, gradually become more distant, removed by stages and gradations; he is the infinitely distant, absolutely a stranger, who has forever placed himself outside the reach of any possible judgment. In the name of what can he be punished, in the order of what discourse and what jurisdiction? To say "crime against humanity" is to plunge into an abyss which, defying the reason, the passion, and the understanding of men, is also a living defiance of all concrete laws, all imaginable codes, all thinkable sanctions. Isn't it granting too much to grant death to the assassin who, in fact and in law, deserves a thousand deaths? By a strange reversal, capital punishment becomes a minimal punishment. Creating the feeling that the crime is expiated and that that expiation has filled in the gap it had made in being, it becomes the most unexpected of methods for erasing the excess of the crime and once more making it banal. This is in substance what the lawyer Serge Klarsfeld thought—that "avenger of blood" with a "cold heart"—when, aiming a revolver filled with blanks at the Nazi Lishka, he had him at his mercy and nevertheless refused to kill him, thereby suggesting that there is no human means of expiating the inexpiable. This is exactly what the philosopher Gershom Sholem meant when, in a famous polemic,[93] he feared that the hanging of Eichmann would create the illusion of an epilogue, a final point, a burlesque and derisive dénouement to an unprecedented tragedy—"Hang him and let's hear no more about it." And this is especially the ultimate meaning of the Genesis narrative in which the enigmatic forgiveness of Cain also has as a motive the fact that, if the sin is too great for the sinner to bear, it is also too grave for Elohim to weigh. Which is why, perhaps, rather than a banal execution—completing the episode, closing the parenthesis, and amounting in fact to an attenuation of the punishment—the chronicler preferred a perpetual exile that would confront the fratricide with his irreducible horror. For a Jew, in other words, good is not symmetrical to or the antonym of evil. To every evil there does not correspond, there is not opposed, a good that is somehow its other side or its just blood price. The just man is also, above all, the one who knows the vanity, the colossal futility of justice. Against the *lex talionis,* the Law.

16

The Oasis of Time

Once again, then, we come back to the Law—between the shores of the covenant and the waves of the senseless. The proper name of the rock and the enamel of its requirements—built from the hard stone that creates the humanity of man. And it is time now, at the end of this trajectory, to recapitulate its figures. At last, we can complete the answer to the question that has constantly haunted this book: What is the meaning, today, of the recourse—not the return—to the biblical tradition? How does this recourse have meaning for all those who place themselves at the service of the imperative of resistance? What is the meaning of the meditation on a Book whose texts tell us that anyone who undertakes it becomes the equal of the highest of high priests?

What is now certain—and what I think I have established—is that there could be no greater misinterpretation than to see in this meditation a legislative concern, a prescriptive paranoia that would make everyone the equal of a grand inquisitor. You remember the radiant bitterness of Isaiah, observing without complaining: "I have toiled in vain, I have exhausted myself for nothing."[1] Deuteronomy says the same thing, taking note of the "small number" of the tribes of Israel, and asserting explicitly that the mission of the Law is not to convert or to master the earth.[2] It hardly matters, adds Ezekiel, whether the peoples "listen" or not, for it is enough that they "know there is a prophet among them," and this prophet never prophesies better than in the solitude of the desert.[3] Even if this prophet of the desert were "false," like those "oracles" whose shadow haunts all the biblical texts and who, we are told, "follow their own spirit without seeing anything,"[4] nevertheless the Torah, according to Jeremiah, "would no more perish for want of priests" than the "word" for lack of a speaker.[5]

For it is indeed to a Word that it must be compared. It derives most explicitly from the order of discourse. From the inscription of Sinai on, it most frequently draws its most insistent metaphors from the form of a language. It is because he shares with his people a language, nothing but that yet entirely that, whether listened to or ignored, that Ezekiel is, all things considered, justified in speaking to them.[6] It is because it is *like* a language—in the image of Hebrew, precisely, which long owed its holiness to its peculiar status as a conservative idiom, living in its dead letter, sacred because it was not used—that the Jewish Law does not have to be engraved in the finiteness of things to prove its legitimacy and its infinite value. It is because a language is always a meta-language, the "competence" for which, modern linguists tell us, antedates any "performance," that the Law is, by analogy, a veritable meta-Law, whose absolute message can, in theory at least, be separated from the relative utterances which men, crowds, and princes carve or not out of the stock of its alphabet. Half articulated, half silent, perpetually mis-spoken even if it is indefinitely repeated, it can only be half spoken, and it would be sacrilegious to claim to embody it entirely. Essentially mis-understood even if it is not at all "incomprehensible" (Ezekiel), ordered according to the symbolic far more than according to the real, it is most constantly inscribed in the register of the prohibited rather than in the order of the political. And this is what it means to come to Judaism today—an ancient Judaism, to be sure, inscribed in the magic spells of the Book, but whose sources are still living, more alive than ever perhaps at a time when great fantasies of complete "liberation" are praised by the present age. This, again, is what it means to think of a commandment which, structured like a language, finally says nothing—before the lesson of Freud—but a colossal wound inscribing on the flesh of every subject the sign of a lack, the brand of the taboo, while at the same time opening him up to the proliferation of meaning.

For it is equally certain that the advent of that Law is rigorously without a source, and that, in order to think of it, we must do without the naïve and naïvely substantialist idea that it has, in past or present time, an author, a guarantor, a master who gives it a name. Jeremiah suggests this, at the end of the verse quoted earlier, when he adds that it no more perishes "for want of a priest" than the "counsel" does "for want of a wise man."[7] In fact, we can find a curious but enlightening definition of that wisdom in a passage of Proverbs which shows that it existed "before the oldest of the works" of Yahweh, formulated "from the beginning, before earth came into being."[8] The text says: "possessed" from the beginning, and not simply "created," as the Septuagint translates, too greatly attenuating the scope of this disturbing and fundamental "precedence." The exact Hebrew word is *quanahi*, the same verb that, in the Pentateuch,[9] played on the name of Cain and the unexpected return of which now seems to indicate a kind of radical character—radical like evil—to this wisdom of the very "beginning."[10] We seem to be dreaming in the following verses when, in the course of an astonishing negative theology, the author makes this wisdom step over the episodes of Genesis one by one to establish it in the days before, at the threshold of heaven, of earth, and of its first mornings.[11] In this case, it is not that the origin is duplicated, split up to infinity in as many beginnings as there are perpetuated covenants; rather, it is literally denied, gone beyond, transgressed by a boundary which was there, always and already there, in a perfectly utopian "there" where things themselves did not exist. But it is not even enough to speak of a boundary, of a "thing hidden from the foundation of the world," since it was predicted, established in the void, in that time before the first day when the entire world had not yet begun to establish itself. It would be saying too much, in the end, to claim to resurrect it with a forceps from memory and from the search for a location, since this before-without-a-before, this truly unconditioned *topos* of non-location, escapes at one stroke both from the category of time and from the *a priori* form of space. Suspended in history and suspending its sequences, the Law is of an age that has seen everything and simultaneously of a youth of which no eye will see the decline—not even God, says Isaiah, who must be rigorously "*kept* mindful"[12] of what he knew at the moment when he could not yet act. We should now call this Law an Arch-Law, but specify that the prefix does not point to an "archaism" but rather to an "anachronism," a non-coincidence with time, which makes the people of the Bible a "people of the past"[13] whose fate is nevertheless conjugated, almost always, in the most modern of futures. And this too is returning to Judaism today at a time when, if we are to believe the general rumor, we have a choice only between the vilest regressions and boundless progressivism: to rely upon the obscure feeling that there are in this world values, principles of ethics and justice, whose origin is so indetectable, so profoundly indeterminable, that they are, in the strict sense of the term, immemorial.

This obscure feeling is the one the Prophets, without exception, strive to clarify. They do so in the most concrete, most brutal, most shattering fashion imaginable. They simply raise—tirelessly—this simple question: What would happen, or rather what would not happen, if, by chance and hypothesis, Creation were destroyed, brought back to that day before, that *archè* without a boundary? The answer is contained in one word, chanted like a litany, apparently quite sibylline: "I will leave a remnant" (Ezekiel),[14] "a remnant will return" (Isaiah),[15] "the remnant of Jacob will be like a dew" (Micha),[16] "the entire remnant of Judah" (Jeremiah),[17] "he granted a remnant to Jacob" (Ecclesiasticus),[18] and, "only the stock remains. The stock is a holy seed" (Isaiah again).[19] But the strangest thing is that this stock does not designate, as one might expect, the survivors—those who by chance or inadvertence might escape from the great disaster. Most of these fragments are set in the context of the holocaust, a total extermination; and in Ezekiel, for example, "whoever" has been "spared" will die "of hunger," for it is written that Yahweh "will satisfy his fury against them."[20] Nor is it a matter of a banal election, a selection, a privilege, according to which God, recognizing his people, would choose to spare them as he once spared Noah.[21] We are now reasoning in the perspective of a universal offense, a cosmic infidelity, a wickedness without exception; Micah, for example, is careful to specify that "the devout have vanished from the land," that "there is not one honest man left,"[22] and that "righteousness" itself has become "like a hedge of thorn."[23] They are thinking even less of a residue, an indestructible reserve, some spring of sacredness or justice that, as in the pagan mysteries, would continue to rise up in the high places, even if all men had suddenly ceased to drink from it. Isaiah, in fact, extends the hypothesis so far that justice, instead of being what remains, becomes literally what "brings down," annihilates, and, "covering all the high places," "plunders the treasures."[24] Neither survival, then, nor election, nor residue; we must conclude that what does not pass is nowhere in this world and that it has neither a status nor an ontological location. No matter how far one searches for it, it remains undiscoverable and escapes by definition from any identity; the puzzle disappears only if we agree to see it as the code name of what must be called a transcendence. Before any dawn, as we have seen, and after any twilight, as we now see. The "remnant" is what remains when nothing remains and when the world itself has come to its very end. Clearly, and to give things their proper names, what this biblical hypothesis suggests—and suggests to us, children of a century so prompt to declare that the commandments of morality are "relative"—is the idea, the conviction, that the immemorial values of the Law, for example, the imperative not to kill or wound, are *valid,* in all places, at all times, in all circumstances, because they are, literally, transfixed by eternity.

Then what is man from the point of view of this eternity? What is man's value; what can and must he do in the face of these values? Inhabitant of a dwelling he has definitively left, to which he knows he will never return, he is, the texts say with ever greater insistence, its living, vibrant, faithful, and scrupulous "witness." The word is to be understood first in the purely passive sense of "giving evidence of." A token and support of God, a trace and a monument on his paths, the subject is an object, barely an effigy, who with his ephemeral being attests to the impassive requirements of the Eternal;[25] and the "stelae" serve this function, as we see in the case of Joshua with the twelve stones of Gilgal[26] of the rock of the desert of Shechem.[27] In a slightly stronger sense, man is the creature who "testifies to." The pride of Yahweh, offshoot of his will, inspired and trembling tribute to his repeated ceremonies, Israel is a "people of witness" created, says Isaiah, "to the glory of the creator," to illustrate his "works";[28] and the Ark of the Covenant also illustrates in this way—Moses calls it, not by accident, the "tablets of the Testimony."[29] Still more profoundly, the witness is, as in a trial, the one through whom the truth arrives, emerging from the silent limbo where it would have remained were it not for him. Biblical man, in this case, is identified with his rock, he is himself the way through which the processions of God pass; it is *"in* Jacob," says the Psalmist, that God has "instituted" the Law so that he might manifest it.[30] And the Law, as such, also manifests itself in this way, as we can see for example in the celebrated "alphabetical psalm," in which it is justly called, twenty-three times, a "witness."[31] Thus, like a stele, an ark, or the Torah itself, the role of the chosen is inscribed in the register of vigilance and commemoration. An effigy, a silent illumination, a wordy and pompous confession, no matter; in each case, but with growing contention, he is the one whose name recalls, preserves, "keeps," say the Psalms,[32] the absent name of the unnameable. Witnessed and bearing witness, a being of flesh or of spirit, no matter, he becomes in his turn like a remnant, the ultimate remnant of the remnant, all that remains of the remnant in a history which, *by nature,* works to forget him. Of an age that has seen everything and reaches back to the threshold of the Word, located in a dwelling of wind in which only breath remains, he has no higher destiny than to raise himself to the height of eternity and to make himself, more than its echo, its metaphysical sentinel. From Ezekiel to Samuel, from Kings to Isaiah, the biblical texts abound in these mysterious "watchers," these "seers" who are sometimes "blind,"[33] who, at the outposts of death,[34] at the confines of what passes,[35] watch for those below the rhythm of what does not pass. And this again is the modernity of the Hebraic message. This is what being a man means for the Hebrew man. And this is, perhaps, the greatest mission that can now be assumed by those who are today called intellectuals: to feel, to think, and to will themselves to be, from the watchtower, older in the world than the world and its disorders.

This knowledge of the "watcher" is very simple—very simple and very obscure, like something timelessly obvious. To the familiar question shouted "from Seir: watchman, what time of night?"[36] he is, in Isaiah, the one who mysteriously answers: "Morning is coming, then night again. If you want to ask, why not ask, turn round, come back?"[37] What does that mean? What can we understand from this "come back" loudly proclaimed "on Dumah"?[38] It means, strangely, what Job can no longer mean, screaming exactly the same words but from the depth of his dereliction: "Lying in bed, I wonder: 'When will it be day?'; risen, I think, 'How slowly evening comes!'"[39] It allows us to hear what, precisely, according to Deuteronomy, can no longer be heard by the condemned man, the "man living in suspension" who is the deported Jew: "In the morning you will say, 'How I wish it were evening!', and in the evening, 'How I wish it were morning!' "[40] On the one hand, a somnambulistic existence in which stupefied men have lost the intimate sense of the succession of days, in a Diaspora whose horror consists less, as is still believed, in no longer having any space than in no longer having any time; on the other, the alert watchfulness of being fully in the world whose happiness consists less, symmetrically, in possessing a land than in having the assurance of a time, expressing and mastering not a plot of land but a calendar. What the former lack—and this fills them with distress—is, more precisely, the law of regularities, the number of repetitions, the measure of turns, returns, and backward flows that would make the finite sequence of twilights something other than a "wandering,"[41] a senseless "shuttling,"[42] a "mercenary" disorder.[43] What saves the "watcher," on the other hand, saves him from "anxiety" and from schizophrenic "terror,"[44] what gives his "close observation"[45] its "grain" of "serenity,"[46] is that he knows the order of the cycles, the persistent circles, the hidden permanences without which the flow is nothing but chaos and the moment a disaster. Further, if we read the texts carefully, Job and the deported know that "day" comes after "night"; but they do not know what they know, they do not know that they know it, they have no way of knowing it, for they have lost, in fact, in the depths of their heart, the principle of unity, of synthesis, of apperception that alone prevents life from being a "breath" and a horrible "dissolution."[47]

And the genius of the watcher, on the contrary, is to be enthroned in a "territory," an intemporal location, a meta-empirical watchtower that is like the fixed point, free from process, from which he can see the mad course of things become organized because he who sees it—and seeing it, measures its rhythm—remains in place. Consequently, two millennia before Spinoza and Kant, the Bible discovered the dual necessity, subjective and objective, for a transcendental ideality that can provide a permanent basis for the apprehension of the ephemeral. Further, the parable means that, left to itself and delivering man to its capriciousness, what is perishable is mortal and a source of misery as long as it is not based, as much in the soul as in being, on an imperishable watchtower. To be a watcher is to stiffen oneself against what passes in the name of what lasts. To preserve, said Hegel, the memory of the truths of midnight at high noon.[48] Time is a calvary, an insupportable way of the cross if, at a time when all nature and all history speak to us only of noon, it is not literally *climbed by the steps of memory.*

For what is the memory of which the Prophets speak? What is the "disease of memory" the modern totalitarian princes regularly speak of eradicating?[49] If memory, as such, is an unequaled weapon of resistance, this is because it is first of all, in fact as well as in the texts, a means of making war against history. The Psalmist does not say yes to what is when he makes memory the first duty of man, but rather no—no to his share of the inevitable, no to his share of the irreversible, no to the quiet death which is his first figure and against which, simply, he presumes that something within his soul not entirely involved in it protests.[50] This protest is never a preservation, a banal resentment creating a mere archive of vestiges saved from nothingness; rather, it is a painful labor, a grandiose reactivation from which no monument escapes without being burned, transfigured by the infinite demiurge who not so much resurrects as transforms it. The opposite of forgetting is not recollection but anamnesis, the "gaze upward" again, by which successions are reconstructed and the most archaic genealogies shuffled and displaced. And this is, finally, the source of the determination of Genesis to rectify filiations and correct the rights of the first-born which Deuteronomy, on the other hand, codifies so scrupulously.[51]

But is it really the past that returns through this artifice? Just as the miracle of Proust's *Temps retrouvé* is that time is lost there, forever abolished in the spaces of meaning carved out by the genius of a language,[52] so the biblical and especially the Talmudic genius is to mourn what has passed, to plunge it into mourning, to submit it relentlessly to what the Freudians now call the "work of mourning." Does this mourning even refer first of all to the past, and does memory point the arc of its stiffness toward the past? Well before Neitzsche and Freud, the Prophets invented the idea of a memory of the future, drawn toward the future, the spring of fidelity and the principle of every commitment, whose essence is less to recall the past of the formulated promise than to remember the tomorrow when it will be appropriate to keep that promise. And this is the deep meaning of the covenant made "with your fathers, Abraham, Isaac, and Jacob."[53] Further, is it still a question of time, everyday time, on the day of this promise? The final lesson of Adam and Cain is that real time, that is, in fact, the instant, is always the time of natural and inevitable sin; and when Yahweh enjoins on the future fratricide the virtues of waiting and patience,[54] he is doing nothing but indicating to him the rhythm of *another time,* an intelligible time, the time of morality, which must be presumed to exist behind apparent time in order for there to be any meaning to freedom, justice, and the values of human universality. "Yahweh," sings the Psalm of David, "your name endures forever":[55] for what this "name" says is that time, as such, is horror; that the spontaneous, spontaneously, is murder; that what passes sweeps along with it only the muck of blood and filth; and that time, therefore, is livable only when it is spun through with an element of eternity.

But also, on the contrary—and by a final reversal—that eternity is thinkable and bearable only if it is paradoxically submitted to the torture of time. It is *in* the world, I said, that man is older than the world. There are bad watchmen who, forgetting this detail, literally disfigure their share of anachronism. "Woe," thunders Yahweh in Zechariah, "to the worthless shepherd" who, breaking the "staff of union" that bound him to men, has broken the "staff of grace" that attached him to heaven.[56] Shame to the "wandering shepherd" who, abandoning his flock to their destiny of wandering and to the chaotic temporality that is their fate in this world, is no longer worthy of his anointing nor of the august "hair cloak"[57] which served in Kings to identify "Elijah the Tishbite."[58] A curse even on Abel, Abel the just, whose name also means "vain thing,"[59] and about whom we can now understand that he displayed too much scorn for the laws of the earth not to find death at the very instant when he came to the "field."[60] Was he not already a "worthless shepherd," the man who, the chronicler explains, made his sacrifice "on his side,"[61] without regard for his brother, without looking on his brothers, far, so far, from the real time of men where alone his divine breath could effectively find expression?[62] Didn't he thus share responsibility for the crime, and isn't this the reason why his name never reappears in the Bible after the fateful episode? Isn't this especially the reason why he is mysteriously included, in the "praise of the ancestors" in Ecclesiasticus, along with his brother the assassin, among the men "without glory," without "legacy," without "memory," who have "disappeared as though they had not existed"?[63] The truth is that the good watchman—the one who, again according to Ecclesiasticus, "leaves a name" and whose "praises are still sung"—[64] is also the one who knows how to remain, to "fix" his descendants, and finally to overcome the split between earth and heaven, the farmer and the shepherd. Amos, for example, "one of the shepherds of Tekos,"[65] began to "prophesy"[66] only after God had "taken him from herding the flock"[67] and, thus torn away from his original singleness, he "looked after sycamores" as well as being a simple "herdsman."[68] In the first lines of Isaiah, the "guardian" is like a "shed"; but that shed is "in the vineyard," it "surveys" the "city," and it has no city but this modest "melon patch."[69] In Book 52, he does not sit in the clouds but on the walls of the city, where again, between heaven and earth, he gives God no respite and insolently pesters him to "restore Jerusalem."[70] Is Yahweh offended by so much zeal and arrogance? In the following book, it is the opposite that "dismays" him and unleashes his murderous "wrath"[71]—the shameful spectacle of this apathetic people in whom he finds neither "support" nor "aid" in his troubling task of perpetuating time. For this is indeed the paradox finally established at this point. If, in the order of pure reason, the great age of values could do without any reference to being, in the order of practical reason, it cannot evade the detour through and the rootedness in existence. If it is correct to say that eternity is the metaphysical figure of time, it is decisive to add that time is, concretely, the figure of eternity. And it is this concrete metaphysics, this covenant again between what lasts and what passes, which probably provides the best explanation of the relationship of Jewish man to history and of his inclination to resist it.

Yet we must be very clear here and forget, for that reason, the resources of the commonplace. We in the West live, in reality, on the basis of three distinct conceptions of this problematical embrace. The first comes to us from the Greeks, particularly from Aristotle, and makes duration a physical substance, a murmuring nature that, ontologically forming a part of every body and every particular place, is dissipated into as many fragments as there are occasions in which it is embodied, and allows to spring up in each one something like a dazzling hint of the intemporal. This is that amnesiac sensualism which provides a source in the modern era for all the romanticisms of ardor and the aestheticisms of the pure present,[72] the qualitative materialism in which eternity is nothing but a dusty scattering of instants and the instant reciprocally nothing but a glimmer of eternity. This, again, is what in Genesis was literally the time of murder, and there sprang from it nothing but the shattering confrontation with the horrible passage to action.[73]

The second concept can be dated from the Enlightenment, particularly from Kant, and sees in duration a mathematical *a priori*, a dead and frozen form which, giving every displacement its ontological framework, remains like a stage under the steps of what passes, would persist in being there even if nothing passed over it, and becomes, more than a hint, the sempiternal name of sempiternity. This is the cinematic representation of quantity, in which eternity is like the abscissa of time, and time is what patiently divides up its empty line, the spatializing idealism that for two centuries has sustained the stubborn effort of despots to reduce the duration of men to the low-water mark of the uniform. This is the second panel of the Diaspora of Deuteronomy, and it is the illusion of its permanence that was denied, fundamentally, by the parable of the "remnant."

Finally, the third concept, Hegelian in inspiration, transforms the stage into a construction site and the Kantian platform into a forge where, destined from the beginning to the advent of its parousia, a "soul of the world" is consumed in as many moments as there are stages in its gestation, and ruins all of them all the better because in each one there slumbers, it believes, the promise of the absolute. This is the dialectic of quantity-quality in which there is now no present that is not worth being sacrificed for the future world, the exploratory progressivism in which temporality becomes a disappearing perspective on eternity, and eternity in turn a vibrant overview on temporality—this is also what, above all, the Bible constantly rejects by denouncing those false prophets who continually announce the end of time. For here, in fact, is the point shared by all three conceptions. They join the two terms together only to be better able to abolish them and confuse them on the same horizon. Whether it is a hint of eternity, its proper name, or its promised soul, time is never anything but a dreary inventory, a redundancy of eternity. Whether it haunts time, underpins it, or is revealed in it, eternity is never anything but the hidden and clandestine rhythm of time. And this is why, against these three versions of an identical conjunction, all of which culminate alike in the horizon of death given or received, the monotheist message can only be understood as buttressed by the opposite idea of a fundamental disjunction.

What is this disjunction? If Hebrew man believes in eternity, it is not, as for the mockers, in the hope that one fine day there will no longer by any time at all and wandering will come to an end in the brilliant blaze of a final revolution. On the contrary, it is because there *is* time, will eternally be time, because time, in fact, will never finish coming to its end and will forever draw after it its infinte distress, that eternity has a meaning, imposes itself on the Hebrew's consciousness, and places its seal of majesty on the misery of the everyday. If there is time and he thus comes to terms with it, this is not—as for so many sophists past and present—so that there may be no more eternity at all, and that its sublime self-sufficiency may be exchanged, in things, for a shimmering plurality of dancing positive phenomena. Rather, it is because there is the eternal, and the fate of this eternal is not to be divided up, not to sink into the patch of land of the world, because time remains time, so heavy and chaotic, and because it is, as such, intolerable. If there is time *and* there is eternity, then, if this "and" of conjunction resembles so closely an "or" of alternative, this is because no connivance has promised that they will come together in the glorious wedding whose banns the mystics are so fond of reading in the origin. The conviction of Jeremiah, for example, is that no couple was more ill-suited, no union more badly joined, no bride more unfaithful than the "young flighty camel" called Jerusalem—and yet the Prophet never ceases to whip its croup with the sting of his inaudible Law. Jeremiah is not simply a "defeatist," but literally undone, put to rout by a temporality he experiences first of all in its strangeness and its rebellion.

Would he suffer the thousand deaths recounted in his book if there were the fundamental complicity between the two orders preceived by the optimists? Would the work, the hard labor, of "witnessing" be necessary if everything, here, spontaneously, spoke to us of the beyond, and if prophecy was an ecstacy, blessed by earth and heaven? No. The first experience of Hebrew man is that of a radical separation; of an absolute estrangement; of the absence of heaven on earth and the absence of earth in heaven: of the radical *non-existence* of Him who he calls his Lord.

Notes

1. What is the source of the legend that the Jews did not resist Hitlerism and allowed themselves to be led to the massacre like cattle to a slaughter-house? Although they were 1 percent of the population of prewar France, they made up 15 to 20 percent of the various resistance movements. The first person condemned to death for resistance was a Jew from Bordeaux, Israel Laizer Karp (on August 27, 1940). Outside France, there were many Jewish under-grounds; in the regions of Bialystok, Slonim, and Naliboki, for example. There was a revolt in 1942 of Jewish unskilled workers (Zionists and Communists) requisitioned for work in the Berlin war industry: all were shot. The "Jewish Brigade of Palestine" actively participated in the battles of Egypt, Italy, and Austria, and its members parachuted behind the German lines. There were numerous revolts in the ghettos: Lodz, Zitomir, Vilna (Poland), Nicolaiev (Russia). There were three great revolts in the extermination camps—Treblinka (August 2, 1943), Sobibor (October 14, 1943), and Chelmno (January 1945)—not to mention the "resistance group of Auschwitz." On all these examples, and others too numerous to name, see the *Encyclopedia judaica*; the irreplaceable and superb *Bréviaire de la haine* by Léon Poliakov, to which I shall often refer; and *La Résistance juive en France* by Annie Latour (Paris: Stock).

2. Homage is also due to Vladimir Jankélévitch, a philosopher and moralist whose ardent thought has often helped me. To Albert Camus, the Camus of *L'Homme révolté* and *Actuelles*; we can never repeat often enough that he was and remains an intellectual of the highest order. To the few friends who be-

lieved in this book, encouraged me to write it, or, like Rosalie Dussard, gave it a title. And finally to Françoise Verny, editor and friend, about whom it is enough for me to say that, without her, it would perhaps not have appeared.

PART ONE: LIMIT POLITICS TO MAKE ROOM FOR ETHICS

1. Quoted by Jean Baudrillard, *Oublier Foucault* (Paris: Galilée, 1977), p. 83.

Chapter 1. In Praise of the State

1. Jonah 4:11.

2. *Barbarism with a Human Face*, trans. George Holoch (New York: Harper & Row, 1979).

3. See the beautiful book by Jean Lacouture, *Survive le peuple cambodgien* (Paris: Seuil, 1978).

4. Eric Weill, *Philosophie politique* (Paris: Vrin, 1971), p. 133.

5. Quoted by Camus, *L'Homme révolté*, in *Essais* (Paris: Gallimard, Bibliothèque de la Pléiade), p. 580.

6. *Ibid.*, p. 569.

7. Bakunin, translator of *Capital* into Russian, saw in it a "magnificent," "profound," and "decisive" theory, which he criticized only for being "too metaphysical and abstract" and therefore "inaccessible" to the "workers." For details, see P. Ansart, *Marx et l'anarchisme* (Paris, 1969); Henri Arvon, *Michel Bakounine* (Paris, 1966); V. Dave, *Michel Bakounine et Karl Marx* (Paris: Éditions de l'Humanité nouvelle, 1890); and Bakunin, *Correspondance*, letters to Herzen and Ogareff (1860–1874) (Paris, 1896), Bibl. nat. 8°Z.14347.

8. See *Aux compagnons des sections internationales du Jura*, MS of February–March 1872.

9. We know that Lenin found a conception of the seizure of power based on "rigorous secrecy, the careful choice of members, the training of professional revolutionaries" to be "majestic." Quoted by Camus, *L'Homme révolté*, p. 580.

10. According to the report in the *Frankfurter Allgemeine Zeitung*, December 15, 1972.

11. See Leo Strauss, *Droit naturel et histoire* (Paris: Plon), p. 196.

12. Hobbes, *Leviathan*, E. W. VI, p. 242. Quoted by Pierre Manent in his remarkable work, *Naissance de la politique moderne* (Paris: Payot, 1977).

13. *Ibid.*, p. 68.

14. Montesquieu, *L'Esprit des lois*, 1, 2.

15. Hobbes, *De corpore politico*.

16. It is to be noted that Hobbes consistently speaks of Leviathan as a "mortal God." The commentators have often pointed out the analogy between

St. Anselm's ontological proof and the deduction of this Leviathan; both are based on the relationship between an "unlimited" being and the idea of it held by a "limited" being.

17. Exodus 20:13.

18. See Jean Poutet, *L'Argentine de la peur* (Paris: Plon, 1978).

19. Solzhenitsyn, *The Gulag Archipelago* (New York: Harper & Row, 1974).

20. See Jacques and Claudie Broyelle, *Le Bonheur des pierres* (Paris: Seuil, 1978), p. 101 and *passim*.

21. Ante Ciliga, *Dix ans au pays du mensonge déconcertant* (reprinted, Paris: Champ Libre, 1977), pp. 50–51.

22. Jean Pasqualini, *Prisonnier de Mao* (Paris: Gallimard, 1975), is worth rereading.

23. See Christian Jambet, "La volonté de pureté," in Christian Jambet and Guy Lardreau, *Le Monde* (Paris: Grasset, 1978).

24. For example, the letter to Kugelmann of April 12, 1871, as well as the famous texts on the Paris Commune, of course.

25. Schmitt's first article on the "total state" was published in the early thirties in the *Europäische Revue* of Karl Anton Prinz Rohan, who was close to the "young conservatives."

26. The "Hanseatische Verlagsanstalt" was established in the early twenties around an important union organization tied to the right-wing nationalist opposition.

27. Ernst Forsthoff's book (June 1933) was the only one explicitly entitled *Der totale Staat*, and the idea seems to have come from the publisher, to oppose the threatened Nazi dictatorship. As for *Das werdende Reich*, it was published in August 1932. See Jean Pierre Faye, *Langages totalitaires* (Paris: Herrmann, 1972), p. 270.

28. On the relationship of Wagner to Nazism, see the piece by Philippe Sollers, unanswerable as far as I am concerned, "D'un albhomme de famille," *Musique en jeu*, 1976.

29. *Völkischer Beobachter*, January 9, 1934.

30. Roland Freisler, *Deutsche Justiz*, January 12, 1934.

31. Wilhelm Stuckart, *Der Staatsaufbau des Deutschen Reiches in systematischer Darstellung* (Leipzig, 1934).

32. On the relationship between romanticism and Nazism, see J. Droz, *Le Romantisme politique en Allemagne* (Paris: Colin, 1963), and the concluding pages of Eric Eugène, *Les Idées politiques de Richard Wagner* (Paris: Publications universitaires, 1978). On neo-romanticism and its direct influence on Hitlerism, see Edmond Vermeil, *Doctrinaires de la révolution allemande* (Paris: Nouvelles éditions latines, 1948).

33. A last plea for the "total state": the article by E. R. Huber published in *Aktion* in April 1934. But he took note of Rosenberg's criticisms against Forsthoff's book.

34. Significantly, this publication, which lasted until 1939, was carried out under the aegis of the Hanseatic Editions of Hamburg.

35. Similarly, at the Party Congress of 1935, Hitler said: "It is necessary to understand the goal beyond the forms which are only means," and: "The state is only a form of organization of the people's life, but it is driven and dominated by the immediate expression of the popular will to live"—Hitler, *Speeches* (Munich: Zentral-Verlag der NSDAP, 1928), p. 262.

36. Similarly, for Goebbels's first rally in Berlin, in January 1927, the posters said: "The bourgeois state is nearing its end . . . Theme: the collapse of the bourgeois state."

37. See the *Organisations Buch der NSDAP*, which was the Bible for every member of the party. Hitler wrote in the preface: "Given that the state can be only a means for reaching a goal, the work of the German renaissance is not in a change of form of the German Reich or its constitution. It is a question of reasoned education and a reshaping of the people"—*Organisationsleiter Ley*, p. xxvii.

38. See Castellan, *Le Réarmement clandestin du Reich* (Paris: Plon, 1954), pp. 54ff.

39. September 1934. The SS used heavy artillery as campaign cannons; General von Brauchitsch, military commandant of East Prussia, confiscated them. The party's decision was to rescind von Brauchitsch's order and confirm Lorenz, leader of the SS group, in his functions.

40. Alan Bullock observes: "Hitler was one of the few Germans who had freed himself from legendary Germanic militarism." *(Hitler, A Study in Tyranny)*. And, in August 1940, Hitler himself said: "We will never again tolerate, in the future, that the Wehrmacht . . . be involved [in] internal critical situations. . . . The Wehrmacht is destined, once and for all, to be wholly and exclusively engaged against the external enemies of the Reich." Quoted by Joseph Billig, *L'Hitlérisme et le système concentrationnaire* (Paris: PUF, 1967.)

41. Herman Rauschning, *Das Revolution des Nihilismus*.

42. See the excellent remarks on this point in Leo Scher, *La Société sans maître* (Paris: Galilee, 1977).

43. Rauschning, *op. cit.*, p. 58.

44. Instead of a "constitution," there was to be a "working plan"—a cellular organization of "cooperatives" in which the "worker" would rule.

45. Subordinated to the SA until 1934, the SS was declared autonomous on July 20, 1934, and placed exclusively under the Führer. See H. Volz, *Die historische Daten der NSDAP* (Berlin: Verlag A. G. Ploetz, 1939).

46. For example: demographic policy, occupation policy, or the manage-

ment of the camps. In August 1940, Hitler contrasted the "association proud of its sobriety" (*Sauberkeit*) to the "proletariat." And in September, Himmler summed up the mission of the SS: "To create an order of blood." Quoted by Billig, *op. cit.*, p. 170.

47. On the permanence of the messianic dream of the "Empire of the last days," inherited from the heretical Christianity of the Middle Ages, see Norman Cohn, *The Pursuit of the Millennium*.

48. The organization of the police forces in the Reich is in itself an extremely complex puzzle. State policy, auxiliary police (*Hilfspolizei*), Goering's Gestapo, the Gestapa of Diels and later of Heydrich, Himmler's SS, and of course the SA. They encroached on each other's territory, since, against Goering who was in favor of massive and rapid liquidation of the opposition (see Delarue, *Histoire de la Gestapo* [Paris: Fayard, 1952]), opposition soon developed in Himmler's branch, which saw the camps as a *racial laboratory* (see the decree of September 20, 1937). On the one hand, there was talk of "*state* camps for rectification and work," on the other of a "concentration-camp anti-race." The Gestapo attempted to circumvent as much as possible the raciological complications of the SS, and even tried to give substance to the principle of the review of sentences, while the SS was preoccupied with forming a stable population in the concentration camps. It remains true, finally, that after numerous shifts and conflicts of authority, the system stabilized in the following way: for the Gestapo, strictly police functions (interrogations, executions, gas chambers); but for the SS, overall responsibility for the camps and their daily management.

Chapter 2. The King in Check

1. See A. Schinz, *La Pensée de Jean-Jacques Rousseau* (Paris: Alcan, 1929), which argues the thesis of a reversal on the part of Rousseau. See also Maurice Halbwachs's critical edition of *Du Contrat social* (Paris: Aubier-Montaigne, 1976), pp. 431ff.

2. *Du Contrat social*, Book IV, ch. 8.

3. *Ibid.*, II, 7, "Du Législateur."

4. *Ibid.*, II, 4.

5. *Ibid.*, II, 6.

6. Letter of July 26, 1767.

7. *Du Contrat social*, III, 4.

8. Sixth letter, *Oeuvres complètes*, vol. III (Paris: Gallimard, Bibliothèque de la Pléiade, 1964), p. 808.

9. Pascal: "Nature everywhere shows the sign of a lost God" (*Pensées*); Meister Eckhart: "divine death," "to kill God" (*Tracts and Sermons*); Luther's chorale: "God himself has died."

10. Nietzsche did not "invent" the "death of God"; he was the first to want

to be God's rival. See the letter of February 14, 1883, to the publisher Schmeitzner, in which he presents his *Zarathustra* as a "fifth Gospel."

11. I, 7, where he speaks of the "holiness of the contract." We know, moreover, that the idea of the "general will" and the infallibility associated with it derive from Malebranche. See Émile Bréhier, "Les lectures malebranchistes de Jean-Jacques Rousseau," *Revue internationale de philosophie*, October 15, 1938, pp. 98-120.

12. Hence all the ambiguity of the relationship to Christianity in the closing pages of *Du Contrat social*. See Halbwachs, *op. cit.*, pp. 450-452.

13. IV, 7: "There is thus a purely civil profession of faith whose articles are to be established by the sovereign." See also the *Lettre à Voltaire* of 1756.

14. Louis Althusser clearly saw this circle in a classic article, "Sur le Contrat social," *Cahiers pour l'analyse*, No. 8 (1967), pp. 5-42.

15. *Du Contrat social*, I, 8, which modestly concludes: "But I have already said too much of this question, and the philosophical meaning of the word *freedom* is not my subject here."

16. *Ibid.*, I, 6: "State when it is passive, Sovereign when it is active."

17. In the manuscript, Book II, chapter 8 was entitled "Du Peuple à instituer." (My itals.)

18. III, 1: " . . . it is absolutely only a commission, a function, in which, simple officers of the sovereign, they exercise power in his name."

19. *Ibid.*

20. Ferdinand Alquié, *La Découverte métaphysique de l'homme chez Descarte* (Paris: PUF), p. 309.

21. Rufin: jurist of the early thirteenth century, author of a *De bono pacis*. Quoted at length in Dufourcq, *Histoire moderne de l'Église*, vol. 6 (Paris, 1932).

22. Manegold, c. 1060-1103, author of a *Liber ad gebehardum, ibid.*

23. For the origin of these arguments, see Thomas Aquinas, *De regimine principum* (first two books). And consult H. R. Feugueray, *Essai sur les doctrines politiques de saint Thomas d'Aquin* (Paris, 1957), which remains the best work of synthesis on the question. Simon de Montfort, who was born circa 1210 and died in 1265 at the Battle of Eversham, was the son of Simon de Montfort, famous leader of the crusade against the Albigensians.

24. We need a history of coronations in France and elsewhere. In the fourteenth century, kings were still frequently deposed by their subjects: Edward II of England on January 20, 1327, and even Jean II of France (1358). St. Bernard considered it right to punish with the sword the "oppressors of the poor" (*Bernardi Vita*, II, 8, 52). From St. Thomas to Abbon of Reims, the Church always preferred election to heredity. See Emile Chénon and Olivier Martin, *Histoire générale du droit français public and privé*, vol. 1 (Paris, 1926), and Emile Chenon, *Le Rôle social de l'Église* (Paris, 1921).

25. "Prelibation" is a central concept in Proudhon's politics. See, for example, *Premier mémoire,* chapter 5 (Paris: Rivière), pp. 337–346.

26. For Proudhon, the "sacred right to govern" belongs rather to society, which in its "autonomy" is supposed to organize itself. *Ibid.,* p. 341.

27. Saint-Just was already saying: "We must attack the problem of forming a public conscience: that is the best police"—*Discours et Rapports,* ed. Albert Soboul (Paris: Éditions Sociales, 1977), p. 185.

28. This point has been emphasized by Jacques and Claudie Broyelle in *Le Bonheur des pierres* (Paris: Seuil, 1978), referring to Chancellor Schmidt's speech in the Bundestag after the death of Andreas Baader.

29. See Meister, *L'Autogestion yougoslave* (Paris: Anthropos), p. 257.

30. Charles Bettelheim, *Révolution culturelle et organisation industrielle en Chine* (Paris: Maspero, 1970), p. 40.

31. *La CFDT et L'autogestion* (Paris: Éditions du Cerf), p. 48 and *passim.*

32. *Ibid.,* p. 45. See also, in another perspective, Jean Dru, *L'Expansion,* February 1969. And Proudhon, quoted in J. Bancal, *Proudhon, pluralisme et autogestion* (Paris: PUF), vol. 2, p. 40.

33. *Cahiers du CERES,* no. 11 (January 1972), reprinted in Didier Motchane and Jean-Pierre Chevènement, *Clefs pour le socialisme* (Paris: Seghers, 1973), p. 353.

34. Santiago Carrillo, *Eurocommunisme et État* (Paris: Flammarion, 1973), pp. 41, 47, 50, 63, 65, where you can find a comic use of Althusser's theories. See also the hilarious chapter (pp. 123–130) on "Soviet Thought and the Democratic Path."

35. Louis Althusser, *Réponse à John Lewis* (Paris: Maspero, 1973). And Jean Elleinstein, *Histoire du phénomène stalinien* (Paris: Grasset, 1976).

36. We know that Stalin was the first to speak of "Marxism-Leninism."

37. See Alexander Motyl, "Soviet Dissidents and Eurocommunism," *Dissent* (Spring 1978).

38. Jean-François Revel and Branko Lazitch have emphasized the ambiguity of the relationship of the PCF with Moscow in their article "La vraie vie de Georges Marchais," published by *L'Express* in July 1978.

39. See Gilles Hertzog and Bernard-Henri Lévy, "Jeu de massacre et conflit de légitimitiés," *Le Monde diplomatique* (October 1975).

40. Fustel de Coulanges, *La Cité antique,* III, 18: "On the omnipotence of the state; the ancients had no concept of individual freedom."

41. Benjamin Constant, *Cours de politique constitutionnelle* (Paris: Laboulaye, 1861), vol. II, p. 842.

Chapter 3. Liberal-Libertarian

1. Husserl, *La Philosophie comme science rigoureuse,* trans. Quentin Lauer (Paris: PUF, 1955), pp. 108–122.

2. See the next chapter.

3. Deuteronomy 17:18-20; 8:14.

4. See Deuteronomy 10:8-9; 18:1-2. "Consecrate all the first-born to me," said Yahweh to Moses in Exodus 13:1; see also 22:38; 30:2. In Numbers, the "sacrificial" process seems to be definitely attributed to the Levites: "I myself have chosen the Levites from among the sons of Israel *in place* of the first-born" (3:12; 3:41).

5. Jeremiah 2:36.

6. I Samuel, beginning with Book 8.

7. "Yahweh then said to Samuel: obey their voice and give them a king" (I Samuel 8:22).

8. In the *Fragments*, there is the outline of an ideal city in which daily life is given its rhythm by work and prayer, the day is begun by hymns to the Eternal, sanctions are foreseen for whoever "does not believe in friendship," and good and bad citizens are distinguished by a "white scarf" (old men beyond reproach), a "black suit" (murderers), or a "gold star" (veteran soldiers).

9. Karl Popper, *The Open Society and Its Enemies* (London, 1966), vol. 1, chapter 9; and especially Maurice Clavel, *Deux siècles chez Lucifer* (Paris: Seuil, 1978), which superbly takes apart the mechanism of this "atheist theocracy."

10. I have emphasized this point in "À la guerre comme à la guerre," *Lotta Continua,* January 11, 1978.

11. See Laurent Dispot, *La Machine à terreur* (Paris: Grasset, 1978).

12. I borrow the expression from Guy Lardreau, *Le Monde* (Paris: Grasset, 1978).

13. Quoted by H. de Lubac, *Le Drame de l'humanisme athée,* p. 342.

14. *Ibid.*

15. In my view, this is the great lesson of the magnificent and terrifying *The Radiant Future.*

16. *Nichomachean Ethics* I, 1, 1094a27; also, all of I, ch. 6.

17. Maxim Gorky, article in *Vie nouvelle,* June 10, 1918.

Chapter 4. Resist the Plebs

1. The most recent example, of course, is the Iranian revolution. Is it absolutely necessary to proclaim victory because an obscurantist religious leader has succeeded to a civil autocrat who was sanguinary and paranoid? There were few voices to be heard, among the Western intelligentsia in early 1979, evoking for example the merits of a *democratic* solution.

2. See Gérard Mairet, "Peuple et nation," in *Histoire des idéologies,* ed. François Chatelet (Paris: Hachette, 1978), vol. III, pp. 57-75. In the same volume, I would mention the dazzling article by Evelyne Pisier, "L'obéissance à la loi."

3. *De cive* XII, 8.

4. Grotius, *De jure belli ac pacis* I, 3: "The right of government."

5. Jurieu, sixteenth pastoral letter, April 15, 1689. The identical notion is in Marsilius of Padua, *Defensor pacis,* I, ch. 12 and 13.

6. *Second Treatise* ch. XIV, art. 222.

7. *Ibid.,* XIX, 230; cf. Rousseau, *Du Contrat social,* II, 3.

8. *Ibid.,* VIII, 99.

9. *Ibid.,* XIV, 168. Explicitly contradicted by XIX, 240, 241, 242.

10. *Ibid.,* XIX, 222, 243.

11. C. B. Macpherson, *The Theory of Possessive Individualism from Hobbes to Locke.*

12. For example, *Second Treatise* XIV, 164, 166, 168; XIX, 239.

13. *Ibid.,* XIX, 242.

14. *Ibid.,* XVIII, 208.

15. *Ibid.,* XIX, 230; XVIII, 209.

16. Literally, "the right to act and conclude the rest," *ibid.,* VIII, 95. Similarly, X, 132.

17. Which are always, for Locke, the attributes of the single individual.

18. *Second Treatise* II, 8 and 10.

19. Quoted in G. Lenotre, "Hanriot," *Vieux Papiers,* III (Paris, 1906).

20. May 27.

21. Dispot, *op. cit.*

22. "We speak of the Jewish race because of the conventions of language, for, strictly speaking, from the genetic point of view, there is no Jewish race. . . . The Jewish race is before all a mental race." *Testament politique de Hitler* (Paris: Fayard), pp. 84–85.

23. "All peoples have the right of self determination. In virtue of this right, they freely determine their political status and freely accomplish their economic, social, and cultural development."

24. As with Locke, for whom it excludes the "vagabond," and Hitler, for whom it excludes the "Jew," the idea of popular sovereignty, here too, has a connotation that must be called racist: the Vietnamese, the Cambodians—perhaps the Iranians—are not "made" for democracy.

25. "Foreign policy is only a means to the goal, the goal being exclusively the promotion of our *popular* entity" (*Mein Kampf,* German edn., p. 687, quoted by Billig, *op. cit.,* p. 73). And Joachim Fest clearly points out how, in the twenties at least, the notion of *"Lebensraum"* played no role in the Führer's thought: *Hitler* (Paris: Gallimard, 1974), p. 260.

26. Hitler met Haushofer in 1922, when he was imprisoned in Landsberg, through the intermediary of Rudolf Hess. Haushofer (1869–1946) was deported in 1938. He edited the *Revue de géopolitique* from 1924 on.

27. See Rauschning, *op. cit.,* pp. 249–254.

28. *Western Russia and its Importance for Central Europe* (Berlin, 1917).

29. Quoted by J.-M. Domenach, *Le Retour du tragique* (Paris: Seuil, 1967), p. 148.

30. "Today National Socialism is in the situation of the Girondins," wrote Otto Strasser in his diary on October 30, 1932. At the same time, Wilhelm Kube, president of the Nazi group in the Bundestag, published *Moscow, Monarchy, National Socialism*. The *Neve Prevssische Kreuzzeitung* was alarmed at strikes in which the Nazis took part. And when Hitler delivered his famous speech to the Industrie-Club of Düsseldorf on January 27, 1932, his promises hardly convinced the liberal press, which continued to write that "the boundaries between Nazis and Bolsheviks are more fluid than ever" (*Vossische Zeitung*, November 3, 1937).

31. The uprising lasted from January 1928 to March 1929. There was a boycott of supplying the cities, consumer strikes, bombs, and armed attacks. It was supported by all the Nazi sects.

32. This daily was founded in the little village of Itzehoe and not in Hamburg or Kiel, notes Ernst von Salomon, who sees this as proof of the extreme importance the Nazis attributed to the movement (*Der Fragebogen,* p. 235 of the German edition). It was edited, he adds, by one of "the most extremist and most gifted" of Nazi journalists, "a man named Bodo Uhse." This Bodo Uhse was probably, at the same time, a communist militant (Faye, *op. cit.,* p. 327).

33. The committee was founded in February 1932 by Otto Strasser's right-hand man, Major Buchrucker. The communist "league of peasants" joined the committee, thanks to the good offices of the astonishing Bodo Uhse. Nazis and communists got on well together until the presidential elections, when the former encouraged Heim to become a candidate, while the latter supported the candidacy of Thaelmann.

34. *Der Stadt* saw in this insurrection "the shock troops of a new reality," which "is aiming at a radical transformation of the German situation" (French translation, Paris: Gallimard, 1937, p. 37).

35. *Der Vormarsch*, November 1928, "National-revolutionary consequences." Plaas joined the SS in 1934.

36. Niekisch: see Rauschning, *op. cit.,* p. 86. Hitler: see Billig, *op. cit.,* p. 26.

37. "The struggles between the idealist conceptions of the world have their final causes in the goals and aims provided by *popular existence*" (*Secret Memoir*).

38. Thus, the elections of July 31, organized by von Papen, in which the Nazis took 700,000 votes from the communists; the strike of the Berlin metalworkers in October 1930, in which the most active elements were the followers of Strasser, organized behind the Nazi union leader Johannes Engle; and the

common picket lines in front of the public transit depots at the time of the November 1932 demonstration.

39. See Faye, *op. cit.*, p. 447.

40. This was exactly the case in the transport workers' strike, when the social democratic press unanimously took fright at "proletarian solutions" (Faye, *ibid.*).

41. Published in the early thirties, translated and published in France by the Éditions Saint-Just in 1966. One can also read in it, for example, that the "worker has nothing to lose but his chains." Already in 1925, in number 2 of the *NS Briefe*, the same Goebbels published an "Open Letter to a Friend on the Left" in which he said notably: "You and I are fighting each other without really being enemies." For this he received, shortly afterward, an indignant reply from Rosenberg in the *Volkischer Beobachter* of November 14 (see Faye, *op. cit.*, p. 544).

42. *Standarte*, May 20, 1926. Jünger proposed, in the same article, to deliver "the word revolution from the absurdity that has marked it for the last hundred years."

43. Numerous quotations taken from *Mein Kampf*, in Billig, *op. cit.*, pp. 26–27.

44. A few names among many: Rudolf Rehm, an old Nazi who joined the KPD in 1933; Beppo Romer, founder of the Oberland Freikorps, joined the KPD in 1932; Wilhelm Korn, who made the trip in both directions; Giesecke, who moved from the KPD to the NSDAP in 1932; and the extreme right-wing lieutenant Scheringer, who simultaneously discovered *Mein Kampf* and *Das Kapital* in his Berlin cell.

45. See, in Jean Pierre Faye's book, the complex topography of these "circulations." Already in 1923 Radek was delivering his famous tribute to Schageter.

46. Erich Koch, prefect of Prussia, then gauleiter of the occupied Ukraine, but connected in his youth to the Strasser brothers.

47. The clearest example is Goebbels, who was Strasser's deputy until 1926, close to the SA until 1931, and who in 1925 noted in his diary (October 23): "In the last analysis, it would be better to end our days in a Bolshevik régime than to be slaves of Capital."

48. See Otto Strasser, *Hitler et moi* (French translation, Paris: Grasset, 1940), p. 122.

49. *Ibid.*

50. In 1930, Hitler was *still* proposing that Otto Strasser be his "chief of press" (*Hitler et moi*, p. 119). Gregor was unquestionably the number-two man in the party, the most popular leader after the Führer. In the Reichswehr and in the presidential palace, they counted much more on him than on the ad-

venturer of Landsberg. And the NSDAP was seen as a red, Strasserite party.

51. Faye, *op. cit.*, p. 449.

52. Speech delivered on November 15, 1933, at the inauguration of the Chamber of Culture of the Reich.

53. See Norman Cohn, *The Pursuit of the Millennium.*

54. See Faye, *op. cit.*, particularly pp. 230ff.

55. The first massacres of the Jews took place during the First Crusade. They were carried out by the *pauperes* for whom the elimination of the Moslems and the Jews represented the first act in the annihilation of the Prince of Darkness. And we can find an illustration of this, without the slightest ambiguity, in *La Chanson de Roland*, which was, as you know, the greatest literary expression of the First Crusade: "The Emperor has taken Saragossa: he has a thousand Frenchman thoroughly search through the city, the synagogues, and the Mahometries. With iron chains and axes, they break the images and all the idols: neither evil spells not enchantments will remain. The king believes in God and wants to do his service; and his bishops bless the waters. They lead the pagans to baptism: if anyone resists Charles, the king has him hung or burned or put to the sword" (lines 3660-3670).

56. *Mein Kampf* (Munich, 1942), p. 70.

57. Goebbels's diary, July 21, 1926: "The Jew is indeed the antichrist of world history."

58. Cohn, *op. cit.*

59. When he appeared, every prince was identified with this king. Then, when disappointment set in, he was called a "precursor." The whole history of the resurrections of Frederick, whose traces can be found among the Swabian preachers, is given its rhythm by this movement.

60. Frederick remained a key figure of Hitlerian mythology. See William Shirer, *The Rise and Fall of the Third Reich.*

61. Again the messianic theme, appearing throughout *Der Mythus des 20. Jahrhunderts,* of a worldwide plot supported by the Roman Church and its henchmen, the Jews. We find the same thing in Darré.

62. The work of an anonymous publicist of upper Alsace; the last and most exhaustive of the medieval echatologies. Quoted at length by Cohn.

63. The formula was exhumed by the "neo-romantic" Möller van den Bruck in 1923.

64. Hitler, closing speech at the Party Congress of 1938: "The German empire of the German nation has now been resurrected."

65. Isaiah 9:16.

66. Isaiah 23:19.

PART TWO: ATHENS OR JERUSALEM?

1. André Malraux, *La Tentation de L'Occident* (Paris: Grasset), p. 174. And much later in the *Adresse aux intellectuels.*

Chapter 5. The Pagan Mausoleum

1. H. Rauschning, *Hitler m'a dit* (Paris, 1939), p. 263.
2. Beginning, of course, with the French Revolution in its terrorist phase.
3. See Ricarda Huch, *Les Romantiques allemands* (Paris, 1978), vol. 1, pp. 117–131.
4. Gérard Mendel, *Le Meurtre du père* (Paris: Payot, 1972), pp. 216–276.
5. Charles Maurras, *La Politique religieuse* (Paris, 1900), pp. 4ff.
6. See the interview of Jean-Edern Hallier in *Art Press,* no. 26 (March 1979), in which the claims of "Celtitude" lead to a "metaphysical extermination of Judaism."
7. Alain de Benoist, article in *Figaro* magazine, January 27, 1979. There also seems to be a strange game going on around Georges Dumézil to whom the neo-fascist magazine *Nouvelle École* recently devoted a special issue (nos. 21–22, Winter 1972–1973).
8. Julia Kristeva, "L'antisémitisme aujourd'hui," *Art Press,* no. 26.
9. Dionysius of Halicarnassus, Thuc. 8.
10. The Book of Wisdom 17:11.
11. Revelation 23:1; Timothy 3:9.
12. This legend in fact came into being only in the late sixteenth century, with the neo-Stoic current of Charron, du Vair, and Justus Lipsius.
13. Aristotle, *De Anima,* 403a28: psychology is a branch of physics.
14. "The noble wife of his father, Phaedra, saw him and was, *according to my plans,* stricken with a furious passion"—*Hippolytus,* Aphrodite's first speech.
15. Phaedra does not speak, she "listens" to the noise of the dispute in the palace.
16. *Ibid.*
17. "Trembling and wounded . . . let the unfortunate woman die in silence."
18. "I will reveal it to Theseus."
19. Line 565.
20. Line 770.
21. Line 512.
22. Lines 591, 593.
23. Line 594: "You are destroyed. Those you love have betrayed you."

24. Line 715. The Chorus: "By holy Artemis, daughter of Zeus, I swear never to speak of your fatal secret."

25. Quoted by Jean-Marie Domenach in his fine *Retour de tragique* (Paris: Seuil, 1967), p. 25.

26. *The Women of Trachis,* line 727.

27. Greek morality is also more a morality of the optative than of the imperative. The idea of Law in the sense of "commandment" is almost entirely foreign to it.

28. Which is the literal meaning of Platonic *erotics,* for example.

29. *Metaphysics* B, 5, 1001b33; see also *Index arist.* 495b45.

30. *Metaphysics* Z, 10 103a8; see also *Physics* I, 7, 191a7.

31. *Politics,* Introduction and Book 1.

32. They were no doubt aware of the distinctions between genera and species, which can be found in Diogenes Laertius (VIII, 60). But this hardly entered into their logic or their metaphysics, which are based on simple "individual and concrete qualities." Thus, in Chrysippus's theory of definition (Diog. 60), there is no longer any question of essence at all. Stoicism's strength is that it resolved the Aristotelian contradiction ("there is no science except of the general"/"only the individual really exists") by simply eliminating the first term.

33. Since it is in effect without any root in essence, they were obliged to find another principle in order for the syllogism, and beyond that science, to be possible. And this principle is: the reason that governs the universe is always in agreement with itself and, consequently, *necessary.* A logic of generic essence was replaced by a logic of natural law.

34. Epictetus, *Diss* I, XXIX, 43.

35. On this point, see the analysis of Émile Bréhier, "Sur une théorie de la valeur dans la philosophie antique," *Actes du IIIe congrès des sociétés de philosophie de langue française* (Paris, 1947), sect. IV.

36. *Works and Days,* line 154.

37. See Victor Brochard, *Études de philosophie ancienne et de philosophie moderne* (Paris: Vrin, 1974) p. 496.

38. *Phaedo,* 64c.

39. *Phaedo,* 82e–83a.

40. Marcus Aurelius II, 5, 2: "To free oneself from all preoccupations; now, you will free yourself of them if you accomplish each action of your life as though it were the last." And at VI, 69: "moral perfection" is "to spend each day as if it were the last."

41. *Phaedo* 68de; cf. Spinoza, *Ethics* IV, prop. 63.

42. *Laches* 198–199.

43. Aeschylus, *Prometheus Bound,* 1080–1093 and *passim.*

44. *Agamemnon.*

45. *Hippolytus,* line 105.

46. "Man or God, everyone has his personal friends."

47. "Farewell," says Artemis, "for I am not permitted to see the dead nor even to defile my vision with the breath of the living."

48. Reinhardt's translation, *Sophocle* (Paris: Minuit, 1979), p. 133, is correct in not making "entombed Antigone" the object of the verb.

49. Line 450, Garnier edition, p. 79.

50. *Ibid.,* p. 91.

51. *Ibid.,* p. 88.

52. *Ibid.,* p. 75: "To claim that the gods care for this corpse is a revolting idea."

53. See J.-P. Vernant, *Mythe et pensée chez les Grecs.* Hence the futile dispute and the formidable misunderstanding between Antigone and Creon around the notions of *philos* and *echtros.*

54. Second stasimon, lines 583–625. The word "star," which means "guilty blindness," recurs four times (524, 614, 624, 625). At 584, 597, 604, and 624, she is explicitly condemned *in the name of heaven.* And finally, at 855, Antigone has risen up "against the high throne of justice."

55. *Ibid.,* p. 90.

56. *Ibid.,* p. 79.

57. *Ibid.,* p. 71.

58. *Ibid.,* p. 89.

Chapter 6. The Genius of Christianity

1. Commentary on St. John, vol. 13, no. 28.

2. Gregory of Nyssa, *On the Creation of Man,* ch. 16; John Damascene, *De duabus voluntatibus;* Maximus the Confessor, *Mystagogie;* Gregory of Nazianze, 38th discourse, c. 11; Clement of Alexandria, *Protrepticus.*

3. Bossuet, *Sermon sur l'Annonciation;* St. Thomas's famous formulation: the soul is *"continens magis quam contenta."*

4. We know, however, the obstacle that the reference to Aristotle remained for Thomism; for if it is true, as Aristotle believed, that individuation is brought about by matter, then it is hard to see how the soul, after death, separated from the principle which individualized it, can survive and become immortal. St. Thomas solved the problem by showing, in matter, the "potential" existence of "determinate" dimensions that individualize the soul-form of the body.

5. Which will be the basis for the third and fourth parts of this book.

6. Auguste Comte, *Système de politique positive,* II, 110.

7. A few significant texts: *De div. quaest. ad simpl.* I, 11–13; *De civ. dei* XII, 6–7; and especially Books V, VI, and VII of the *Confessions.*

8. Vitrier was guardian of the Franciscan monastery of Saint-Omer. He was one of the principal figures of the current around Jacques Lefèvre d'Étaples, Charles de Bovelle, Guillaume Budé, and of course Erasmus, which was less concerned with a "return to Antiquity" than with the definition of a *"devotio moderna."*

9. See the dedication of his *New Testament* addressed to Leo X.

10. *Système de politique positive*, III, 550; letters to Henri X. Hutton, 34.

11. St. Ignatius, *Constitutions de la compagnie de Jésus* (Paris: Desclée de Brouwer, 1967), pp. 264–267.

12. Arnauld, *De la fréquente communion*, 1643; see Jean Laporte, *La Doctrine de Port-Royal* (Paris: Vrin, 1951), vol. 1.

13. Chateaubriand, *Vie de Rancé* (Lausanne: Guilde du livre, 1956), p. 145. The author, enumerating the "constitutions," the "rules," and the "general instructions" of the Trappist abbey, reaches this one: "You will never stay alone in any place of darkness." And he comments: "And yet, he placed man alone before his passions."

14. Verlaine, *Parallèlement*.

15. *Confessions*, Book I: "I have shown myself as I was, contemptible and vile when I was contemptible and vile. . . ."

16. And Lacan today: "There is no love but the love of God."

17. Bishop of Lincoln from 1235 to 1253, commentator on Aristotle and Boethius, Job and the Psalms, St. Paul and the Areopagite.

18. Guillaume d'Auvergne, canon in 1223, bishop of Paris from 1228 to 1249. His most important work was *De Universo*.

19. His position can be summed up as follows: Against Aristotle and Averroes, the association of a spiritual substance with matter is not the only principle of individuation of beings; in themselves, "following essence and truth," souls, spiritual substances, each have their own individuality. See Noël Valois, *Guillaume d'Auvergne, évêque de Paris, sa vie et ses ouvrages* (Paris, 1880).

20. Duns Scotus was probably born circa 1274 in Ireland, and he died in Cologne in 1308. A Franciscan in the monastery of Newcastle, he was the author of the two monumental *Commentaries on the Sentences* of Peter Lombard. In 1304, in a solemn argument, he upheld the thesis of Mary's immaculate conception.

21. Unlike Duns Scotus, Occam does not say that a thing is an "individual" in virtue of an "individuating determination" which is added on to a common nature in it. He takes one further, decisive, step: a thing is an individual by the simple fact that it is. *"Nihil est a parte rei nisi singulare determinatum"* (In *Sent.* I, dist. xxv). See Maurice de Gandillac, in Fliche and Martin, *Mouvement doctrinal de IXᵉ au XIVᵉ siecle*, pp. 432 and 435–436.

22. "Avertissement" to *Phèdre*.

23. See Thierry Maulnier, *Lecture de Phèdre* (Paris: Gallimard), whose quality I would be ungracious not to recognize.

24. Sainte-Beuve, *Port-Royal* (Paris: Gallimard, Bibliothèque de la Pléiade), p. 576.

25. Berdiaev, *Un Nouveau Moyen Age* (Paris: Gallimard), p. 21.

Chapter 7. The Death of God

1. See, in *L'Homme revolté*, the commentary on Saint-Just's indictment at the trial of Louis XVI (*ed. cit.*, pp. 526ff.).

2. *Libres propos sur la guerre et la paix*, collected under the direction of Martin Bormann (Paris: Flammarion), vol. 1, p. 8. We can find the same theme in *Bolshevism from Moses to Lenin: Dialogue between Hitler and Me* by Dietrich Eckart, published a year after his death. Already in 1887, a *Haudbuch der Judenfragen* was published in Leipzig (Hammer Editions) by Theodor Fritsch; it had sold 145,000 copies by 1933, and its central argument was that "never in history has there been a spiritual, political, or economic power which, on the one hand, has declaimed so much against Judaism and, on the other, has intervened so much to protect it." On all this, see the next chapter.

3. *Op. cit.*, vol. II, p. 306.

4. Clavel, *op. cit.*

5. André Gide, *Dostoïevski* (Paris: Gallimard, 1970 edn.), p. 223.

6. Gérard de Nerval, *Aurélia*, in *Oeuvres* (Paris: Gallimard, Bibliothèque de la Pléiade), vol. 1, pp. 111–114.

7. Domenach, *op. cit.*, p. 200.

8. And especially with more genius.

9. *Le Temps retrouvé* (Paris: Gallimard, 1945 edn.), vol. 2, p. 112.

10. *Albertine disparue*, vol. 2, p. 118.

11. By Cocteau, 1931.

12. The theme of "flight" is one of the principal motifs of Philippe Soupault's *Bon Apôtre*, which was considered at the time as the key book of the new generation (see the article by François Mauriac in the *Nouvelle Revue Française*, November 1923).

13. Maurice Betz, *L'Incertain*, 1931.

14. By Pierre Drieu La Rochelle, 1931.

15. By André Obey, 1920.

16. By Robert Desnos, 1930.

17. By Paul Morand.

18. *Op. cit.*, p. 57.

19. *Journal* (Paris: Gallimard, Bibliothèque de la Pléiade), p. 108.

20. *L'Annonciatrice*.

21. Montherlant, *Aux fontaines du désir* (Paris: Grasset, 1927), p. 33.

22. René Crevel, *Détours* (Paris: NRF, 1924). With, as a bonus, scenes exalting a butcher who plunges his arms in blood (p. 27), or a "pretty drowned woman" fished out of the Seine (*ibid.*).

23. *Les Nouvelles Nourritures* (Paris: Gallimard, Folio), p. 193.

24. See, for example, "Lettre à Barbusse," *Art Libre* (January 1922).

25. *L'Annonciatrice*, vol. 2, p. 58. Of this book, Radek said: "It is our greatest victory" (speech to the Congress of Soviet Writers, August 1934).

26. Quoted by Maurice Nadeau, *Documents surréalistes* (Paris: Seuil, 1948), p. 14.

27. Breton recalled the surprise of this conversion in the *Entretiens* with A. Parinaud (Paris: Gallimard, 1962), pp. 164-166. *Hourra l'Oural* (Paris: Denoël, 1931).

28. *Vie de Staline, Le Couteau entre les dents, Russie.*

29. Romain Rolland, *Quinze ans de combat* (Paris: Rieder, 1935), p. lvi.

30. Quoted in the excellent work by Micheline Tison-Braun, *La Crise de l'humanisme*, vol. 2 (Paris: Nizet, 1967).

31. Maurice Bardèche, *Lettre à François Mauriac*, p. 178.

32. See *Mes idées politiques* (Paris: Fayard, 1937), *passim.*

33. Romain Rolland, *Robespierre* (Paris: Albin Michel, 1939), p. 62.

34. *Cent heures chez Hitler*, in *Notre avant-guerre* (Paris: Plon, 1941), pp. 182-183.

35. Gide, *Les Nouvelles norritures*, p. 245.

36. The theme can also be found in Maurice Genevoix (*Ceux de 14*), G. Bonnet (*L'Ame du soldat*), Adrien Bertrand, who was close to Barrès and Bordeaux (*L'Appel du sol*). As Micheline Tison-Braun shows very clearly, the whole age was living in the wake of this question: How did men "stand up" to, resist, the horror of the war? And the answer was unanimously repeated: because of a hidden, organic, filial bond to the earth.

37. *Lettre à François Mauriac*, p. 43.

38. *L'Annonciatrice.*

39. Tison-Braun, *op. cit.*, pp. 302-303.

40. *Retour d'URSS* (Paris: NRF, 1936): Communist man is one who "withstands the heat of the furnace, and this test strengthens him. In him, something *superhuman* is coming into being, something robust and unexpectedly glorious" (p. 9, my itals.).

41. Tison-Braun, *op. cit.*, p. 373.

42. *Ibid.*, pp. 259-261.

43. I quote from memory.

44. See, earlier, *L'Enfer* or *Les Suppliants.*

45. *Journal des années de guerre* (Paris: Gallimard), p. 1586. *Jean-Christophe, le Buisson ardent* (Paris: Ollendorf, 1912), p. 324.

46. See particularly *La Gerbe des forces*, 1937; *La Brière*, 1923.

47. Heidegger says of "religiosity" that it is not at all ruled out by "de-divinization" (*Holzwege*).

48. Quoted by Christian Jambet in *Le Monde*.

49. Solzhenitsyn again, the Dante of our time.

50. Quoted by Billig, *op. cit.*, p. 40.

51. It can hardly be stressed enough that the publication of the *Cours de philosophie positive* was completed in the same year that Feuerbach published *The Essence of Christianity*.

52. *Système de politique positive*, 2, 134.

53. Comte says exactly that the positive state is the reestablishment of the "normal state interrupted during the Western transition or rather in its last phase" (*Système de politique positive*, 4, 22).

54. Or else, and this amounts to the same thing, the return to what he calls, in Book V of the *Cours,* the "religion of the Middle Ages," that "eminent political masterpiece," which he elsewhere calls the heir of ancient polytheism (*Système de politique positive*, 2, 112).

55. See note 1.

56. Quoted by Michel Spannent, *Permance du stoïcisme* (Paris: Duculot, 1978).

57. *Discours et rapports à la Convention,* ed. Marc Bouloiseau (Paris: U.G.E., 10/18, 1965), p. 131.

58. Imprisoned in June 1793, Manon Roland, the "would-be Lucretia," as the indictment of the Comité de sûreté générale calls her, came to her trial on November 8 entirely dressed in white. During her imprisonment, she wrote fevered *Mémoires,* which end: "Nature, open your breast. Receive me. At thirty nine" (published in the year III under the title *Appel à l'impartiale postérité*). Garat, a revolutionary minister under suspicion, tells of his admiration for Seneca, who "teaches us to die" *Mémoires de Garat* (Paris, 1962). As for Laclos, precious details can be found in C. Dard, *Le Général Ch. de Laclos, auteur des "Liasions dangereuses"* (Paris, 1936).

59. The same Naigeon was the author of some of the anti-Semitic articles of the *Encyclopédie* (see the next chapter).

60. Spannent, *op. cit.*

61. Bernardin de Saint-Pierre, *Études de la nature* and *Harmonies de la nature*.

62. Shaftesbury, *Principles of Moral Philosophy*.

63. On the definition of the body, see Cicero, *De finibus,* Book III, chapters 5 and 6. The definition of "uneasiness" in the *Second Treatise* again brings Cicero to mind: *Tusculanes* IV, 7. Compare, with reference to Locke's sociability, *De Oficiis* 1, 7, and 16. And finally, on the obligation to preserve oneself, compare with *De finibus,* III, 5 art. 16.

64. It was only at Molyneux's request that Locke added to the second edi-

tion of the *Essay on Understanding* a twenty-seventh chapter in Part Two to clarify this point and finally to name his "subject."

65. The great difference between the French and American Declarations is probably that the latter explicitly calls on the "Creator."

Chapter 8. Critique of Political Paganism

1. I don't care, said the Führer to Rauschning, about "those ignoramuses who construct Nordic myths"—*Hitler m'a dit* (Paris, 1939), p. 66.

2. See Gérard Mendel, *La Révolte contre le père* (Paris: Payot, 1972), chapters 4 and 5.

3. William Shirer, in *The Rise and Fall of the Third Reich,* clearly describes the transferences of sanctity by which the book became a Bible and its author a Messiah.

4. See J.-J. Goux, *Les Iconoclastes* (Paris: Seuil, 1978), p. 56.

5. Hitler was initiated into the Indo-European "mysteries" by Lanz von Liebenfels.

6. "The vermin will be definitively eradicated from Europe"; "I have lanced the Jewish boil"; "People will be eternally grateful to National-Socialism for having *obliterated* the Jews in Germany and Central Europe"—*Testament politique d' Hitler* (Paris, 1959). This language of erasure and prophylaxis is not an effect of mere madness, but a will to *leave nothing* of a people in history. And when the text ends with the incredible order addressed to the "government of the nation" simply to observe the "racial laws" and to "resist pitilessly" against a Judaism already largely decimated, we sense clearly that this is not "ordinary" hatred or "ordinary" extermination.

7. Montherlant, *Le Solstice de juin* (Paris: Grasset, 1941), p. 294. Montherlant, to do him justice, was not an ordinary collaborator. He wrote and spoke little during the four years of shame. But in *Le Solstice* there are nevertheless remarks of this kind: "And I said to myself, lifting my gaze toward the exterminators: why am I not with them! Why is it not licit for me to join in their joy! And my heart was swollen with joy" (p. 89). Or, even worse: "One should do everything necessary to annihilate the adversary, but once he has shown that he has the upper hand, one should become his ally with the same spirit" (p. 288). This is the literal formula for collaboration, and stoicism.

8. Drieu La Rochelle, "Mauriac," *Nouvelle Revue Française* (October 1941). It is true that Drieu also believed in a reconciliation of the two traditions, as indicated, for example, in his *Notes pour comprendre le siècle* (Paris: Gallimard, 1941), p. 26. In November 1941, he even discussed Montherlant's position in an article in the *Nouvelle Revue Française* entitled "Christianisme et Paganisme" in which he hoped that fascism would bring about the resurrection of a "virile Christianity." But it is clear that Christianity had little to do

with the message of the Scriptures, and a good deal to do, on the other hand, with fascism.

9. Let me be clear. I use "romantic" in the very broad sense that goes from Schelling though Wagner to Spengler and Jünger. I am thinking of the "ideologues" of this current and not of its "poets" who, precisely as poets, are worth what their works are worth. But I simply think that it is hardly possible to exonerate the Schlegels, for example, for their concrete traces in history, any more than it is possible to exonerate Marx and Engels for the effects of real socialism.

10. Precious details can be found in Michel Le Bris, *L'Homme aux semelles de vent* (Paris: Grasset, 1978).

11. *Fragments from the Athenaum:* "Everything ancient is full of genius." Freidrich Schlegel, *Ideen:* "Plato's philosophy is a majestic preface to the relition of the future."

12. Ricarda Huch, *op. cit.*

13. For France, see Paul Sérant, *Romantisme fasciste* (Paris: Fasquelle, 1960).

14. Ernst Jünger, *La Guerre notre mère* (Paris: Albin Michel, 1934), p. 232.

15. *In Stahlgewittern;* French translation, *Orages d'acier* (Paris: Plon, 1960), p. 126.

16. *Ibid.*, p. 183.

17. Schlegel, *Ancient Fragments,* fgt. 38.

18. See Laurent Dispot, "Wagner, charron politique," *Art Press,* no. 25 (1979).

19. Quoted by Léon Poliakov, *Histoire de l'antisémitisme, de Voltaire à Wagner* (Paris: Calmann-Lévy, 1976), p. 462.

20. See Poliakov, *op. cit.*, pp. 363–377. And notably his remarks on the reactivation of the myth of the wandering Jew.

21. From Epictetus to Marcus Aurelius, the metaphor of "man the actor," which is found again in the "theater" of the Hegelo-Marxist dialectic.

22. See Caicidius, in plat. tim. 142 *(Chrysippus)*.

23. On the idea of "exegesis," see, for example, Epictetus, *Diss.*, I, vi, 19.

24. *De vita beata*, XV, 5; Ep. 107, 11.

25. Marcus Aurelius, *Thoughts*.

26. Cicero, *De finibus*, III, 9, 31.

27. Marx, *A Contribution to the Critique of Political Economy*.

28. Kant, *Idea of a Universal History from a Cosmopolitan Point of View*, fifth proposition.

29. I venture the hypothesis—which I will demonstrate in Part III, chapter 11—that totalitarianism begins with the myth of a total being. With Seneca's

struggle, for example, against the *turba causarum* (Ep. 65, 11), which is another name for modern materialist monism. We can therefore see that anti-Marxism as such is a derisory position, and that the stakes are much greater.

30. *The Jewish Question*, in Karl Marx, *Early Writings*, trans. Rodney Livingstone and Gregor Benton (New York: Vintage, 1975), p. 241.

31. *Ibid.*, p. 236.

32. *Capital* (Harmondsworth, Middlesex: Penguin, 1976), vol. 1, ch. 4, p. 256. This image and others of the same kind were preserved by Marx in the three editions of volume 1 published in his lifetime.

33. Quotations taken from E. Silberner, *Sozialisten zur Judenfrage*, pp. 136–148.

34. See the recent work by Mark Mitine referred to in *Le Matin*, January 30, 1979.

35. See Roderick Stoltheim, *The Mystery of Jewish Success* (1934), quoted by Henri Arvon, *Les Juifs et l'idéologie* (Paris: PUF, 1978).

36. See Wilhelm Bockelmann, *From Marx to Hitler* (1944), quoted by Arvon, *op. cit.*, p. 98.

37. Speech delivered after the Six Day War at the CGT congress, published in *L'Humanité*, June 17, 1967.

38. M. Thorez, "Rénégats et politique d'Union sacrée: Léon Blum tel qu'il est," *Internationale communiste*, no. 2 (February 1940, Moscow).

39. Quoted by Arvon, *op. cit.*, p. 56.

40. *Ibid.*

41. Bruno Bauer, *Christianity Unmasked*, 1843.

42. See Poliakov, *op. cit.*, p. 422.

43. *Encyclopédie*, article "Judaïsme." An article full of quotations from and references to Seneca; in order to prove, by contrast, the infinite poverty of biblical language and thought and the sublime eminence of the only religion that can match the measure of paganism—the civil religion which orders us to bow to the state and its laws.

44. This petition followed one from the Jews who wished to practice "commerce and the arts" in Paris. It was composed by the lawyer Goulleau at the request of merchants of the city. "One can," he says, "compare the Jews to wasps who enter the hives only to kill the bees, open their bellies, and draw out the honey from their insides." But nowhere, I repeat, is there any mention of the crime of deicide.

45. Posthumous publication, nine years after the author's death, sponsored by d'Holbach.

46. *L'Esprit du judaïsme*, pp. xix–xx, 200, 201.

47. Voltaire, *Dictionnaire philosophique*, article "Anthropophage." "Job" finds grace in Voltaire's eyes, for he is not a Jew but an Arab. The article

"Juif" is the longest in the *Dictionnaire*, thirty pages; and it concludes, after a series of insults rarely equaled at the time, with this recommendation: "But they ought not to be burned."

48. Voltaire, *Traité sur la tolérance*, in which we read the usual accusations about the Jewish taste for murder and the fact that Hebrew is to Greek what the language of a peasant is to that of an academician.

49. Éditions Sociales.

50. P. Charbonnel, *D'Holbach, textes choisis*. See the jacket copy.

51. See Poliakov, *op. cit.*, p. 107.

52. Voltaire, *Lettres de Memmius à Cicéron*, 1771.

53. *Dictionnaire philosophique*, article "Abraham."

54. Letter to the chevalier de Lisle, December 15, 1773.

55. Consult the excellent work by Arthur Hertzberg, *The French Enlightenment* (New York: Schocken, 1968), p. 305.

56. *Ibid.*, p. 301.

57. Quoted by Arvon, *op. cit.*, pp. 32–33.

PART THREE: THE MIRACLE OF THE NAME

Chapter 9. The Name of the Law

1. For this play on "re-mark" and the circle of dereliction, see the very fine book by Philippe Nemo, *Job et l'excès du Mal* (Paris: Grasset, 1978).

2. Thus, we should note in passing, the usual discourse on the paucity of the master's reality is the worst enemy of resistance, as we shall soon see in more detail.

3. Maine de Biran, *Oeuvres* (Tisserand), vol. 1, p. 144.

4. The modern notion of human nature came into being, as we know, with the question of the relationship of the West to the Indians. Appointed "attorney for the Indians" by Charles V, Las Casas began a battle in 1516 which ended in the middle of the century with the prohibition of expeditions of conquest. But it was above all Francisco de Vitoria, theologian of Salamanca, who, in the course of two "lessons," affirmed the notion of a "nature" independent of faith and the hazards of the religious struggle, irreducible to cosmological nature and its laws. The Indians are Men because of the simple fact that they are men, and that is true beyond any assurances of science or Christian militancy. On this question, read the work of synthesis by J. Baumel, *Les Problèmes de la décolonisation et de la guerre dans l'oeuvre de Francisco de Vitoria* (Montpellier, 1936).

5. Nietzsche, *The Will to Power, passim.*

6. Maurice Clavel, *Ce que je crois* (Paris: Grasset, 1976).

7. In a famous passage of *L'Homme révolté:* "The particular sensual de-

light of which Epicurus speaks lies above all in the absence of pain; it is the happiness of stones."

8. Or, as Kierkegaard also says, by recognizing in the Kantian imperative a version of the Decalogue, a dialogue between myself and God.

9. I take the phrase from Philippe Sollers's commentary on a fragment of *Paradis* delivered at an international colloquium on psychoanalysis in Milan in November 1978. He would probably agree that there is no ethics but a Freudian ethics, that is, in fact, a monotheist ethics.

10. Franz Fanon said this in the opening pages of *Les Damnés de la Terre* in which he analyzed the discourse of the "colonizer" about the "colonized."

11. Albert Cohen, *Solal* (Paris: Gallimard, 1936): "Yes, we Jews are a monster of humanity."

12. Malachi 2:9.

13. Exodus 32:33.

14. According to the Midrash, God offered the Torah to Edom and Ishmael, who refused it; one because his hands were stained with blood and it is written: "You shall not kill," and the other because he lived by plunder and it is written: "You shall not steal."

15. Israel, on the contrary, accepted without any preliminary conditions.

16. Isaiah 49:1.

17. Jeremiah 1:1.

18. Genesis 6:9.

19. Ezekiel 3:2.

20. Proverbs 7:3.

21. Quoted by Emmanuel Levinas, *Difficile Liberté* (Paris: Albin Michel, 1976), p. 48.

22. See Levinas, *ibid.*

Chapter 10. Destroy the Sacred Groves

1. Plato, *Philebus* 35ab. This is what makes for the extraordinary and lucid melancholy of the *Philebus:* an *infinity* of pleasures and the *finite* capacity we have to enjoy them (*Philebus* 27e). Compare *Phaedo* 58e, 61d, 63a, 64a.

2. Rousseau, *Rêveries du promeneur solitaire.*

3. "Since death, if we consider it well, is the true goal of our life . . . its image, far from being frightening for me, is entirely sweet and consoling! I thank my God for having given me the grace to recognize death as the key to our true beatitude." See H. de Curzon, *Lettres de W. A. Mozart* (Paris, 1928), letter of April 4, 1787.

4. *Barbarism with a Human Face,* Part One.

5. In late 1978, the weekly *L'Express* published a conversation of Philippe Ganier-Raymond with the former high commissioner for Jewish affairs, Louis Darquier de Pellepoix. There followed a strange collective psychosis, which

proved once again that the real division in France remains that between the Stalinists and the Pétainists, and that all the terms with which we are still living, whether we like it or not, were established in those few crucial years.

6. In late 1978, again, there was a polemic between myself and the secretary general of the PCF. Having accused him in an interview with Maurice Szafran in *Le Matin* (November 1, 1978) in which I noted the "discreet phantom" of "anti-Semitism" that continued to "lurk" in "some" of his "declarations," I was honored, along with Claude Perdriel, director of *Le Matin*, with a public reply as absurd as it was ignoble. Claude Perdriel retorted with great dignity *(Le Matin,* November 3, 1978). And, for my part, I thought it right to recall the constancy, in the PCF, of an anti-Semitic temptation that obviously went beyond the case of its secretary general *(Le Matin,* November 3, 1978). Permit me to refer the reader to that text in which I recalled some obvious facts and raised some "questions" that, as I write these lines, have remained unanswered.

7. *Charlie Hebdo,* June 1978: "Comment écrire un article de droite."

8. Mussolini, Hitler, Stalin, Pol Pot. And suppose "red fascism" were a pleonasm. This is the question raised by Laurent Dispot in *La Machine à terreur.* See also Ernst Nölte, *Les Mouvements fascistes* (Paris: Calmann-Lévy), p. 62.

9. For which the masterwork remains the book by Gilles Deleuze and Félix Guattari, *L'Anti-Oedipe* (Paris: Minuit, 1970).

10. I take the expression from the title of the book by Mariella Righini (Paris: Grasset, 1978).

11. This point has been emphasized by Guy Lardreau and Christian Jambet, *Le Monde.*

12. See, for example, in France, the fact that the feminist movements have fallen back on judicial and repressive weapons: rape cases, etc.

13. It is also significant that the Jews of the Bible gave themselves the name B'nai Israel, "children of Israel." Whereas in the case of the Egyptians, the Hittites, or the Assyrians, the expression is always "people." This clearly means that the idea of being chosen presupposed neither a bond of *blood,* nor a biological *root,* but a covenant, whose structure will be presented later (Part Four, chapter 14).

14. Malachi 2:9.

15. Genesis 2:21–23. I recall the passage: "So Yahweh God made the man fall into a deep sleep. And while he slept, he took one of his ribs and enclosed it in flesh. Yahweh God built the rib he had taken from the man into a woman, and brought her to the man. The man exclaimed: 'This at last is bone from my bones, and flesh from my flesh! This is to be called woman, for this was taken from man.' "

16. Genesis 1:27.

17. Genesis 5:1–2.

18. Genesis 2:7. The verse relies on a play on words between *"'Adâmâh"* which means earth and the etymologically similar *"'âdâm"* which means man. This *'âdâm* becomes a proper name at 4:25 and 5:1,3.

19. Genesis 1:5–24.

20. Emmanuel Levinas, *Quatre lectures talmudiques* (Paris: Minuit, 1976).

21. Deuteronomy 29:13–14: "Not with you alone do I make this covenant today and pronounce these sanctions, but with him also who is not here today, as well as with him who stands with us here in the presence of Yahweh our God."

22. Jeremiah 12:15. And, says the Prophet, it is only after they have been "torn out" that "I will take pity on them again and bring them back each to his heritage, each to his own country."

23. Isaiah 1:29.

24. Zechariah 2:8; Ezekiel 4:2–6.

25. Jeremiah 50:21–27.

26. See, for example I Kings 13:18.

27. "Fill the earth and conquer it," says Genesis 1:28.

28. The category of exile is so thoroughly attached to the biblical tradition that it has lasted into modernity, at the very heart of the idea of a "nation." It was only in the sixteenth century, with Rabbi Loewe Ben Bezalel, that there appeared for the first time, the possibility of thinking of a nation against exile, a "nation" of which exile would not be the basic constituent. Then and only then came into being the Zionist idea of attachment to a land. It is therefore possible to think that exile became an obstacle to Jewish national life only with the awakening of "nationalisms" in Europe. And beginning at that point, with the denial of Jewish national identity, modern anti-Semitism, from Voltaire to Hitler, also came into being.

29. Genesis 17:5: "You shall no longer be called Abram; your name shall be Abraham, for I make you father of a multitude of nations." Genesis 17:15: "As for Sarai your wife, you shall not call her Sarai, but Sarah." Genesis 32:39: "Your name shall no longer be Jacob, but Israel, because you have been strong against God, you shall prevail against men."

30. See the remarkable article by Guy Scarpetta, "Éloge du cosmopolitisme," *Art Press*, no. 26 (March 1979).

31. Smolensky.

32. Quoted by Levinas, *Difficile Liberté*.

33. Noces.

34. Vladimir Jankélévitch, interview in *Le Nouvel Observateur*, February 16, 1979.

35. In late 1978, *Pravda* hailed Jim Jones as an American "dissident."

36. Jean Seznec, *The Survival of the Pagan Gods: The Mythological and Its Place in Renaissance Humanism and Art* (New York, 1953).

Chapter 11. We Are All Children of Israel

1. This is why the classic argument, which moves backward from the Inquisition to the Revelation, and denies the validity of the latter because of the excesses of the former, is absolutely irrelevant. And the great difference with Marxism, for example, and the impeccable logic that traces the Gulag back to *Capital,* is this: while Marx and Engels never tire of saying that practice is the criterion of every theory and that no theory is valid outside its vocation to *transform* the world, the Christian is one who believes in a spiritual message which, even if it is distorted, denied, and betrayed, continues by definition to be valid in the absolute.

2. Read the excellent work of synthesis by Claude Lepelley, *L'Empire romain et le christianisme* (Paris: Flammarion).

3. *Les Martyrs* was badly received by Hoffmann as well as Sainte-Beuve, Flaubert as well as Benjamin Constant, by Taine, Faguet, and all the critics of the nineteenth century. Constant, for example, in *Le Mercure de France* of May 31, 1817, criticized the author for having contrasted "the religion of Homer, a religion which disappeared many centuries ago, to Bossuet's Catholicism" (quoted by A. Vinet, *Études sur la littérature francqise au XIXe siècle,* vol. 1, pp. 398ff).

4. Is it an accident, then, that Chateaubriand confesses in Book II that he prefers Tasso to Dante; that already in *Le Génie du christianisme* (Part Two, Book IV, ch. vii: of "Saints"), he was so "certain" that "the poets have not taken from the Christian supernatural everything it can provide for the muses"; that, in the *Examen des Martyrs,* he declares: "I adore the Ancients and look upon them as our masters; I completely adopt the principles established by Aristotle, Horace, and Boileau"; that, in the *Préface,* he quotes so abundantly from Aristotle, Dionysius, and Strabo, and refers to the century of Louis XIV only insofar as it was "nourished by Antiquity"? The truth is that we find in this first great romantic the motif common to all of a *return* to the ancient world.

5. Mosaic Law, in effect, distinguishes between "converts of the door" and "converts of justice," who are completely converted to Judaism. See Elie Banamozegh, *Israël et l'humanité* (Paris: Albin Michel, 1977), pp. 282ff.

6. A Noachid has the possibility of observing some of these prescriptions; the sabbath, for example. See Isaiah 56:3–7; 66:23.

7. Of course there are many passages pointing in this direction. For example: "All the tribes of the earth shall bless themselves by you" (Genesis 12:3),

and: "In those days, ten men of nations of every language will take a Jew by the sleeve" (Zechariah 8:23).

8. Raschi, commenting on Deuteronomy 20:18: "we conclude that if they repent they will be accepted" (Benamozegh, *op. cit.*, p. 274).

9. We can find a catalogue of this minimal law, less religious than ethical, in the Talmud Sanhedrin, for example (48b): "Our Doctors have said that seven commandments were imposed on the sons of Noah: the first orders them to have judges; the six others prohibit: (1) sacrilege; (2) polytheism; (3) incest; (4) homicide; (5) theft; (6) the use of a member of the living animal."

10. Jeremiah 35:12–18.

11. Exodus 9:20; 12:38.

12. Circumcision, for example. Benamozegh, *op. cit.*, p. 72.

13. Tyrian or Phoenician symbols.

14. Sanhedrin 91b; Pesahim 90.

15. Benamozegh, *op. cit.*, p. 65.

16. See André Chouraqui, *Juifs d'Afrique du Nord* (Paris: Hachette, 1976).

17. Traditional and no doubt etymological meaning.

18. Spinoza, *Tractatus Theologico-Politicus.*

19. The Hebrew word is *"Nâbî',"* which comes from *"Nâbâ',"* to call.

20. In Greek, *apo-stellein.*

21. Levinas says this well in *Difficile Liberté.*

22. Mallarmé, lecture delivered at Oxford and published in *La Musique and les lettres.*

23. The "drama" of assimilation is well known; Gershom Sholem has analyzed its origins and, for my part, I am inclined to see it as a specific form of voluntary servitude. We should not forget that, when Lenin recognized and theorized the rights of "nationalities," he denied them to the Jews, who have, so he said, neither language nor territory.

24. See Lardreau and Jambet, *L'Ange* (Paris: Grasset, 1976).

25. Isaiah 56:6,7.

26. Numbers 11:26–27.

27. Numbers 11:28, 29.

28. Joel 3:1, 5.

29. Talmud Sanhedrin 99a. With reference to Jeremiah 30:21, where it is written: "Their prince will be one of their own."

30. Talmud Berkhot 61a. Commentary of Genesis 2:7.

31. On exile, the metaphysical exile in which one leaves "by daylight when they can see you," see Ezekiel 12:3. On the letter that kills, see Isaiah 10:1, which explicitly says that the greatest evil is to write "infamous laws."

32. Numbers 33:9.

33. *Oeuvres complètes* (Paris: Gallimard, Bibliothèque de la Pléiade, 1959), vol. 1, p. 363.

34. This is the question raised by Jean Starobinksi, *Jean-Jacques Rousseau: la transparence et l'obstacle* (Paris: Gallimard), p. 54.

35. Whatever Saint-John Perse's later quarrels with General de Gaulle, the fact remains that Perse was among the first to be banished from Vichy. Personally opposed, from 1938 on, to the policy of appeasement of Hitler, he was denounced as a warmonger at the time of the armistice. Replaced as secretary general of the Quai d'Orsay, he refused the position of ambassador to Washington offered to him by the "French State." On June 16, in the Gironde estuary, he boarded an English freighter sailing for England. Invited to Chequers by Churchill to discuss the fate of France and the rallying of French forces, he then sailed for New York on July 14, 1940. In October, he learned that the Vichy government had stripped him of French nationality, confiscated his possessions, and stricken his name from the order of the Légion d'honneur.

36. Quoted by Claude Vigée, "Saint-John Perse, parole de vivant" in *L'Art et le Démonique* (Paris: Flammarion, 1978), pp. 28ff.

37. "Dante, ce rebelle-né," opening speech at the international congress of Florence for the seventh centenary of Dante.

38. Hobbes, *De Cive* I, 5; *Leviathan* IV.

39. Destutt de Tracy, in 1796, in a *Mémoire* presented to the Institut national des sciences et des arts.

40. Hence, the publication by Didot, in the year IX, of *Projets d'Eléments d'idéologie*. In the preface (p. xvii), he explains how man can now, armed with this concept and its clear definition, be assured of always reasoning perfectly and of having his reasoning follow the straight and faultless path of science. This science of ideas is then assimilated to natural science, in the purest mechanistic tradition (p. xix). Thus Destutt rediscovers the theme common to the whole century, and which took the form we know in the following century, of a necessary, linear, and mathematical progress of knowledge (p. xx).

41. Stendhal an ideocrat? No, of course not. But a representative, in any case, of the spirit of the age. *Les Eléments d'idéologie*, *La Grammaire générale*, and *La Logique* were his Bible. His whole *Correspondance*, his *Journal* of the time, and his *Pensées* (published by Henri Martineau under the title *Filosofia nova*) attest to this imprint. He thought in substance that the whole problem of thought, of ethics, and of action was to know what spring should be set in motion, when, and how. And even in his literary work we find the taste for nomenclatures, catalogues of character types, repertories of peculiar traits; and we know from the *Correspondance* that he begged his younger sister Pauline to help him establish them.

42. Hitler, *Mein Kampf* (French translation, Paris: Nouvelles éditions latines, 1934), p. 585.

43. Stalin, *Voprosy Leninizma*, 2nd edn., p. 545. See also Gramsci, *Oeuvres choisies* (Paris: Éditions Sociales, 1959), p. 74.

44. Article in *Les Temps modernes*.
45. See Camus's last interview, in the Pléiade edition.
46. Roland Barthes, *Sollers écrivain* (Paris: Seuil, 1979).
47. Talmud Sanhedrin, quoted by Levinas, *Difficile Liberté*.

Chapter 12. The Kulak and the Commissar

1. See the fine analysis by Jean-Paul Dollé, *Le Désir de Révolution* (Paris: Grasset, 1977).
2. Locke, *Second Treatise*, II, 4, 6; IV, 39; V, 27, 44.
3. *Ibid.*, IV, 23; XI, 135.
4. *First Treatise*, IV, 86.
5. *Second Treatise*, V, 27.
6. *Ibid.*, V, 26, 28, 36.
7. *Barbarism with a Human Face*.
8. Thomas More, *Utopia*, quoted in Pierre Mesnard, *L'Essor de la philosophie politique au XVIe siècle* (Paris: Vrin, 1977), p. 165.
9. *Ibid.*, p. 171.
10. *Ibid.*, p. 176.
11. To the point that it is only then, with this right of property, that a system so concerned, we remember, with "people" and "sovereignty," succeeds in really thinking of the *individual*. The clearest example deals with the right of people in war, *Second Treatise*, XVI, 193.
12. I am of course distorting its meaning; in the Prophets it designates rather rebellion against God.
13. Isaiah 26:20. The exact text is: "Go into your rooms my people, shut your doors behind you. Hide yourselves a little while until the wrath has passed."
14. See Maurice Bardèche, *Stendhal*.
15. I, 5.
16. V, 2.
17. *Ibid.*

PART FOUR: THE BIBLE OF RESISTANCE

Chapter 13. The Seven Commandments

1. "The proof of the pudding is in the eating," said Engels. We have eaten the pudding and the proof has been produced.
2. You have recognized the holy family: Leibniz, Hegel, Marx.
3. The Gaullist movement included at most 7,000 men in July 1940, and 35,000 at the end of the year, where it remained until November 1942 (Robert O. Paxton, *Vichy France*).

4. See André Beaufre, *Le Drame de 40* (Paris, 1965), p. 265. This was not an isolated event.

5. See Gérard Miller, *Les Pousse-au-jouir du maréchal Pétain* (Paris: Seuil, 1975).

6. Paul Reynaud resigned. Lebrun called on Pétain to form a new government. This government was a model of national union in the style of the Third Republic. There could not have been a less spectacular, a more *legal* revolution.

7. Among the eighty: thirty-five SFIO, thirteen Radicals, and others from various parties. The majority of socialists and Radicals voted yes; Édouard Herriot abstained. See Robert Aron, *Histoire de Vichy* (Paris: Fayard, 1954).

8. See Poliakov, *Le Bréviaire de la haine* (Paris: Livre de poche, 1974), pp. 257–277.

9. I am of course not talking about the many isolated acts (isolated as always) of those who, risking their lives, refused to become heroes of *Le Chagrin et la Pitié*, and I do not underestimate what we owe them. But the fact remains that, during those years of shame, the sacrosanct working class and the good people of France in its depths never undertook the smallest strike, the smallest mass demonstration, against the wearing of the yellow star.

10. See *La France de Darquier de Pellepoix* (Paris: Syros, 1979).

11. See the implacable *Histoire du Parti communiste français* by Jacques Fauvet (Paris, 1965), which quotes extensively from the communist press of the time. For the posters, see A. Rossi, *La Guerre des papillons* (Paris, 1954).

12. Jacques Soustelle, *Envers et contre tout* (Paris, 1947).

13. Paxton, *op. cit.*

14. Ecclesiasticus 18:22.

15. Genesis 21:14–21.

16. Genesis 21:16.

17. Genesis 21:20.

18. Quoted by Levinas, *Difficile Liberté*. Similarly: "There will be no further delay in the fulfilling of any of my words" (Ezekiel 12:28). See also Deuteronomy 23:24.

19. After the appeal launched in late 1971 by André Malraux.

20. I still remember the subtle strategists of the "left" who, in the spring of 1977 in France, were afraid that the voice of the dissidents "would perturb their local elections" (Clavel).

21. "Un appel de Marek Halter pour lutter contre la barbarie," *Le Monde*, October 19, 1977; *The New York Review of Books*, November 18, 1977. "Une rage que je boudrais faire partager," *Le Matin*, October 4, 1977. "Pourquoi l'Argentine," *Le Monde*, February 4, 1978. On January 12, 1978, the Socialist Party, through its spokesman Lionel Jospin, adopted Marek Halter's position.

22. See Nicolas Grimaldi, *Le Désir et le Temps* (Paris: PUF, 1971).

23. Hegel, *Aesthetics.*

24. Ecclesiasticus 3:23. Along the same lines, Isaiah 8:10.

25. This committee, led notably by Claudie and Jacques Broyelle, set itself the task of outfitting a ship to fish Vietnamese refugees out of the South China Sea. Among the signatories were Raymond Aron *and* Jean-Paul Sartre.

26. Robert Hersant, open letter to Olivier Todd, *Le Figaro*, December 10, 1978.

27. Olivier Todd, interviewed on Antenne II the same evening.

28. Hence political itineraries which seem tortuous only to the malicious: the Maoists or my friend Philippe Sollers, whose alleged "apostasies" are perhaps nothing but the movement of a continuous antifascism.

29. Another example of the rejection of the "logic of alternatives": Camus's attitude during the Algerian War.

30. Isaiah 49:4. Similarly, Isaiah 50:2: "Why did I find no one when I came? Why did no one answer when I called?"

31. Marx, *A Contribution to the Critique of Hegel's Philosophy of Right. Introduction.*

32. *Euthydemus* 290c, 291a.

33. A quotation from Aeschylus's *Seven Against Thebes.*

34. *Phaedrus* 266b–c.

35. Like Hobbes in *Leviathan,* Spinoza in the *Tractatus* raises the question: What is the word of God? Who prophesies it? Who are the true and the false prophets? Hobbes answered (*Leviathan,* ch. 38): It is the Anglican Church which sanctifies the sacred books. Spinoza answers in the same way *(Tractatus,* ch. 19): "The eternal reign of God" can be established only if positive law and decrees strengthen natural intelligence. And this is the real reason, beyond any preoccupation with "free will," why he attacks sects and churches.

36. With the possible exception of Kant.

37. In 1924, it was Stalin himself who denounced social democracy as the "moderate wing of fascism" and declared the two tendencies "not antithetical but twins." Numerous and spectacular examples of the concrete effects of this line and its impact in the rank and file can be found in Jean Valtin, *Sans patrie ni frontière* (1941; reprinted, Paris: Lattès, 1975).

38. See *Frankfurter Zeitung,* August 26, 1931: in the face of the strange conjunction of slogans, the identical clamor about *"nazionale und soziale"* liberation, this newspaper printed the headline: "The Ring Is Closing." See also Joseph Rovan, *L'Allemagne n'est pas ce que vous croyez* (Paris: Seuil, 1978).

39. The expression can be found, literally, in the issue of Otto Strasser's weekly dated August 26, 1930.

40. See *Frankfurter Zeitung,* October 30, 1930.

41. See Jean-Pierre Faye, *Langages totalitaires.*

42. At least in electoral terms.

43. German anarchist, early anti-Nazi, quoted in Eve Dessarre, *Les Sacrifiés* (Paris: Olivier Orban, 1978). See also Trotsky himself, to whom Neumann's line seemed so frightening that he felt the need to publish *Against National-Communism* in 1931 (published in France by Marcel Rivière with the incorrect title *Contre le national-socialisme*).

44. Hannah Arendt, *Eichmann in Jerusalem.*

45. Léon Poliakov, *Le Bréviaire de la haine* (Paris: Livre de poche, 1974), p. 344.

46. André Gide, *Voyage au Congo* (1927) and *Retour du Tchad* (1928), in which he accused the concessionary companies of subjecting Africans to forced labor. There was a trial for libel which he won and after which the monopoly of la Forestière was not renewed.

Today again there are a few men who, amid the great uproar of the partisan order, have the audacity to express the virtues of lucidity. Thus, Jean Daniel ("Le retour de la belle âme," *Le Nouvel Observateur*, 1977), whom I consider one of those who, over the last twenty years, have saved the honor of the French left.

47. French translation, *Traité du rebelle* (edn. du Rocher, 1957).

48. For example, the "union of public safety" of pastors against the German Christians.

49. Quoted by Eve Dessarre, *op. cit.*, p. 165.

50. With the same determination, Goerdeler protected the Jews of his city. He resigned in 1936 when the Nazis removed the statue of Mendelssohn against his will.

51. Ossietzky: director of *Die Weltbühne*, Nobel Peace Prize in 1936, died on May 4, 1938, in a Berlin hospital. Erich Mühsam: excluded from the KPD in 1925, poet and incomparable orator, arrested on February 26, 1933, he died in a concentration camp in 1934. Ludwig Quidde, Nobel Peace Prize in 1937, director of the "German Society for Peace," also died in a camp.

52. Dessarre, *op. cit.*, p. 170.

53. Arrested in 1933, he survived the war and chose voluntary exile in Paris.

54. Dessarre, *op. cit.*, p. 180. This shattering account contains countless anecdotes and portraits that illustrate the scope of this internal resistance.

Chapter 14. The Order of Evil

1. Leibniz, *Théodicée*, 196–213.

2. Official thesis of the French Communist Party on the eve of its twenty-third congress.

3. Descartes, *Discours de la méthode.*

4. Epictetus, *Diss.* III, 17; III, 9, 3–4; IV, 7, 36–39. Marcus Aurelius, XII, 16, 2; VIII, 4, 6.

5. This is no doubt the function of the so-called liberal intellectuals in the Western parties. Among the worthies, Jean Elleinstein and the authors of *L'URSS et nous* (Paris: Éditions Sociales, 1978).

6. Simone Veil, *Le Matin,* November 1, 1978, on the Darquier de Pellepoix affair.

7. Dominique Desanti, *Drieu La Rochelle ou le séducteur mystifié* (Paris: Flammarion, 1978). In spite of our disagreement, I would like to emphasize the rigor and talent of the book.

8. Thus, whether we like it or not, Malraux is not Drieu, nor is Nizan Aragon.

9. Malebranche, *Recherche de la vérité,* I, 1, 2; *Traité de morale,* I, 3, 15.

10. Henri Amouroux, *Les Collabos* (Paris: Laffont, 1978).

11. Shirer, *The Rise and Fall of the Third Reich.*

12. Chateaubriand, *Vie de Rancé* (Guilde du Livre), p. 214; same theme in Montaigne, *Essais,* I, 18.

13. *L'Espoir;* see also Tchen's "to die at the greatest height possible" in *La Condition humaine.*

14. On this point, see the magnificent analyses of Vladimir Jankélévitch in *La Mort* (Paris: Flammarion, 1976), pp. 188ff.

15. Ecclesiastes 8:8.

16. Job 19:8, 10, 20.

17. Genesis 4:3–16.

18. Genesis 4:6–7.

19. Genesis 4:8.

20. *Ibid.*

21. Genesis 4:7.

22. See Ecclesiasticus 3:29.

23. Genesis 4:15.

24. Paul Ricoeur, *Finitude et Culpabilité* (Paris: Aubier-Montaigne), vol. 2, p. 74.

25. Genesis 4:11.

26. Hosea 4:12; Jeremiah 9:14; 2:23; Ezekiel 23:20.

27. Jeremiah 5:23; 31:33; Ezekiel 11:19, etc., etc.

28. Guy Lardreau has emphasized this point in the preface to *La Mort de Joseph Staline* (Paris: Grasset, 1977).

29. Except for Paul Ricoeur, *Finitude et Culpabilité,* p. 222.

30. Genesis 2:15.

31. Genesis 3:1.

32. Genesis 2:19.

33. Genesis 3:14.
34. Genesis 3:12–13.
35. Genesis 3:6–7; on this point, see Ricoeur's commentary, *op. cit.*
36. Isaiah 51:17, 22; Jeremiah 25:15–16; 51:7; Lamentations 4:21.
37. Amos *passim,* notably 8:3 and 10.
38. Isaiah 27:1.
39. Isaiah 24:3–6; 28:22, 49:19; Jeremiah 4:27; Ezekiel 5:9.
40. Isaiah 5:1, 7; Ezekiel 7:10.
41. Micah 2:7–9.
42. Habakkuk 1:2.
43. Plato, *The Statesman.*
44. See Philippe Nemo, *Job et l'excès du Mal.*
45. This is the very definition of the "philosophy of history."
46. Jeremiah *passim.*
47. Genesis 4:26.
48. Genesis 3:5.
49. Isaiah 5:20.
50. Deuteronomy 15:11; commentary in Talmud Derachoth 34b.
51. Is this dispossession not the abuse of power which Ezekiel mentions when speaking of those who "capture the souls" of men to "assure the life of their own soul"?—Ezekiel 18:8.
52. Psalms 18:3; Isaiah 51:1; Psalms 18:32; Habakkuk 1:12; Deuteronomy 32:18, II Samuel 22:3; Psalms 144:2; Isaiah 44:8; Psalms 73:26.

Chapter 15. Thus Spake the Stones

1. Ezra 1, 5, 6; Daniel *passim,* notably 10.
2. Isaiah 51:1; Deuteronomy 32:18.
3. Jeremiah 18:6; Lamentations 4:2.
4. Isaiah 51:1.
5. Aristotle, *Metaphysics.*
6. Isaiah 51:1.
7. Isaiah 51:2.
8. Isaiah 51:1.
9. The Hebrew word *"Maqqêbéth,"* cavity, evokes *"neqêbah,"* woman.
10. Isaiah 51:3.
11. Genesis 6:6: "Yahweh regretted having made man on the earth, and his heart grieved. 'I will rid the earth's face of man, my own creation,' Yahweh said 'and of animals also, reptiles too, and the birds of heaven for I regret having made them.' "
12. I take the word from Jean-Joseph Goux, *Les Iconoclastes* (Paris: Seuil, 1978).
13. *Mein Kampf.*

14. Genesis 2:6.
15. Isaiah 51:23.
16. *Ibid.*
17. Genesis 4:1.
18. Genesis 4:2.
19. "I have acquired [*qanîti*] a man," says Eve at Genesis 4:1. As for Abel, his name comes from *hebel,* "breath."
20. Genesis 25:21.
21. Genesis 25:22.
22. Genesis 28.
23. Genesis 25:27.
24. Isaiah 51:13–14: "What has happened to the fury of the oppressors? The captive is soon to be set free."
25. Psalms 18:1.
26. *Ibid.*
27. Isaiah 51:4.
28. Isaiah 51:10.
29. Nahum 1:4.
30. Genesis 6:7.
31. Ezekiel 36:36.
32. Psalms 104:1–4, 10–15.
33. Jeremiah 13:9.
34. The Book of Wisdom 19:6.
35. Exodus 31:18.
36. Exodus 32:15.
37. Jeremiah 31:31–32.
38. Joshua 8:32. Similarly, Deuteronomy 17:18: "When he is seated on his royal throne he must write a copy of this Law on a scroll for his own use at the dictation of the . . . priests."
39. Genesis 32:3.
40. Exodus 19:9.
41. Exodus 19:12.
42. For example, Jeremiah 19:15.
43. Jeremiah 33:22.
44. Zephaniah 1:15; Psalms 12:2, etc.
45. See Levinas, *Difficile Liberté.*
46. Habakkuk 1:4.
47. Jeremiah 2:8.
48. Deuteronomy 34:10.
49. Jeremiah 8:5.
50. Jeremiah 31:31.

51. Ezekiel 3:3.
52. Ezekiel 3:1.
53. Ezekiel 34:2, 4–5.
54. I Samuel 8:5.
55. I Samuel 10:22.
56. I Samuel 16:14.
57. Deuteronomy 29:14.
58. Exodus 34:12.
59. See Anders Nygren, *Eros et Agapè* (Paris: Aubier, 1962), vol. 1, p. 58.
60. Luke 10:25ff.; Mark 12:28ff.
61. Matthew 28:38ff.
62. Exodus 34:12.
63. John 17:11.
64. Matthew 5:44–45; 2:17; 10:8; Luke 15:4, 11–32.
65. Job 34:11; Psalms 12:13; Proverbs 24:12; Jeremiah 17:10; 32:19.
66. Matthew 20:1–16.
67. Jonah 4:11.
68. Matthew 5:38ff.
69. Psalms 17:8–9.
70. Psalms 18:21–22.
71. Psalms 9:9; 31:4.
72. Genesis 4:14.
73. Jonah 4:11.
74. Proverbs 3:32.
75. Proverbs 3:31.
76. *Ibid.*
77. Ezekiel 14:3–8.
78. Deuteronomy 19:14.
79. Exodus 20:5; 34:7; Numbers 14:18; Deuteronomy 5:9.
80. Jeremiah 31:39; Ezekiel 18; Deuteronomy 24:16; Isaiah 59:18.
81. Psalms 42; 44.
82. Genesis 4:15.
83. Numbers 35:19.
84. Deuteronomy 19:6.
85. *Ibid.*; Dhorme translates simply "lest he strike him dead."
86. Deuteronomy 19:2; Numbers 34:6, 11, 13.
87. Deuteronomy 19:3.
88. Exodus 34:7; see also Jeremiah 30:11.
89. Psalms 37:21.
90. Numbers 14:18; Psalms 78:38; Exodus 34:6; Nahum 1:3.
91. Exodus 34:7.

92. Psalms 32:1–5; 103:10.

93. Polemic with Hannah Arendt; reprinted in *Fidélité et Utopie* (Paris: Calmann-Lévy, 1979).

Chapter 16. The Oasis of Time

1. Isaiah 49:4; 48:4; 50:2.
2. Deuteronomy 7:17.
3. Ezekiel 2:5.
4. Ezekiel 13:3; Deuteronomy 18:10.
5. Jeremiah 18:18.
6. Ezekiel 3:5.
7. Jeremiah 18:18.
8. Proverbs 8:23; compare Job 40:19; Ecclesiasticus 1:4; 24:9.
9. Genesis 4:1.
10. Proverbs 8:23.
11. Proverbs 8:24–31.
12. Isaiah 62:6.
13. Isaiah 44:7; 43:10.
14. Ezekiel 6:8.
15. Isaiah 10:13–23.
16. Micah 5:6.
17. Jeremiah 44:28.
18. Ecclesiasticus 47:22.
19. Isaiah 6:13.
20. Ezekiel 6:12.
21. Genesis 7:1.
22. Micah 7:2.
23. Micah 7:4.
24. Isaiah 10:13.
25. This is the proper meaning of "creature."
26. Joshua 4:20–24.
27. Joshua 24:25–27.
28. Isaiah 43:10; 44:8.
29. Exodus 31:li; 32:15; 34:29.
30. Psalms 78:5.
31. Psalms 119:32.
32. Psalms 119:2.
33. This is the case of Eli "sitting on his seat beside the gate watching the road, for his heart trembled for the ark of God" (I Samuel 4:13). And the chronicler adds: "Eli was ninety-eight years old; his gaze was fixed; he was blind" (I Samuel 4:15).

34. Ezekiel 3:16–21.
35. II Kings 9:17–20; II Samuel 18:24; I Samuel 14:16; Isaiah 52:8.
36. Isaiah 21:11.
37. Isaiah 21:12.
38. Isaiah 21:11.
39. Job 7:4.
40. Deuteronomy 28:63–68.
41. Job 7:4.
42. Job 7:6.
43. Job 7:1.
44. Deuteronomy 28:65.
45. Isaiah 21:7.
46. Isaiah 21:10.
47. Job 7:7–9.
48. *Phenomenology.*
49. "Disease of memory" is an expression of the new masters of Cambodia, one of whose first concerns was, as is well known, to destroy every archive.
50. Psalms 44.
51. Deuteronomy 21:15–21; see also Genesis 25:31, 34; 27:36; 43:33.
52. See Jean-François Revel's remarkable *Sur Proust.*
53. "Modernism" again.
54. Genesis 4:7.
55. Psalms 125:13; 102:13.
56. Zechariah 11:7, 17.
57. Zechariah 13:5.
58. II Kings 1:8; Matthew 3:4; Mark 1:6.
59. Abel: *Hebel.*
60. Genesis 4:8: "while they were in the fields."
61. Genesis 4:4: "Abel for his part brought the first-born of his flock and some of their fat as well."
62. Zechariah 13:5: "I am no prophet, I am a tiller of the soil."
63. Ecclesiasticus 44:9.
64. Ecclesiasticus 44:8.
65. Amos 1:1.
66. Amos 7:14.
67. Amos 7:16.
68. Amos 7:14.
69. Isaiah 1:8.
70. Isaiah 62:7.
71. Isaiah 63:3–6.
72. See, for example, Barbey d'Aurevilly, *Du dandysme et de George*

Brummel, in *Oeuvres romanesques complètes* (Paris: Gallimard, Bibliothèque de la Pléiade, 1966), vol. 2, pp. 694, 689, 703, 687.

73. See also Isaiah 49:7: "Their feet run to do evil, are quick to shed innocent blood."

Index

Polytheism, 100
  Greek, 75 (*See also* Greek religion)
  See also Paganism
Poor people, body of, 165
Popular Front, French, 184
Possessed, The (Dostoevsky), 38, 90
Power (political power), 27, 32
  naturalist illusion and, 4–5
  western European communist parties
    and, 27–28
Priests, 153
  as offerings (sacrifices), 34
Prince, the, 22, 23, 31–32
  in a theocratic system, 34
  See also State, the
Principles and Commandments (Jesuit
    text), 82
Propaganda, 57
Property, right to, 44, 45, 167, 168
  as first human right, 170–74
Prophetic model (or deal), 157, 159, 162
Prophetic relationship to the truth, 155
Prophets
  apostles contrasted to, 153–56
  atheist, 155
  in the Bible, 155–56
  Christian, 154–55
Prophets, Books of the, 130, 141, 143,
    246
Proselytism, 150, 152
  See also Apostles
Proust, Marcel, 92–93, 245
Proverbs, 231, 239
Psalms, 222, 233, 234, 242, 243
Psyche, Greek concept of, 66, 67
Psychoanalysis, Freudian, 210
Psychology, 81
  in Euripides, 63–64

Racine, Jean Baptiste, 64, 85–87
Rancé, Abbé Armand de, 82–83, 206
Rauschning, Herman, 14, 15
Realphilosophie, 33
Reason, the People and, 46
Rebellion, 117–19
  See also Resistance

Religion
  civil, 18, 102
  Greek, 71, 73–75
  of politics, 21
  Rousseau on, 18, 21
  of the state, 3, 8, 102
  the state and, 16, 18, 19
  See also Christianity; God; Judaism;
    Monotheism; Paganism; Polytheism
Religiosity of intellectuals, 97–100
Remnant after destruction of all
    Creation, 240–43, 249
Republic, The (Plato), 67
Resistance, 22, 26–27, 57, 58, 172
  a priori conditions for, 217–18
  Christianity and, 80, 230
  cogito of, 119, 124
  Comte on, 80, 82
  desire and, 132, 134, 135
  as freedom, 58
  the future and, 188–90
  justice and, 230–36
  monotheism and, 36, 179
  in Nazi Germany, 199–200
  of the Stendhalian hero, 176
  without a theory or a revolutionary
    party, 195–98, 204
  See also Dissidence; Rebellion
Resistance movement, French, 183–84,
    197
Revolution
  Lenin on, 107
  totalitarian, 4, 10
Revolutionary party, resistance without,
    195–98
Revolutionary politics, 36
Rights of man, 27, 43, 44
  See also Declaration of the Rights of
    Man; Human rights
Right to property, 44, 45, 167, 168
  as first human right, 170–74
Robespierre, Maximilien, 101, 174
Rock, image of the, 219, 224, 226, 227,
    229–31, 242
Roland, Manon, 101
Rolland, Romain, 93–97